Also by Pauline Barclay

Magnolia House

Satchfield Hall

Sometimes It Happens…

Storm Clouds Gathering

In The Cold Light of Day

Next Christmas Will Be Different – a 20 minute e-read

The Wendy House

Pauline Barclay

www.paulinebarclay.co.uk

The Wendy House

A CIP catalogue record for this title is available from the
British Library.

Dedication

This book is pure fiction. The people and places are from my imagination and bare no relation to anyone living or dead. However, I could not have written this book without the help of a special person I met some years ago. What this lovely, brave lady shared with me, not only broke my heart, but will live with me forever. Yet despite the pain of her years of abuse, she wanted me to write a book on this subject. For this courageous, beautiful lady, I dedicate, The Wendy House.
This is for you lovely with all my love.

-

Very Special Thanks to…

Cathy Helms
Jo Field
Elaine Denning
Elaine Hensel
Sue Beveridge

A grateful thank you to you the reader for buying a copy of The Wendy House, it was not the easiest of books to write, but I hope that you will find it a worthwhile read.

And last, but not least, a huge huggy bear hug to my fabulous husband for being the best.

Chapter One

'Mum can I have a word?' Nicola asked, in a voice that hinted she'd had more to drink than was decent. She approached her mother with a half empty glass of white wine clutched in her hand and a sardonic smile twisting her lips as she glared at the person her mother was talking to. She watched as her mother turned from the man in the wheelchair and as their eyes met, Barbara Knight frowned. Nicola could almost taste her mother's disdain as she took in the brightness of her mother's eyes and flushed cheeks.

'Don't you think you've had enough?' Barbara hissed, as she moved closer to Nicola and reached out to grab at the glass. Nicola pulled her hand away, slopping a few drops of the contents onto the gold-patterned carpet. 'Today of all days, can't you behave?' Barbara took hold of Nicola's elbow and with unnecessary haste, guided her out of the room and into the large hall where they could be alone.

'I *am* behaving and that's why I'd like a word with you. Today of all days is perfect.'

Barbara bit down on her lower lip. 'Why do you always have to do this, Nicola? Do you not have a sensitive bone in your body? We've just cremated your father, the man who loved us. He made our lives what they are today and we're never going to be the same without him.' Tears pooled in Barbara's eyes and she dabbed at them with a tissue.

Nicola took in her mother's grief and felt her resolve weaken. The moment of courage she had struggled to find, slowly evaporated. What she needed to say had waited for so long, it could wait a while longer. She loved her mother, but they were permanently at odds with each other, neither able to hold onto the closeness they once had. Nicola wrestled with all the emotions that flooded her, each jostling for pole position. Right now she just wanted to run; run until she was far enough away from everything and everyone. The urge to disappear had been with her for so long that it was like a second skin, but as much as the desire to leave it all behind shadowed her, she knew she could never leave her children; they were all she had. Knowing the moment was now lost, she moved forward and wrapped her arms around her mother. Her wine glass tilted precariously down her mother's back as she looked into her mother's face and saw a reflection of her own pain. 'I didn't mean to upset you, but ...' she said, her voice brimming with emotion as she left the rest of the sentence unsaid, finishing it under her breath. *I really do need to talk to you... there's so much you need to know.*

'Darling, I know,' Barbara said. 'We will all miss him. I don't know how I'm going to get through without him.' Barbara gazed into Nicola's eyes and with her damp tissue, wiped at her daughter's face. Seeing the glass of wine still clutched in her hand, she added, 'Please don't drink anymore, it will only add to your sadness. I know what you're like with drink inside you.'

Nicola bristled at her mother's insinuation, the moment of closeness evaporating, hugs and words forgotten at her mother's need to criticise. 'Are you saying I'm a lush?'

'Good God, I'm not going to walk on egg shells today, Nicola. There are family and friends in the room next door, here to pay their last respects to a man who was a pillar of strength and offered genuine friendship in this community; a man that everyone trusted.' Barbara pulled her hand away. She ran it across her forehead, adding, 'Today is not about you!'

It never is, Nicola thought and took a large gulp of her wine.

'I'm going to ask you again to behave. I've ignored the outfit you've turned up in, but I will not put up with your outbursts today. Now, please go and wash your face and make sure everyone is fine, including your children.'

The anger that lived in Nicola's heart was bursting to spill out. She took a deep breath and was about to ask what, exactly, was wrong with her outfit when, from the corner of her eye, she spied *him* in his wheelchair, entering the hall.

'Barbara, are you all right?' The concern in Bob Wakefield's voice was evident in every syllable.

Nicola didn't miss the piercing look he shot her, but for the first time she saw fear in his eyes and it made her feel euphoric. She glugged down the rest of her wine and watched him over the top of her glass.

'Yes, thank you. I just needed to hug my daughter,' Barbara replied, casting a warning sign to Nicola that clearly meant, *don't push me any further*.

'I understand,' Bob said. He pressed the lever on his right armrest and swivelled the wheelchair out of the hall.

Barbara placed a firm hand on her daughter's shoulder. 'I'm going back to join the others and I suggest you do the same.'

'*He's* the one who should have been cremated today,' Nicola said, her stare taking in the space Bob had left.

Turning sharply, an exasperated sigh escaped Barbara's lips and a mixture of shock and sadness filled her face. 'Nicola, why are you angry with everyone and everything? At twenty-seven you should not only have grown up, but you should show some respect!' As if exasperated, Barbara thrust her arms in the air in a gesture of defeat, and strode down the hall, calling over her shoulder, 'I can't take anymore of you today.'

Nicola hadn't meant for the conversation to go this way, it wasn't how she had planned it. She peered down into her empty glass. She was angry, very angry, and she wanted someone to know why. She had almost told her mother and hopefully one day she would find the courage to go through with it. Why should she have to hold in all this pain and knowledge? She wished her father was still here because she would have liked to have seen his face when she did eventually speak.

9

Nothing had prepared her for his death, but unlike the rest of the so-called friends here today, she was not crying. She wanted to, but knowing it had been because of her father, she couldn't.

In an act of defiance she had carefully chosen her outfit for today: a black and pink suit, white blouse and matching two tone shoes, black for respect and the pink to remind *him*. She had known her mother would be livid at her garish outfit and that, amongst many more reasons, was why she had worn it. The colour would always remind her of that day years before and she wanted it to be a reminder again today. She would never know if her father knew, but she knew *he* did, and here he was as if nothing had ever happened. She couldn't even think *his* name, let alone say it; for her *he* could only ever be *"him"*.

'Hey Nic, what are you doing on your own? I've been looking everywhere for you.'

Startled, Nicola looked up from a button she had started to fiddle with and a broad smile lit up her face as her eyes met Tony's. 'I just needed a minute on my own,' she said.

Apart from her children, Tony was the best thing that had ever happened to her. He had made her feel normal and clean, as if she was someone different; someone special. He knew all her flaws, every single dirty one, and yet he still loved her and wanted her in his life, never questioning all she had told him, only listening and helping. It was because of Tony that she now knew it was time to try and talk to her mother; he was certain it would help her. Maybe if she had another drink she could forge a path to start the conversation she should have attempted years earlier.

Fingering the stem of her empty glass, she was painfully aware that she was drinking too much, but what she had to say needed a strength she could not find anywhere else. No matter how much she drank, though, it would never deliver the pain relief she longed for, but she needed to try.

Chapter Two

Barbara watched as Nicola weaved her way unsteadily to the bar and wondered why her eldest daughter felt the need to drink so much. For what must have been the millionth time since she had given birth to her, Barbara asked herself the question: where did I go wrong? Even the birth hadn't been easy; she had been in labour for thirty-six hours before Nicola had finally arrived. As soon as the midwife had gathered the tiny bundle up in her arms, the newborn had shrieked at the top of her voice, announcing her presence to everyone within earshot. In that respect, she had not changed much at all, today being no exception. The outfit she was wearing was in poor taste, shrieking attention, the same as she had on the day she was born.

As a baby, Nicola had been beautiful and, although wilful, she had not been a particularly difficult child, but then it all started to change and before they knew it Nicola had turned from a self-assured, confident little girl into a pouting and moody eleven-year-old. By contrast, Becky, Barbara's youngest, had transformed from the shy little toddler who followed in the steps of her elder sister into a girl who knew what she wanted. School, for Becky, was a breeze. A smile filled Barbara's face as she remembered Becky announcing she was going to be a doctor when she left school. By contrast, Nicola saw school as rubbish. 'It's a waste of time. We can't all be like *her*,' she had snapped, flicking a contemptuous gaze at her sister before storming out of the house.

It seemed Nicola had had other ideas on educating herself: drugs, alcohol and smoking, until they had found out and put a stop to it. They had grounded her for a month and to their surprise she had settled down. Nicola had actually managed to talk without pouting or complaining, even staying in to do her homework, but it hadn't lasted long. If they thought those times were stressful, worse was waiting just around the corner.

Barbara snapped her mind closed on what had happened next. No way could she think of going there today of all days. It was painful enough to know it had broken Terry's heart. Barbara dabbed at her eyes as they brimmed with tears, the memories of Nicola's behaviour threatening to overwhelm her and she just wished, at this time, that her eldest would try and act like a grieving daughter instead of being provocative and causing rift and pain. She squeezed at her tissue. Just thinking about Nicola caused an imaginary dark cloud to hover over her head. She knew she had failed, but she just wanted today to be about Terry, not Nicola. It had been barely hours since she'd had to say goodbye to the only man she had ever loved, and instead of being comforted by Nicola she was engaged in fighting back bitter memories. Why couldn't Nicola just try and think of someone else instead of herself for once?

Lost in her heavy-hearted ruminations, Barbara was startled at the sound of a familiar voice and swung round.

'You look miles away,' Bob said, moving towards her.

Dragging her mind back from a past she hadn't wanted to visit, Barbara forced a smile as Bob brought his wheelchair to a halt at her side. He reached out for her hand and taking hold, he gently squeezed it. 'Are you all right?' he asked, looking up into her face. Taken aback at the unexpected gesture of care, a sense of relief surged through Barbara and her smile widened as the unpleasant memories slowly slipped away.

'As well as can be expected,' she replied, looking down at him. 'Thank you,' she said in a voice that was barely above a whisper. Where would she be without him? Bob had been Terry's best friend since the children were small. He had been there when others had let them down. Thinking about it, she couldn't remember a time when he hadn't been there. Even after his accident all those years ago, he still came to the house. He was unable to help physically with any one of the many of the projects Terry had kept coming up with, but instead he offered his advice. He had even been there to teach the girls to swim when they had gone away on one of their many summer holidays to the seaside. Terry hated the water, but Bob had been on hand when the girls had screamed to learn. It was odd that Bob had never taken a wife, though he had never been short of admirers, but none, it seemed, had stolen his heart. Over the years she had grown fond of Bob and, like Terry had, she saw him as part of their family.

'You know, I don't know how we would have managed without you, not just now, but all the years we struggled with Nicola. You've always been there for all of us,' she said, feeling the warmth of his hand over hers. Life without her wonderful Terry was going to be very painful, but knowing Bob was there for them all, she knew they would get through, eventually.

'And don't you think about how I would have managed without you, my adopted family?' he said, squeezing her hand. 'I saw Nicola with her new man, Tony. She looks upset.'

Barbara nodded, noting the change of subject, back to her recalcitrant daughter. 'She's no doubt sulking; she wanted to talk to me. You know what Nicola can be like. Today of all days, she wants to talk,' she huffed. 'I told her today was about her father not her. Unfortunately, my eldest believes everything revolves around her.'

Barbara pulled her hand free from Bob's. 'She'll be fine and will no doubt forget about her behaviour tomorrow when she's nursing her hangover,' she said tartly. What was going on in her daughter's head was a worry, but not today, she simple couldn't do it; aiming for the summit of Mount Everest in flip-flops would be easier to achieve than reaching Nicola these days. 'As for me, there's no need to worry, I'll be fine too.'

Barbara turned from Bob and with heavy steps and a head filled with memories, she walked away.

Chapter Three

The pain was so intense, Nicola felt as if her head were about to explode. Slowly she opened her eyes and in a fuzzy blur of vision, looked around the room and tried to take in the pastel-coloured painted walls and cream blinds at the window, where light streamed in. For several seconds she had no idea where she was. With panic rising, she tried to move. It was only after she had managed to turn over and saw the bedside lamp casting a soft glow over her that she realised she was in bed, in her own room. Relief flooded through her, but was immediately replaced with horror because she could not remember how she had ended up there.

With shaking hands she pushed back the duvet and, with as much effort as she could muster, nudged herself upright until she was able to rest her head against the headboard. The coolness of the rosewood on the back of her neck did nothing to alleviate the pounding inside her head. The bitter taste of bile rose in her throat and reluctantly she swallowed, grimacing at the vile taste. The last thing she needed right now was to be sick and make her head pound even more. What she really needed was a mouthful of paracetamol or, better still, a lethal injection to put her out of her misery. What had possessed her to drink so much? Nicola closed her eyes to keep the light from searing at her retina. It didn't matter what the reason was, all the answers in the world would never take away the throbbing in her head or the wrenching pain in her heart.

She thought about the en-suite and wondered if she could will the packet of painkillers to jump from the bathroom cabinet and drop into her lap. Knowing this could never happen she pushed the duvet back and eased her legs out of bed. Her feet sank into the thick pile of the rug and at the same time a rush of dizziness swept over her. She grabbed the side of the mattress to stop herself from falling. 'Whoa!' she groaned and flopped back against the pillows. She flicked the duvet back over her and feeling the safety and warmth of the thick cover, she gently massaged her throbbing temples, her short nails digging into the skin. As she attempted to ease the pain, it then slowly registered where she had been to end up with such a hangover. Tears slipped down her face at the memory.

'Oh no,' she sobbed, the bile rising again in her throat and with an energy she had no idea she possessed, Nicola scrambled out of bed and raced to the toilet. Making it just in time, she heaved into the bowl.

Several minutes passed whilst she retched. Only when there was nothing left to bring up, did she sink down on to the cold, tiled floor and weep. Not until she was spent did she tug at the toilet paper. Ripping several sheets off, she wiped at the snot dribbling from her nose and the tears that cascaded down her face.

She tossed the sodden paper into the toilet and vowed that she would never drink too many again. Disgusted with herself, she reached over and pressed the flush button. As water swirled round the bowl, she dropped the lid and sank down on it. These last few months she had worked hard at reducing her alcohol intake to the point that there were days when she had managed to live on little or no alcohol at all. Of course, all of this had been thanks to Tony. A beautiful man who cared for her and loved her like no one had ever done before. Just thinking of Tony brought fresh tears to her eyes and once again the shame enveloped her. She had let him down. How he must hate her.

Slithering onto the tiled floor, Nicola huddled down and wrapped her arms around her knees. Resting her head on her tearstained hands, she thought back to yesterday's funeral and the days before.

Her mother had been her usual self: laying the law down, comparing her to Becky and always making sure she was seen as the one who constantly let the family

15

down; the one who disgraced the name of "Knight" on more occasions that her mother cared to count.

Her mother's latest verbal attack had been brought about when Nicola had foolishly mentioned that she didn't want her girls going to the funeral. 'It would be too upsetting,' she had reasoned, adding that she had made arrangements for them for the day. But that wasn't good enough; her mother had insisted they needed to say their goodbyes to their granddad. 'For heaven's sake, Chelsea's nine years old and Mya's seven. You can't deny them a final goodbye,' she had argued.

Nicola had taken several deep breaths to keep her cool and had explained, calmly, that she didn't want them there. 'I don't care about their age; I don't want them to go. I still feel it would be upsetting.' It was then that her mother had rounded on her.

'Nonsense! You can't protect them from death! You'll live to regret not allowing them to be there. It's their grandfather, for goodness sake!'

Trying to keep her patience in check, Nicola had volleyed back, 'Yes, but only when it suited you.'

'That's rubbish and you know it. It's you that keeps everyone at bay. Anyway, I'm not going down that road now. Your father would want them there and they should be.'

'They're my girls and I'm not having them upset when there's no need,' she had said through gritted teeth not missing the steely look in her mother's eyes.

'It's called respect!'

Respect, she screamed silently, and as usual she had felt the familiar feeling of defeat. Her father was dead and no amount of arguing would bring him back. She still loved him, even if he had let her down. Knowing she hadn't the strength for further confrontation, she had reluctantly agreed that the girls would be there. She had never had the capacity for arguments and would always end up backing down afraid that what really needed to be said would gush out at the wrong moment.

'I don't agree with your reasons, but okay you win,' she had said, hurt creeping into her voice and feeling defeated. 'As Tony's taking the day off, we'll come as a family.'

'Whatever for? We hardly know him, do we Nicola?' her mother had snapped back, ignoring her climb-down on the girls attending the funeral. 'Let's be honest, he's one of several men who've been in your life and in my book he needs to prove he's worthy. Good heavens, the last one certainly wasn't,' her mother had tutted in a way that conveyed her utter distaste for the father of Nicola's daughters. 'But now is not the time to go down that murky road...' Her mother's voice had trailed away.

If Nicola had been slapped across the face it would not have stung more. And, as easy as it would have been to lash back, *if only you knew...* she had bitten down hard on her tongue, like she always did.

Unable to take any more, Barbara had reached down and grabbed her handbag. Tucking it under her arm, she had added. 'There will be no eulogy. Becky is far too upset to say anything and has asked me to excuse her from standing up and speaking at the funeral.' Her mother had glared at Nicola before adding her *pièce-de-résistance*, 'And I don't want you speaking either. We can't take the risk that you'd not be three sheets to the wind, slurring your words and swaying all over the place.'

How could a mother be so cruel? Nicola asked herself. It had taken all the effort she could muster to prevent herself from lashing out and doing the unthinkable. Itching to slap her mother's arrogant face, she had clasped her hands together behind her back to restrain them, so tightly that her fingers had tingled from the pressure. At the same time her mother's cornflower-blue eyes had locked onto hers. 'You do understand, don't you Nicola?'

Unclasping her hands to let the blood flow again, Nicola knew she never would understand. But one day her mother would understand where her daughter was coming from, and then she would see just how turbulent had been the water that had passed under the bridge; not so much a flow as a raging torrent! She had opened her mouth to speak, but the words had stuck to the roof of her mouth. In the silence that hung between them, their eyes had stayed locked on each other. Breaking the gaze, Nicola had turned and headed out of the living room.

'Nicola,' her mother had called, stomping behind her, 'I'm talking to you.'

She had ignored the plea, wrenched the front door open and stormed out of the house. As the door had hit the door stop, she had run to her car parked at the kerbside. She had needed to put as much distance between herself and her mother before she really did let rip and then all hell would break loose. Reaching her silver Golf, she had fumbled with the key fob before she had managed to unlock the door and drop into the driver's seat. Yanking the door shut and with her hand shaking, she had slotted the key into the ignition. The car started first turn and with a squealing of tyres she had pulled away.

'Nicola!' her mother's voice drifted above the roar of the car engine.

Glancing into the rear view mirror, Nicola had seen her mother standing on the pavement, her arms waving like a windmill, her words lost in the distance between them. Would there ever be a time when she could talk to her without a scene, Nicola wondered. Moving up to third gear, she sighed. She had not missed the emphasis on her name either. It was always *"Nicola"* when her mother was angry or against something she did, or was going to do. In the past, she had been referred to as "Nic" or "Nicky", though she had not heard either of those names for a very long time; years in fact.

She had flicked the indicator to turn left, the sound of her mother's voice yelling *'Nicola'* still ringing in her ears. It spoke volumes about her mother's feelings towards her. As difficult as her life had been over the years, she was at last getting everything sorted out, now she had Tony. She hoped her mother could see this, but if she did, like everything else to do with her, she appeared to ignore it. Tony was there for both herself and the children - a sensitive, loving man who knew how it was to live with pain. It would have been wonderful to have told her mother how important he was and the difference he was making to her life, but the mere mention of his name had caused her mother to go off on one of her rants. Right now, words about how she was moving forward would only fall on deaf ears. For years her wish had been for her mother to accept her for everything - the past and how her life was now - but it was a wish that would never come true. And, as she always did after these outbursts, she blamed herself for being weak and stupid. But one day she would be strong; very strong. She had to believe this because, when that day arrived, she would answer her mother back and would let rip, and the years of anger and abuse would burst out of her. It would be a dangerous day and her mother's world would rock violently on its axis. She, Nicola Knight, would stand back, hands on her hips and watch how her words cut and slashed, destroying her mother in the same way she had been destroyed.

Seething silently, she had driven across town heading for home. Upset and hurt and wishing she had the nerve to speak to her mother, she had kept the confrontation to herself and had said nothing to Tony. She didn't want him to know just how vindictive her mother could be.

The night before the funeral Nicola had had nightmares, the ones that returned time and time again; the ones that stalked her sleeping hours and threatened to suffocate her with fear. By the time she had managed to drag herself out of bed, she had been wrung out feeling more dead than alive: a corpse like her father. How she was going to get through his burial had panicked her. Before they had left the house for the funeral she had downed a whisky, a small one, telling herself it was for medicinal purposes. With the whisky inside her, the children smartly turned out and Tony at her side, Nicola had been convinced she would be able to cope.

Tony had driven in silence to the Chapel of Rest. To her surprise it was full, with many mourners standing at the back. She and the children had sat at the front with her mother and sister. Tony had dropped a kiss on her lips and after acknowledging her mother, who had curtly nodded at him, he had headed to the back of the hall, where he had stayed throughout the service. She had wanted him at her side for comfort and support, but he had insisted it would be best if he left the front rows for family.

Knowing that there was to be no reading of a eulogy from the family, it never occurred to her that the person her mother would ask to remember her father would be Bob Wakefield. Nicola had almost passed out with shock when, gripping his sticks, he had stumbled to his feet.

Bob Wakefield had leant on the lectern, having been assisted to the privileged area by the vicar. From his vantage point he had peered down at the assembled congregation, a pair of reading glasses perched on the end of his nose and genuine sadness filling his face as her father's coffin rested on the covered table next to where he stood. As he spoke, his gaze flicked between Becky, herself and their mother, his voice sombre as he reminded everyone of the happy family man who had enjoyed life to the full. He talked about the famous parties her dad had organised, the projects they had done together and how proud Terry was of his family. Nicola wasn't sure if she would pass out of throw up when he had mentioned the projects and parties, but like all the other times in her life when she'd had to control herself in situations she could not escape from, she remained still, shutting down all her emotions. But what had been almost her downfall was how her mother had hung on to his every word.

After the service, feeling emotionally battered, they had made their way to Griffin Hall, which was no more than a five-minute walk from the crematorium. She had been grateful for the fresh air, Tony had held her hand and the girls followed by her side. She had tried to keep her composure, but the shock of Bob Wakefield talking about her father had unbalanced her and her resolve not to have a drink crumbled.

Entering Griffin Hall, Nicola had made her way straight to the bar area and ordered a large wine. With the chilled glass in her hand, she had passed pleasantries with her sister. Becky had glared at her with a disapproving look and was obviously on the brink of voicing her objection when one of dad's friends had interrupted. Relieved, Nicola had watched as Becky happily moved away, knowing they had nothing to say to each other. In truth, they had nothing in common these days. Becky was married to a consultant in a teaching hospital and she was a junior doctor at the same place. No children, no pets, they lived in a luxury penthouse apartment overlooking the English Channel. By contrast, Nicola lived in a rented three-bedroom semi-detached on the edge of a large housing estate, with three children and a partner she had known for less than a year. She had no fancy doctorate or degree, though she had a medical record: two abortions, a miscarriage, treatment for depression and self-harming. Not quite the same as her sister and her brother-in-law. Becky's husband had not been able to attend the funeral due to an emergency at the hospital, but Nicola knew all about emergencies and the need of medical staff. She was not angry with her sister, envious perhaps, because had things been different then maybe she would have had a life similar to Becky's. She too would have had the pride of place photograph on her parent's sideboard of her graduation, or walking down the aisle with a handsome, successful man. Instead, she had other events to remind them of her; none that warranted photographs.

Now, leaning against the toilet in the en-suite, Nicola took a deep breath and tried not to think about what might have been. Yesterday, she had made a fool of herself and created a scene at her dad's funeral. Shame washed over her and she wished she could turn the clock back, not just to yesterday, but right back to when she was young, to see if she could have done everything or anything different.

Right back to just before her tenth birthday, the day her childhood had ended…

Chapter Four

Nicola pulled down one of the Venetian blind slats and stared out of the lounge window. Through the double glazing she heard laughter from her parents. She watched them hurry, arms linked, towards the taxi waiting by the kerb. Before sliding into the car, her mother turned and waved. Nicola waved back, a smile filling her face, she loved it when her parents when out to parties. And like all the other times when her parents went out, Uncle Bob babysat. She like him, he was funny and he always let her stay up long after the time her parents' said she needed to be in bed. And if that wasn't enough, he always brought her treats; chocolate, ice cream and sometimes he even went out to get them a pizza. By then, Becky would be snuggled down in bed fast asleep. Sometimes Nicola wished her parents went out more often because she loved being spoilt by Uncle Bob.

Watching the taxi speed off down the road, she released the blind slat and as it sprung back in position, she padded over to the sofa.

'Right, I'm having a beer do you want your milkshake now?' Bob called out as he headed through to the kitchen.

About to sit down, Nicola changed her mind and followed him. 'I think I'll have it a bit later? It's not time for bed yet,' she said checking the time on the oven clock.

'Too early for that,' Bob said, pulling a beer from the fridge. He flicked the door shut with his elbow, then reached over to one of the tall cupboards and grabbed a large packet of crisps. 'Come on Nic,' he said, heading back to the lounge, 'let's watch TV.'

Dropping down in one of the large armchairs, Bob tossed the bag of crisps to Nicola now sitting with her legs curled underneath her on the sofa. 'Open these,' he said, grabbing the remote control. 'So what do you want to watch?'

Bob pressed the on switch and the TV screen burst into life.

Nicola pulled open the packet of crisps, instantly the whiff of salt and vinegar filled her nostrils, she sniffed and plucked out two and stuffed them into her mouth. Crunching on her favourite flavour, she knew her parents would be furious if they could see her filling her mouth with crisps, but that was part of the fun when Uncle Bob babysat. She beamed and took another two.

'I've got a few films here if you want to choose one,' Bob said and leaned over the side of his chair to pick up a carrier bag. 'Here, take a look at these,' he said, reaching over towards her. Nicola stretched out her hand and took hold of the bag and as her fingers curled round the handle, she felt his warm fingers touch hers and she let out a soft giggle.

'Thanks,' she said feeling her cheeks burn at how Uncle Bob's eyes roamed over her. Uncle Bob was very kind, even if he did look at her with a faraway look in his eyes from time to time, she thought, placing the crisps to one side and peering into the bag.

'Have you ever tasted beer?' Bob asked, as she pulled out one of the films.

'Well once, when Dad wasn't looking,' she admitted, reading the label on the cover.

Keeping her attention on the film cover, she thought Uncle Bob looked just like the young doctor on the television, the same one all the nurses were trying to get to notice them and take them out. But unlike the doctor in the programme, who looked very young, she knew Uncle Bob was old. She had heard her mother once say that he was two years younger than her dad, which would make him thirty-eight, though she could see he didn't have grey hair yet and his face was still chiselled. One of the nurses had said that about the doctor's face. Nicola had looked the word up in the dictionary and decided it was a great description and now, as she slyly gazed over at Uncle Bob, she could see it suited him. He might be old, she thought, but he still resembled the young doctor and his face *was* chiselled. Dreaming about growing up, she wondered if one day she would marry a handsome doctor who looked like Uncle Bob.

'Would you like a taste then?' Bob asked, brandishing his beer can at her. Abandoning his chair he moved over to the sofa and sat next to Nicola, his thigh brushed against her leg.

Looking up at him, Nicola smiled. Even his eyes were the same colour as the doctor's: grey, like a dark pebble on the beach. Being grownup would be amazing, she thought, especially if her life was to be like the nurses'; full of smiles and handsome doctors.

'You'll be ten in a few weeks, so I'm sure having a taste won't hurt you. Anyway, I'm hardly going to let you drink the lot, am I?' Bob said, winking at her. 'Here, take it.' He chuckled and held the can in front of her.

Still thinking about being a grownup, Nicola reached out and took hold of the beer. Slowly she placed it to her lips and cautiously sipped at the amber liquid. It fizzed on her tongue and as it slipped down her throat, she tasted its bitterness. She pulled a face. She couldn't ever remember the nurses pulling a face at the doctor when he'd bought them a drink. Maybe she should try another sip. This time she took a mouthful, but instead of swallowing it, the bubbles caught in her throat and she found herself choking. Eventually, she managed to gather her breath and gulp it down.

'Hey, you're not supposed to swig it down in one go,' Bob cried, wrapping his arm around her and gently slapping her back. Nicola coughed and spluttered as the bitter taste lingered in her mouth.

Taking the can back, Bob removed his arm from around her. 'I'll get you some water. It seems you're not ready for this adult stuff yet.'

'I am,' she said, sniffing, feeling she had let him and herself down.

'I'll still get the water,' he said with a smirk. Perhaps if she stopped day dreaming about television programmes she wouldn't have choked and made herself look childish.

'Here you are,' he said a few moments later, handing her a glass of water.

'Thanks,' she said and tried not to see the doctor's face reflecting in Uncle Bob's.

'Cheers,' he said, clinking his can against her glass.

'Cheers,' she said, then downed the water. Placing the empty glass on the carpet, she said, 'Can I have another taste of your beer?'

'I don't think that's a good idea, do you? What if your mum and dad find out? I won't be allowed to babysit again and worse still, your dad won't be my best friend.'

'They'll never know, will they?' she said, knowing Uncle Bob always let her have her own way and she would really like to try again without behaving like a baby. She giggled inside knowing she could wrap him around her little finger.

'Okay, but only on one condition.'

This time she didn't miss the change of tone in his voice and suddenly she wasn't too sure. He had never said *on one condition* before when she had asked to stay up late or eat crisps and chocolates, so why now? Then she remembered the films. That was it; he wanted to watch his favourite rather than hers. She laughed at the fact she had worked out his *one condition* and nodded. Taking the can from him she drank down all that remained. Then, with the back of her hand, she wiped it across her mouth, just like she had seen the men doing on TV, and belched loudly.

'Very lady like!' Bob laughed and took the can from her. He tossed it on to the floor. 'Now young lady, you should be getting your nightie on.'

'But it's not time for bed yet,' she said, feeling a little sick after drinking the beer.

'That's not what I said. You just need to get undressed and then you can sit here in your nightie and we can watch the film. I'll go upstairs and get it while you take your clothes off.'

Nicola watched him leave the room and listened to his footsteps on the staircase. She tried to stand, but fell back on the sofa. She knew she was going to be in trouble if her parents found out she had been drinking beer. The next time she attempted to stand she managed to stay on her feet and after unbuttoning her top, she slipping it off. She tugged at her jeans. Flopping down onto the sofa, she wrapped her arms around her knees and wished Uncle Bob would hurry up with her nightie.

'Got it,' he said, waving it in the air as if it was a flag. Standing in front of her, he dangled her pink nightie from his fingertip. 'You're still half dressed.'

'I'm not,' she argued, staring up at him.

'To me you are, so take of your knickers and I'll give you your nightie.'

'Turn away! You shouldn't be looking,' she said, wobbling as she got to her feet. When he faced the other way she quickly pushed down her underwear, but before she had a chance to step out of her knickers, Bob swung round and gently pushed her down onto the sofa. Still clutching the nightie, he picked her up and placed her on his knee. 'You know, you're such a pretty girl, but I want to see just how beautiful you are.' As he spoke, he slid her knickers over her ankles and dropped them on the floor.

A wave of panic trickled through her as he ran his fingers slowly down the length of her body, tracing all her little curves. This wasn't right, he shouldn't be doing this. Silently she screamed for him to leave her alone and tried to wriggle out of his arms, but he was strong and held her tight. 'Please can I have my nightie?' she squealed, in a voice that sounded strangled.

'In a minute you can,' he said. Smiling at her he squeezed the top of her legs to make them part. Before she could say or do anything, she felt his fingers touching and probing a place that he shouldn't. Holding her breath for fear of being sick, she wanted to tell him to stop, but she couldn't. The words stuck in her throat along with the bile she had brought up.

'You're even more beautiful than I thought,' he said, removing his hand. Then as suddenly as it all began, it stopped.

'Here, let me put your nightie on,' he said in a voice she didn't recognise.

Too shocked to resist, she let him place her nightie over her head. Pulling it down over her body, he added, 'You know you must remember this is our secret, Nic. Nobody must ever know. I'll never tell anyone and you mustn't either, because if you do, then they'll know you drank my beer and said you wanted to be treated like a grownup.'

Nicola pulled her nightie further down, unsure of how it had all happened. What he had done was wrong and she knew that, but who would believe her? Drinking the beer and her stupid fantasy about a television programme had made him touch her. It was all because of her. Hadn't she looked at him just like the nurses looked at the doctor? What had she done? Knowing she was to blame, she had to accept she could never say anything and, as frightened as she felt, she agreed. 'I won't tell anyone, I promise,' she said, slipping off his knee and standing away from him.

Reaching out to her,' he added, 'surely you enjoyed me touching you?'

She shook her head, already feeling a strange soreness between her legs and on her thighs.

'Then you will next time,' Bob said, with a smile.

Chapter Five

A surge of happiness swept through Barbara as she looked from her husband to Bob, and as Bob's eyes smiled back at her, she was reminded that he was more than a good friend, more than Terry's best friend, importantly, he was part of the family. Not only did they all love him, but he loved the girls as if they were his own and was proud to be called their Uncle Bob. It had been a lucky day when Bob Wakefield had walked into her husband's life all those years earlier. And if having him as part of the family wasn't enough, he had given endless hours to construct this beautiful Wendy House.

'Thank you,' she said turning her attention back to Terry and this time felt the prick of tears at the back of her eyes.

The Wendy House had been Bob's idea after the girls had harped on incessantly about how their friends now had large plastic play houses to have sleep overs in and friends round to play.

'Please, please can we have one,' Becky had begged enough times to sound like a record. In a half-hearted way, Nicola had chorused it too in support of her sister's appeal. Worn down by all the pleading and talk of a Wendy House, Bob had come up with the idea of making one.

'My workshop is plenty big enough to make it up and then we can put it together here. Make a big surprise for the girls,' he had added. Barbara had straight away warmed to the idea and could think of nothing else, especially as the school summer holidays would be upon then before they knew it. After talks on how it could be achieved as a surprise, Bob and Terry had set about making a Wendy House. Terry had drawn up the plans and between them they had constructed it together in their spare time. Last night it had been erected at the bottom of the garden. To guarantee the surprise they had planned, Barbara had organised a sleepover with Jenny, knowing her girls got on well with Jenny's two.

Now, as she swept her gaze over the shingled pitched roof and the honey-coloured tongue-and-groove planking, the pink floral curtains that hung at the little windows, and the tiny planters perched on a shelf outside them, Barbara's excitement bubbled up. She pictured the girls' excitement as they barrelled out into the garden on their return later that morning.

'Come on, let's have a final peep inside before the girls fill it with all their things,' Bob, said placing a screwdriver into the pocket of his trousers. He pushed the painted yellow door open and stood to one side.

Barbara transferred her gaze to Terry and saw the pride in his eyes at what had been achieved in secrecy. Filled with happiness, she entered the little house. Immediately the redolence of new timber assailed her nostrils and she inhaled its fragrance. Standing in the middle of the Wendy House, her breath caught in her throat as she marvelled at the detail. In the right hand corner was a small fitted kitchen. She counted three little wall cabinets and floor cupboards and a wooden oven with a smoky Perspex door. A wooden hob was fitted over the oven and the soft glow of red on the rings added a little realism. Two chairs, a small sofa with brightly coloured cushions and a miniature wooden coffee table sat to the left. All the pieces of furniture had been constructed by the two men. Her own contribution had been the cushions and the curtains. It just now needed to be filled with the sound of laughter, she thought, to make it complete.

'What are you thinking?' Terry asked, as he slipped his hand around her waist.

'So many things,' she said, seeing his wide smile. 'You two are amazing and I love you both. I can't wait for the girls to come home they are going to be so excited.' As she spoke a lump of emotion rose in her throat for the two men who had given so much time to making this beautiful play house.

Three months it had taken to organise and build and with just a week away from school breaking up for the summer, the timing was perfect. Barbara took another long look around and this time allowed her happy tears to spill out. Wiping them away, she made her way back to the garden. In her mind's eye she could picture Becky clapping her hands and squealing with delight. Nicola, she hoped, would be just as happy. It hadn't escaped her notice, of late, that her eldest daughter had been a little subdued. She had tried talking to her, but there was nothing Nicola would say to her words, simply shrugging her shoulders and telling her all was fine. During the times Bob had babysat, she had asked him to keep an eye on her daughter and to let her know if he thought there was anything bothering her, trouble at school, perhaps. He was close to the girls, and especially Nicola. After the last time he had babysat, he had reported back, saying Nicola seemed like her usual self and had not said anything about school. In the end Barbara had put it down to the likely onset of hormones. It seemed children, girls in particular, appeared to mature so much earlier these days. She didn't like the idea of her little girl growing up too fast and had made a special effort to pay more attention to Nicola, reminding her that she was always there to talk and listen to her about anything. The Wendy House was just one of the ways to show her daughters how much she loved and listened to them.

'I think we are all set to go,' Bob said, 'which means, I'm out of here.'

'I don't think so,' Barbara and Terry said in unison. 'You are part of this present,' Terry added, placing his hand on Bob's shoulder, 'and we want you here to see their faces.'

'Sorry, but this time I'm not listening to you both. I'm leaving you to enjoy your girls' excitement. My part is done.' He nudged Terry's hand off his shoulder then slapped his friend on the back. 'Sorry mate, but I do need to be somewhere else,' Bob added before dropping a kiss on Barbara's cheek. 'Take plenty of photos,' he called, walking down the garden path to the gate.

Disappointed, Barbara watched their friend walk away from the celebration yet to come. She turned to Terry, 'He can be strange sometimes,' she said.

Chapter Six

Barbara groaned as the doorbell resonated through the house. After admiring the Wendy House earlier she knew she had plenty of time to finish her baking, so why was her door bell ringing? She glanced at the clock and saw it was only ten-thirty, she wasn't expecting the girls back from their sleepover until after eleven. As if their early return wasn't bad enough, Bob was not staying for the celebrations. She felt he more than deserved to see the girls' faces when they saw the Wendy House and his unexpected departure had disappointed her. The bell chimed again. 'Damn,' she muttered, and after glancing at the muffins in the oven and wiping her hands on her apron, she hurried down the hall.

'Sorry we're early,' Jenny gushed, pushing past Barbara as she opened the door, a beaming smile filling her face.

'Morning Jenny.' Barbara stepped back and looked at the bubbly, rotund woman with the blonde corkscrew curls, who now stood in the middle of her hallway.

'Why does everything happen at once?' Jenny said, beckoning the girls inside. 'Come on darlings, you know I've got to rush back.' She turned to Barbara, 'I'm all of a fluster. We have a viewing on the house at lunch time. Would you believe it? The call came in last night. Heavens, don't people go home on a Friday? Anyway, as we don't want to miss any opportunity to sell, we agreed they could have a look and the place looks like a bomb site. So you can guess I'm in a mad panic,' she said, taking a breath.

Barbara stifled a chuckle. Jenny's life ran at maximum speed with everything constantly on full throttle. Just having her in the house for a few minutes already had her head spinning.

'That's great news,' Barbara replied, unsure if Jenny would be listening. 'Let me know how it goes. I hope my two haven't left any mess for you to clean up.' She smiled at Nicola and Becky, who stood at her side with their overnight wheelies, giggling.

'Good heavens no, they're a treat to have. Anyway, mustn't stop,' she said, bending down and kissing each girl on the cheek, leaving behind a pink bloom from her lipstick. 'Catch up with you later, Babs. Oh, by the way,' she said, reaching the door, 'the nasty bruise on the top of Nic's leg was there when she arrived. There's no accidents on my watch! And be warned, they might need a nap. None of them closed their eyes much before midnight.'

'Right,' Barbara said, feeling like she'd been flattened by a steam roller. No matter how few minutes she spent with Jenny, she always felt wrung out afterwards.

'See you all soon!' Jenny called, heading down the path. 'And wish me luck with the viewing.'

Barbara watched in amusement as Jenny almost tripped over her own feet in her haste to get to her car parked at the bottom of the drive. She wondered if the mother of two had a pause button. Probably not, she mused, watching as Jenny pulled away.

Barbara closed the door and turned to her girls. 'Come here darlings,' she said, her arms outstretched. Dropping to her knees, she wrapped her arms around them. 'Did you have a good time?'

'It's a mad house,' Nicola said, 'but we always have fun.'

'What about you, Becks? Was it fun?'

'It was,' she sighed, looking up at her mother with dreamy eyes. 'Sammy's got a big plastic Wendy House too and we played in that for most of the time.'

'Has she now,' Barbara said, turning back to Nicola. 'What's this bruise Auntie Jenny mentioned?'

The happy smile slipped from Nicola's face and with her eyes downcast, she mumbled, 'It's nothing, I hurt myself doing gym at school, that's all,' and wriggled out of Barbara's embrace.

'But Nic...' Barbara said, reaching out her hand to her daughter, then paused in mid-sentence as she jumped to her feet. 'Oh no,' she groaned, as the smell of muffins wafted through the air. 'Sorry girls, but if you're going to have your favourite treat, I've got to get back to the kitchen.' She sprinted down the hall and snatched the tea towel from the surface top. Wrapping the cloth around her hands, she pulled open the oven door and to her relief saw the muffins were not burnt, but perfectly baked.

'They smell scrummy,' Nicola said, the pout of moments earlier replaced by a smile that lit up her face. Giggling, Becky skipped into the kitchen.

'What's so funny, Becks?' Barbara called over her shoulder as she pulled out the tray.

'I'm just thinking that if Nic eats all the muffins there'll be none for me and I'll have to have chocolate instead.'

'There's more than enough for you, Miss Piggy,' Barbara said, wondering how sisters could be so different - Becky a podgy, cute six-year-old and Nicola, soon to be ten, slender with fine features. She'd be beautiful in a few short years. Steeling a glance at her pretty girl, she felt her heart twist with love at the sight of her smiling again. During the last few weeks her concern had grown over Nicola's moody behaviour. On several occasions she had attempted to talk to her, but had been brushed off with, *'I'm okay.'* Thankfully, whatever it was seemed to have passed. Having a sleepover at Jenny's always made the girls happy and she was certain the surprise at the bottom of the garden would add to their happiness.

Laying the hot tray down on one of her chopping boards, Barbara sidled over to Nicola. Placing her arm around her shoulders, she gazed into her daughter's eyes. 'You know I love you and I'm always here. You can talk to me about anything, any time. When things upset you, they upset me too.'

Meeting her mother's eyes, Nicola smiled. 'I know Mum, but I'm fine, honest. I've been worried about you too because sometimes you seem too busy to smile.'

'You never need to worry about me, I'm a grownup, but I worry about you. As long as you're fine though, then I'm happy too. As for smiling, I promise to try more,' she said.

Nicola smiled, 'I love you Mum.'

'And I love you my gorgeous Nic Nac,' Barbara said, hugging Nicola close.

'Now,' she added, reaching out her hand to Becky, 'I want you both to come with me, we've got something special to show you.'

'What about the muffins?' Becky piped up.

'They're for later, but first we have a surprise.'

'Surprise? What surprise?' Becky squealed, skipping round the kitchen like an excited puppy.

'If you'll just stand still for a moment I'll show you,' Barbara said, taking hold of Becky's hand. 'Come on, Nic,' she added, unfurling her arm from around her eldest and reaching out her hand.

Barbara stepped out onto the terrace first, blocking the view of the garden. 'Now close your eyes,' she said. Becky squeezed hers closed and a large grin filled her chubby face. Barbara glanced over at Terry, who was standing in front of the Wendy House still admiring his handiwork. Looking back at her and the girls, he beamed and stood to one side. Barbara let go of their hands. 'Okay, you can open them,' she whispered, stepping aside.

Becky let out an ear piercing squeal. 'Nic, look!' she cried, clapping her hands in excitement and tearing off down the garden. Nicola stared at the Wendy House. 'Wow,' she said, her eyes wide.

'Off you go,' Barbara said, 'it's yours as well.'

'Mum?' Nicola said quietly, and looked up at her, hesitating.

'Yes love?'

Shrugging, Nicola smiled. 'It's nothing,' she said, and set off down the garden after her sister, leaving her mother bewildered. She frowned, hoping her daughter was all right. She would be ten in a few weeks and Barbara hoped against hope she was not starting her periods yet; she was still a little girl. The cries of Becky's delight filled the air and pushed away her sombre thoughts.

Returning to the kitchen, Barbara slipped the muffins onto a tray. Satisfied they were cool enough to eat, she took hold of them and made her way to the Wendy House, safe in the knowledge her girls were happy, with not just a loving family, but a special uncle too.

Chapter Seven

How long ago it seemed, that sunny day when her daughters had been little girls, screaming with delight at their new Wendy House. And now they were all grownup and their father had gone forever. 'Of all the days your sister should choose to show me up,' Barbara said to Becky, tight-lipped, as she dabbed at her mascara with a tissue. 'I shudder to think what your father would be thinking.' She looked skyward. 'God rest his soul,' she added, a mixture of emotion and anger thick in her voice. Swinging round, she slid open a top drawer from one of the kitchen units and pulled out a packet of Paracetamol. Her hands trembled as she drew out a foiled sheet, then punched out two tablets and popped them straight into her mouth. Filling a tumbler with tap water, she washed them down. As the tablets slipped down her throat, she wished there was such an easy remedy to take all the pain away that her eldest daughter had caused. When she wasn't worrying why Nicola had turned out the way she had, she was fretting about what she was up to and worse, who she was getting involved with. Over the years, once the apple of her father's eye, she seemed to have gone out of her way to befriend the least desirable. How had it all come about? She shuddered as the tablets settled in her stomach, but the tremor was more at the knowledge that Nicola had disappointed them on so many levels. Even for her father's funeral she had defied protocol, turning up in a ridiculous outfit and drinking too much. Today should have been about Terry and yet here she was fuming over her eldest. Why? 'Thank God you didn't turn out like her,' she said, turning to reach out to Becky.

'Don't let her upset you again,' Becky said. 'You know what Nic's like; drinking too much is what she's good at these days.' Becky took hold of her mother's hand

and squeezed it affectionately, the dark red nail varnish appearing garish against her pale fingers.

'You always did stand by your big sister, no matter what she did,' Barbara said, remembering how Becky had idolised her. These days they were distant, but it hadn't always been that way. Three years younger, Becky had protected her sister when she'd started to go off the rails, covering for her when she'd stayed out until the early hours of the morning. Insisting Nicola was sick or had a bad period pain when in fact she'd drunk too much or was doped to the eyeballs after trying some trendy drug. Once they knew what the little madam was up to, they had grounded her. It had been a waste of time, instead of it teaching her a lesson, to their dismay it had had the opposite effect as Nicola slowly headed for destruction. Why had their eldest turned to such a lifestyle? That was the question that had filled Barbara's days and haunted her nights for the last fifteen years.

Lost in her thoughts, it took Barbara a few seconds to realise Becky was gazing at her tearstained face. 'She's not perfect, Mum, and having Chelsea at seventeen must have been a nightmare for her. We're not close these days, but I still think about her.'

'If only all the worrying would change things,' Barbara said, despair creeping into her voice. 'But difficulties had begun long before little Chelsea was born. Your sister is a very troubled soul,' she admitted, letting go of her daughter's hand.

She rubbed the tips of her fingers across her forehead, feeling as if there were more lines there than there should be for a woman of her age. She was fifty-eight, young these days, she reminded herself as she tried to ignore the ravages of time, though there were moments when she felt she had lived her life several times over with the troubles that had been dropped on her doorstep. Caressing the lines of age and worry, she asked silently if it had really only been hours since she had buried her husband. Her head throbbed and right now all she wanted was to lie down, close her eyes and try and forget all the pain. But, as if to torment her and deprive her of a moment to grieve, her mind stumbled down memory lane, tripping from one crisis to another as if it needed to pick through the murky waters of the past few years. *Oh Terry, why did you have to leave me?* She silently sobbed, feeling the force of his absence and wondering how she was going to cope without him.

'The word *troubled* barely scratches the surface,' Barbara suddenly found herself saying, as if the words had manifested themselves as she mentally sifted through the pieces of a jigsaw which, no matter how many times she tried, would simply not slot together.

Nicola was more than troubled and all the counselling she'd had appeared to have done no good at all. Her heart ached as she recalled Nicola's first session. It had been after the nightmare time they'd had with her. She had been just fifteenth. Who would have believed a young girl who had been surrounded by love, caring parents, and a sister who worshipped her, would ever need professional help? She sighed deeply at the memory of those times because whilst Nicola's contemporaries talked about clothes, the latest crush, which boy band they should be screaming over or the possibility of university one day, Nicola sulked and rebelled against it all. A happy young girl had slowly turned into a pouting, moody young woman. By fourteen she had tried drugs and alcohol and, as if that wasn't enough, she had ventured into sex. The consequences of that foray had been devastating.

Barbara felt more tears rolling down her cheeks. What had she done wrong? And more disturbing, what had she missed? The memories of those harrowing times still had the effect to make her feel sick; not physically sick these days, but mentally ill. As angry and hurt as she was, she was also broken, because she had failed her daughter.

'Are you all right?' Becky asked, reaching over and placing her hand on her mother's arm.

Barbara took in the concern etched on her daughter's face. 'As right as I can ever be on such a day, my love,' she said, looking at Becky and seeing a successful woman, one she was very proud of. *I must have done something right*, she reminded herself, in an attempt to soothe the pain in her heart. 'As much as I fume over your sister, I still worry about her. She might be a mother, but her behaviour is still questionable. There are times when I wonder if she'll ever behave like a responsible woman. Today was an example of how quickly she can blow between hot and cold. I know she has lost her father, but...'

Her words trailed off as she thought about how Terry had quietly worried about Nicola and far too often found he could no more reach her than his wife could. It didn't matter how many roads he had travelled down to try to find a way back to her, he was always faced with a dead end. Barbara sighed, 'I'd like to think she is grieving in some way, but if her display today was of grief, then...'

She trailed off again. She had been down that path so many times, trying to understand what was going on in Nicola's head, and had failed. What she should be doing was grieving for the man she had loved beyond words; the same wonderful man with whom she had conceived twice. And now she had lost him. Her heart skipped as she felt that somewhere along the way she had lost her eldest daughter too.

Over the years, the distance between them had fluctuated. At times, Nicola had needed her. At others she had treated her mother like a stranger. She knew there were occasions when Nicola saw her as interfering, domineering and opinionated, but when she was needed, she was expected to pick up the mess of whatever Nicola had embroiled herself in, dust her down and get her back on her feet. There had been times when Barbara had felt the pressing urge to wash her hands of her eldest once and for all, but instead, in fear of saying or doing something she would later regret, she had distanced herself. She had thought it would help, giving the cracks in their

41

relationship a chance to heal, if only for a short time. It didn't.

Today, despite what she had said to Nicola about her father's funeral not being about her, it *had* turned out to be about her. Here she was, her thoughts ploughing through the detritus of her daughter's life in the knowledge that the years of pain and humiliation had added to the strain Terry had had to shoulder. And try as she might, it was impossible not to lay some of the blame for his death at her daughter's feet. Nicola's conduct of the last few years had slowly chipped away at them both, until the final nail had been hammered home into his coffin.

There had been pain and shocks that they'd had to come to terms with, but there was one incident that ranked as one of the worst nightmares any parent would have to deal with. Looking back, she understood that had it not been for Bob, they probably would never have got through it. He had been there for Terry, taking him out for a drink and talking man to man with him. And, of course, stepping in to mind the house and the girls when everything had all become too much. Even today he was there and had been a pillar of strength, despite his own disability.

'Whatever did I do wrong?' she asked Becky, the pain in her head reaching crescendo heights.

'I don't think you did anything wrong, Mum,' Becky said, wrapping her arms around Barbara's shoulders. 'Come on, let's go and sit down,' she insisted, steering her through to the conservatory.

The sun was setting and shadows from the tall pine trees in the garden created a sombre atmosphere in the large, domed glass room. 'Sit down, Mum, and I'll make us both a cup of tea. Or would you prefer something a little stronger?'

'A very large brandy would be best, I think,' Barbara said wearily, perching on a cane chair with soft, pastel cushions. 'If it hadn't been for you and Uncle Bob, I'm not sure I'd have got through the day,' she added, as Becky flicked on a tall lamp, which immediately lifted the gloom from the room.

Settling back into the chair, Barbara was aware the day had taken its toll on her body and the sting of tears reminded her how close to the surface her emotions were. She wiped at her eyes with the back of her hand, her tissue now scrunched up and soaking. No matter which way she viewed it, she had failed Terry because he was no longer here. She had failed Nicola, but then Nicola had failed them too, and on top of all of this, she had even failed at being a grandmother. As she let these thoughts torment her, she recalled how Nicola's children had been perfectly well behaved today. How they were not affected by Nicola's unstable mind, she had no idea. Perhaps now she should find a way to be a supportive grandmother? Though it would be a long time before a sustainable bridge could be built between her and Nicola. As for the latest man in Nicola's life, she had little knowledge of him other than the fact he was a widow with a young boy. It appeared he had patience and time for the children and from what she had witnessed they were comfortable in his company. At least he had been polite and civilised when he had spoken to her, and he had turned up smartly and respectfully dressed. Thankfully, he had taken Nicola in hand and had whisked her out of the hall before she had collapsed on the floor, the two girls following behind as if it was the most natural thing in the world to witness their mother three sheets to the wind.

'Here you are,' Becky said, placing a large brandy balloon, indecently filled, into Barbara's hand. 'Sip this. It'll help. I'm staying tonight, so I'm having one too,' Becky added, relaxing in the chair next to her mother. Reaching over, she clinked her glass with Barbara's. 'To Dad,' she offered up, 'the very best anyone could have.'

'To Terry, the best husband and father,' Barbara added, her voice faltering.

A silence filled the conservatory as mother and daughter gazed into their cognac before sipping the fiery liquid. Over the top of her glass, Barbara took in her daughter and didn't miss the tear that slipped down Becky's face.

'Come here, love,' she said, her arms outstretched. Nodding, Becky placed her glass on the low table and moved over to her mother, who wrapped her arms around her. 'He loved us all so much, even Nic, after all she had done,' Barbara whispered, breathing in the fragrance of lilies from Becky's hair, 'but there's a lot you don't know.'

Becky gently pulled away. Wiping at her tears with the tips of her fingers, she looked down at her mother with an unspoken question.

'We tried to keep as much of the anguish from you as we could,' Barbara said, biting her bottom lip in an attempt to control her voice. 'The drug carry on when she was thirteen we had put behind us, but when we found out she was pregnant, it almost killed your father.'

'Pregnant?' Becky perched on the edge of her chair, her eyes wide. 'When?'

'When she was fourteen. She was still a child and there she was expecting a child herself.' Barbara took another gulp of her brandy and as it burned the back of her throat she grimaced, aware that the shock of that day still had the power to send a shiver down her spine. 'The day I learned Nicola was pregnant was the day the school rang to ask if we would go to see them to discuss something. I thought it was to do with her retail project. One morning I saw her in the shopping centre, she didn't see me and for reasons I still don't understand, I scooted into a shop and hid. Over the coming weeks I saw her several times there. I asked her what she was doing instead of being in school and she told me it was something to do with a retail project. I wanted to believe her, I wanted to believe she was doing something worthwhile at school and so I let it drop. At the same time her moodiness was getting me down. I approached her and tried to talk to her about what was making her so unhappy. It was obvious she had lost weight and that bothered me, and so I made an appointment at the doctors in the hope he could offer some medication for the mood swings, but Nicola refused to go. Then, to our surprise, she began to behave like the normal daughter she used to be. She even started eating what I put in front of her. So when the school asked to see us, I could only think it was to do with her project. Unfortunately, that day your dad was unable to go so I went on my own. The head teacher told me more or less what we already knew, that Nicola was moody and at times disruptive. But that wasn't all she told me.'

Barbara placed her glass to her lips and swallowed the remainder of her cognac, knowing no amount of alcohol would dim the shock of that visit which now replayed in her mind.

'Thank you, Mrs Knight, for coming,' Mrs Hargreaves, the head teacher said, as she held the door open to her office and beckoned Barbara to enter. 'Please take a seat,' she offered, a chubby hand pointing to a straight-backed chair. Closing the door with a soft click, Mrs Hargreaves strode to the other side of the desk, cluttered with papers and exercise books, and lowered her large bulk into her brown leather swivel chair.

Keeping her questioning gaze on the head teacher, Barbara clutched her handbag to her chest and perched on the edge of the chair she had been instructed to take. 'I assume you want to talk about the retail project?' she said nervously. Even as a mother of two, she still felt intimidated at being summoned to the head teacher's office. Did you ever grow out of that feeling, she wondered.

'Project?' Mrs Hargreaves said, surprised, her eyebrows arching. Shaking her head as if confused, she continued. 'Nicola is not assigned to a project. No, Mrs Knight, I fear what I have to talk to you about is a little delicate,' she said, her double chin wobbling as she spoke.

Not missing the grave tone in her voice, Barbara felt the hairs on the back of her arms stand on end and wished

Terry was by her side. Fiddling with the strap on her bag, her mind raced with what Nicola could have been up to and she tried not to think the worst. After all, the school was still standing, as the fact that she was sitting in one of the rooms proved, so there had been no fire. Though to her knowledge, her errant daughter had not played with matches... yet. Not wanting to go down the route of drugs, Barbara prayed fervently that Nicola had not been caught taking them. She had promised, crossing her heart, that it would never happen again and to Barbara's knowledge, her daughter never lied. So what could be so terrible that the head teacher had summoned her today? It then struck her that if there was no project, and she had seen Nicola at the shopping centre on numerous occasions, that she had obviously been skiving when she should have been in class. Barbara's spirits plummeted and, with a sinking feeling, she repeated, 'Delicate?' At the same time a flush crept up her neck and her heart rate increased to such a pitch, she was convinced Mrs Hargreaves could hear it beating above the background noise of the school.

'Mrs Knight, does Nicola have a boyfriend?'

Stunned by the question, she snapped, 'Goodness no, she's only fourteen.'

'You are sure?' the head teacher asked, creases appearing on her forehead, making her half-moon reading glasses slip down her nose.

'Of course!' Barbara replied, shuffling almost off the chair. 'Nicola has had a few problems of late, but thankfully boys have not been one of them. She has so far shown no interest in boys. I can tell you that, Mrs Hargreaves.' Nerves had not stopped her tongue as she gabbled on. 'I'm relieved on that score as they grow up far too quickly these days,' she gushed, eager to stop any thoughts that her daughter was up to no good, but she wondered what it had to do with the school if Nicola *did* have an eye on a boy.

'You are absolutely certain?'

'What is this?' Barbara bristled. 'We both know Nicola can be difficult, but I thought you called me in to discuss Nicola's work, because if not, I don't understand why I'm here.'

'So you are not aware of anyone Nicola might be seeing secretly?' Mrs Hargreaves pushed, peering over the half lenses of her steel-framed spectacles.

Barbara wondered if people in authority glared at you over their glasses to intimidate. If so, it was having an effect as she was perspiring and about to lose control. Taking a deep breath, she tried to ignore it.

'Secretly!' Barbara exclaimed. 'We are a happy and open family,' she said, knowing that on both counts it was not strictly true. These days they were divided; Nicola seemingly against the rest of the family and at times, the world, as her moods swung. Trying to reach her these last couple of years had been difficult and there were occasions she'd have had more luck trying to hug the moon than get close to her daughter. More than aware they were difficult times, she tried to reassure herself they were no different to other families with teenage girls. As for secrets, she didn't believe there were secrets; not ones that a head teacher would know or need to talk to her about. With a feeling that the school was crossing the line in its suggestion of Nicola being with boys, Barbara added dryly, 'It seems to me you have something to say and I suggest you spit it out rather than keep asking me questions. I take it that's why I've been summoned here.' Despite her burst of bravado, an uneasy feeling settled in the pit of her stomach at the scorching look Mrs Hargreaves shot her.

'I'm sorry if you think this is a summons, but you see, what I am going to say will be upsetting. I believe Nicola may be pregnant,' the head teacher said, her voice soft, almost a whisper and dripping with regret.

Barbara gasped at the implication and emitted a noise that sounded like a strangled cry. For a moment she thought she had misheard. 'What are you talking about?

That is *not* possible. Where on earth did you get such an idea?' she cried, her voice now filled with disbelief and disgust. 'As I said, she's only fourteen and a long way from getting involved with boys. No, you are very much mistaken,' Barbara said, as shock turned to anger. Pushing at the chair with the back of her legs, she stumbled to her feet.

'Mrs Knight, please sit down,' the head teacher begged, her hand raised and her palm facing Barbara, indicating for her to stay.

With an urge to flee, yet needing to put this woman right, Barbara felt her legs buckle and reluctantly dropped onto her chair. 'What you're saying is ridiculous. Whatever makes you suggest such a thing?'

'I do hope I am very wrong, but you see I have been reliably told that Nicola was in the toilets vomiting when one of her class mates walked in. It appears that Nicola panicked at being seen, grabbed her school bag and clutching a handful of toilet paper pushed against her mouth, she hurried to the door. Before she could reach the door, the contents of her bag spilled onto the floor and amongst the items was a pregnancy test. The other girl, in an attempt to help, tried to gather up Nicola's things and saw the test, but before she could speak, Nicola snatched it out of her hand, telling her to mind her own business.' Mrs Hargreaves paused long enough for Barbara to absorb what she had said, then continued. 'The class mate, who I shall keep nameless, came to me because she had no idea what to do and was deeply worried about her.'

'But...' stammered Barbara, trying to take in what she had heard.

'I didn't want to alarm you and so I asked Nicola to come to my office,' Mrs Hargreaves cut in. 'She looked very pale and it was clear something was far from right so I didn't beat about the bush and asked her outright about the vomiting and the test kit in her bag. With her head bowed, she simply shrugged her shoulders.'

'That's hardly surprising, you probably scared the life out of her because it wasn't anything to do with her!' Barbara snapped, anxious to get out of the office, go home and speak to her daughter, because this teacher was barking up the wrong tree. Nicola had problems but this was going too far.

'If you would be kind enough to let me continue,' Mrs Hargreaves said, her voice modulating to reflect the situation.

Aghast, but remaining silent, Barbara glared at her.

'I asked if it was a test for her and she simply nodded. Was it positive, I enquired, and again she nodded. From this I continued with more questions, but none elicited an answer. I could see she was in shock and I put my arms around her and asked if someone had done anything to her she hadn't wanted them to. She shook her head. I also asked about a boyfriend and like all the other questions, Nicola refused to answer. I am sorry, Mrs Knight, I called you in to the school not to be judgemental, but as a responsible teacher. I felt it was my duty to inform you. I believe Nicola is in shock. You can rest assured I have spoken to no one other than Nicola. As for the other pupil, she has given me her word that she will remain silent, though that I cannot guarantee. I am very sorry, but please understand that I am here if I can do anything for Nicola and your family.'

The sound of Becky's gasp brought Barbara out of her reverie. Rolling the empty bourbon glass between her hands, she couldn't remember leaving the head teacher's office or driving home that day. The days that followed were a blur. Now, as she looked at Becky, she saw the tiredness of earlier that had dimmed the sparkle from her daughter's eyes, along with the sadness and shock of what she had just heard. 'I'd no idea she'd even thought about sex,' Barbara said, 'let alone tried it. To this day, Nicola has never told me who he was. I had my suspicions, but without Nicola sharing what had happened, I could do nothing.'

A silence descended on the room and the only sound that filtered through the hush was the evening song of a sparrow perched in one of the trees in the garden.

The quiet lengthened and Barbara felt Becky's discomfort as if it was tangible. She reached out and took hold of her hand. Clasping it in hers, she could still remember the smell of fear that had emanated from Nicola when she had told her, later that day, that she had been called into the school by the head teacher.

'Are you pregnant?' Barbara asked, without preamble, praying with every fibre of her being that Nicola would have a temper tantrum and scream that she was evil to think such a thing.

'Yes,' Nicola snapped back.

'Oh my God, Nicola,' Barbara cried. Feeling as if the earth had shifted on its axis, she gripped the kitchen table to steady herself. She tried to absorb Nicola's single word reply and wondered how it could have happened and how a teacher knew more about Nicola than she did. 'So Mrs Hargreaves was right. Why didn't you tell me?' Even as she asked the question, she could see a blank look glaze over Nicola's eyes. A look that warned her that the shutters were coming down and her daughter had no intention of answering any more questions. Well, if she thought this was the way to deal with this disaster, she had another thing coming, Barbara silently fumed, and swallowed hard in an attempt to keep the panic down.

'How far are you gone? Who's the father?'

'I don't know,' Nicola retorted, shrugging her shoulders.

'This is important, Nicola. You're fourteen years old! It's illegal to do what you have done. You do understand that, don't you?'

'I'm nearly fifteen,' Nicola said, her head bowed as if she were studying the pattern of the floor tiles.

'What, so you think that will make a difference?' Barbara snapped, and a wave of emotion swept over her. She wasn't sure if she wanted to wrap her arms around Nicola and hug her tight or shake the answers out of her.

Describing this scene to Becky, she ended, 'All I could think of was how I was going to tell your father,' she said, nursing her empty glass.

'I think we need a refill,' Becky whispered, as if the power of her voice had deserted her. Getting up from her chair, she placed a hand on her mother's shoulder.

'Thanks,' Barbara said, her voice strained. She watched as Becky padded, in an old pair of her slippers, across the cool, tiled floor through to the kitchen.

'Here,' Becky said, moments later, clutching the bottle of brandy. She pulled the stopper out and poured a generous amount into Barbara's glass, then sloshed a large brandy into her own.

'You're shocked and I understand,' Barbara said, her reflection staring back at her through the conservatory window as darkness fell. 'I was numb with what I'd just learnt and all your sister could do was shrug her shoulders. It was as if she'd been caught smoking in the school toilets rather than being found pregnant. It was then I decided not to tell your dad. I thought if I could deal with it myself then he'd never need to know. I didn't want him to know, in case it changed things between them. I'm still not sure who I was trying to protect, him or Nicola, but I felt I needed to keep it contained. I told Nicola it would be our secret and we would never say anything to anyone, it would be between us. It was then she started to cry, slow tears at first and then racking sobs. I scooped her in my arms and hugged her tight. All she kept saying was that she was sorry. I told her not to worry and that it would help if I knew who the father was, but no amount of asking would loosen her tongue. Of course, I drew my own conclusion, knowing how Nicola had been friendly with that Nat Weston, but she denied it was him. I didn't believe her, but I said nothing. Instead, I spent the coming days visiting a private clinic to organise an ...'

'Mum, no!' Becky cried, as the word teetered on Barbara's lips.

She shot a look at her daughter. 'What choice did we have? Nicola was four months pregnant and only fourteen! How could she bring a child up? She was a child herself. I was protecting her and saving your dad from knowing. And on top of all of that, I had no idea who the father was. Apart from that moment of emotion, Nicola had little to say, she just crawled back into her shell. The day I took her to the clinic, she looked so young and vulnerable. All I wanted to do was find the person who had done this to my little girl and harm them badly enough so that they'd never father another child, but Nicola maintained a wall of silence on who he was, so there was nothing I could do. At the clinic, the procedure was classified as simple and safe.

'We arrived at nine in the morning and left at three thirty, but three days later Nicola was taken to emergency, she was bleeding heavily. Thankfully, it was dealt with quickly and with no consequences for the future, but of course by then I had to tell your dad. I won't go into details as to how he reacted, but it was the start of a distance that would grow between the two of them. After that terrible time when I wondered if I'd lose her, Nicola not only returned to being moody, but seemed to be set on a path of self-destruction. To our horror, she started to self-harm and that's when the regular trips to casualty began and her first session of counselling started. I'd do anything to turn the clock back to see if I could have done something different that would have changed the course of her life.'

With tears rolling down her face, Becky stared at her mother. 'Poor Nic.'

Chapter Eight

Still sitting on the tiled floor in the en-suite, Nicola had not moved for the last twenty minutes. No matter how tightly she closed her eyes or hugged her knees, she couldn't stop the past from playing over and over in her mind. It was as if the play button had stuck and the events that had shaped or ruined her life were there in glorious 3D. The bruise, which was the beginning of what was to change her life forever, had been in a secret and private place and yet on the sleepover at Claire and Sarah's, to her horror, Auntie Jenny had spotted it.

'Come on girls you should be in bed,' Jenny said as she breezed into the bedroom just as Nicola and Sarah slipped into their nighties. 'What's that?' she cried pointing at the multi-coloured mark at the top of Nicola's leg. 'It looks painful.'

Embarrassed, Nicola pulled her nightie down frightened Auntie Jenny would guess how it had got there. Thinking quickly, she replied, 'I hurt myself in PE.' She knew Auntie Jenny's attention span was less than a nano-second, the woman was permanently in a spin and everything was carried out as if there were only ten seconds left to live.

'I see, well into bed, the pair of you,' Jenny said, pulling back the duvet, 'It's gone midnight, blimey, the owls will be going to bed before you at this rate.'

Nicola shuffled into bed and pulled the duvet over her and as Claire slipped in beside her, she wondered how her friend lived in such chaos. It was a crazy house. Auntie Jenny behaved like someone on medication, or something equally as mind blowing, but even so, she had spotted the bruise and Nicola was so worried she found it hard to get to sleep.

The following morning, she had found herself checking the bruise. She had no idea how to hide it, but a few days later it had disappeared.

She would never forget that bruise as long as she lived. Of course, Auntie Jenny had not forgotten about it, but thankfully, her mother had been too preoccupied and had only casually asked about it. At the time Nicola had been grateful for the distraction of the Wendy House. It would be the only time in her life that she would be and looking back as an adult, the irony of that did not escape her. Of course, back then her mother had still been caring and loving and she and Becky were given equal affection. The bombshells that would change their lives had yet to be dropped and she had yet to commit the many heinous crimes that would further rock the lives of the Knight household. If she could have changed the events that were to shape their lives, she would have, but she could no more stop them than she could hold still a wild animal. She had lied so easily about the bruise; the words had tumbled out of her mouth as coherently as if it were the truth. Yet despite the lie that had formed so readily on her lips, deep down she had wanted to tell her mother how she had got the bruise. And just like always, fear had silenced her; afraid she would be seen as the one who had encouraged *him*.

As images of the Wendy House flashed before her, Nicola's mind reeled with the events that were to start a catalogue of actions that would ruin her forever. She stifled a sob at what had happened in that pretty little cabin. All her dreams for when she grew up had been blown away; not so much gone with the wind, but blasted out of the universe. Going to University and travelling, even being a normal teenager, had been taken from her. There was not a day that passed when she wished she had been able to stop it and seek help. Even now, she was just as paralysed by the fear of what had happened and the consequences of revealing it. In a perverse way, she knew she must have encouraged him, though how she had done so she had no idea, apart from being a girl and liking an actor on the television who looked a bit like him. Oddly, all the television programmes and articles in magazines and newspapers designed to encourage young people who suffered abuse to seek help, were all very commendable, but those who made the programmes and wrote the articles had no idea how paralysing fear was. Pain she could deal with, but fear had silenced her then and still did.

Chewing on her bottom lip, the cold of the en-suite tiles seeping into her bones, Nicola wished her mind would still, because just thinking about what he did brought fresh waves of shame and loathing. Huge, heavy tears of self-pity spilled down her face, splashing onto her bare legs. She swiped the back of her hand over her running nose before flicking at the wet patches that pooled on the floor. Through misty eyes she stared down at her legs which, unlike her arms, held no scars. The many bruises that had regularly covered the tops of her legs had long since faded and disappeared, though that first one would forever be etched in her mind as the day she lost not only her innocence, but the ability to feel normal again. To her it was the deepest scar of all.

Pulling several sheets off the toilet roll, Nicola wiped at her face. She tried to push away the dark times at what had happened after they had been given the Wendy House and instead forced herself to concentrate on the laughter and love of that happy day. It was the last day of true happiness she could remember.

The weather had been perfect. The sky azure blue and cloudless and a hot sun beat down on them. Back then, they were a united and happy family. The work that had gone into the Wendy House, both in its construction and secrecy, had added to the excitement. She remembered how her dad had insisted on relaying how it had all been achieved without Becky or her knowing.

'You have no idea how we schemed to make sure you had no idea, though it was tough at times when you, Becks,' Terry bent down and wrapped his arm around his daughter, 'kept nagging wanting a Wendy House like your friends, but we got there in the end.'

'It is so much better than everyone else's and I love it Dad,' Becky said excited, clapping her hands as she stared at the wooden structure.

'What about you Nic?' Terry asked.

'It's amazing,' Nicola said, feeding off Becky's excitement, 'I love it too and I can't wait to have sleepovers in there. Just perfect.'

'Sleepovers, parties. It's space for you girls to enjoy with each other and your friends,' Terry said, and Nicola could already picture the long summer days and nights staying in the Wendy House even if Becks had to share it with her.

'What you don't know is that this wonderful surprise has all been down to both your dad and Uncle Bob,' Barbara said, her voice filled with pride as her gaze swept between Nicola and Becky. 'They've spent weeks designing, planning and building it just for you two.'

The realisation that Uncle Bob had been involved hit Nicola like a flying rock and she stumbled back. For a moment it felt as if the rug had been pulled from under her feet. The bubble of happiness she had basked in, not so much burst as exploded. The image of him touching her flashed into her mind and at the same time a dark shadow draped itself over her. *Why did he have to be involved?* she cried in silence.

'Believe you me girls, had it not been for Uncle Bob you might not be staring at a finished house,' Barbara said, turning to Terry.

'Yes, it was a joint effort,' Terry added, 'but I'll concede he's the skilled one with the hammer and saw.' He held up his hand to show off the scars. 'Me and the tools kept falling out with each other,' he said, chuckling.

Nicola glanced at her dad's hand and saw the redness from the wounds and thought about her own scar: the bruise. As if the sun had disappeared behind a cloud, the joy of the day evaporated as her father continued to enthuse about his best friend's abilities, and as he spoke, Nicola wondered what he would think about Uncle Bob's other handiwork.

'So, as we all love it, then we will have our first picnic in the Wendy House,' Barbara said, breaking into Nicola's thoughts. 'We've all those muffins and a pile of sandwiches to eat.'

'That's yummy,' squealed Becky, rushing into the Wendy House as if it was the most important thing to do.

'You've gone quiet all of sudden,' Barbara said, turning to Nicola, 'feeling a bit too grown up for a Wendy House?'

'No, just thinking, Mum.'

'If you like you can have your tenth birthday party in there. Would you like that?'

Nicola forced a smiled at the idea and tried to push away the thoughts of what Uncle Bob had said about "next time". So far there hadn't been one and hopefully he had forgotten about it. She just wished she could.

'Come on,' Terry called, gripping his video camera, 'I'm going to record our day.'

Terry filmed every action. 'Don't you think you've filmed enough? Barbara said, sighing. 'Anyone would think we're visiting a National Trust Hall!'

'You might mock, my love, but we'll look back on this day and remember the fun we had. And, who knows, one day we might get to show our grandchildren,' Terry said, smirking, 'though what they'll make of Becks running round like a lunatic, heaven only knows,' he added, laughing as he pointed the camera at Barbara. 'Final smile and then I'll stop. You too, Nic, I promise it really is the last. Go on give your dad a cheesy grin, you'll regret it if you don't when we replay it in the future.' Nicola pulled a face which she hoped was a good enough smile and crossed her fingers that her dad was right and they would look back with happiness.

Now, as she crushed the toilet paper in her cold, damp hand all she could think of was how clever Uncle Bob had been and try as she might, she could not blank her mind to stop the memories coming...

Chapter Nine

'Becks is soundo,' Bob said triumphantly as he strode into the lounge, a smile filling his face and his steely grey eyes staring straight at her. A shiver ran down Nicola's spine as she coiled her bare legs under her and pulled at her skirt to cover her knees. And although it had been over a week since the happy day of the Wendy House surprise, it still saddened her that he had been involved. Thankfully, he had not been to the house in that time, which was unusual; something about him having to go away on a course. She didn't care why he was away, just relieved. Her cheeks grew hot with embarrassment at the memory of the last time he had babysat. Even her dreams were filled with him touching her and as much as what had happened frightened her, she had kept her promise and said nothing to anyone. She had even stopped watching the programme with the doctor and nurses.

'Sleeping like a baby,' Bob added, as he dropped into the armchair nearest the television. 'What about you giving me a grand tour of the Wendy House? He leant forward and gazed at her as he rested his elbows on his knees.

Feeling his eyes roving over her, Nicola swallowed down a lump of apprehension and tried not to look at him. The last thing she wanted was to behave in a way that would encourage him to do something else to her.

'What's the matter with you?' Bob asked, irritation creeping into his voice, making her jump as he patted the arm of the chair he sat in.

Not moving, Nicola picked at the skin around her fingernails. Her index finger was already sore from days of worrying it, yet she could not help picking at the skin until it bled. She licked at the droplet of blood that oozed out.

'I only asked if you'd give me a VIP tour, I thought we were friends?' he said, reaching over to her and then, as if changing his mind, withdrew his hand. 'I'm not going to hurt you, why would I want to do that? You must know it was me and your dad who made the Wendy House, right?'

Keeping her gaze on her bleeding finger, Nicola nodded. 'I know, thank you,' she said. 'I think it's best if I go to bed,' she added, casting a surreptitious glance at the door that led through to the hall and seeing an opportunity to escape.

'I couldn't agree more, you look bushed. I won't stop you, though I would still love it if you and me could go and admire the Wendy House first.'

'You've already seen it when you were building it,' Nicola said in a petulant voice, this time lifting her head just enough to sneak a glance at him.

Bob nodded in agreement. 'That's true. I just thought we could have a little celebration, just you and me. I've brought two Turkish Delights and a bottle of coke knowing you love these.' He smiled at her and, as wrong as it seemed, her mouth automatically smiled back.

'That's better,' he said, a grin filling his face. 'Then I'll have a beer and no, before you ask, you can't have any this time.' He emphasised the last words as he raised his right eyebrow.

Nicola blushed further at the memory.

Ignoring her flushed face, Bob leaned over the side of the chair and lifted a white plastic carrier bag from the floor. 'Here, this is for you,' he said, holding the bag in front of her.

Nicola hesitated and saw the smile he had flashed when he had first babysat all those months earlier, the one that said, *"You're safe with me."* She took a deep breath and realised she was being silly; Uncle Bob only wanted to be friendly and kind. 'Thank you,' she said and reaching over took hold of the bag. Gripping it, she swung her legs down and dropping it onto her lap, peered inside at the bars of chocolate and can of drink. For the first time since the night of the bruise, she began to believe she had been worrying needlessly. Maybe she had imagined what had happened, after all, the beer had made her head feel fuzzy and she had felt strange. And, just now he had mentioned only the beer, he had said nothing else about touching her. 'Thank you,' she repeated sheepishly and was grateful he couldn't read her mind. For the first time since he had arrived, she felt safe; the fear she had worried about was all in her imagination. Relaxing, Nicola pulled out one of the Turkish Delights.

'I know what you like, Miss Knight, so come on. I'll get a beer from the fridge and we'll have a picnic in The Wendy House. What do you say?'

Nicola remembered that day along with all the others. She had eaten both Turkish Delights and Uncle Bob had clinked his beer can against her bottle of coke. Afterwards she had felt sick, but thankfully she hadn't been. And just as he had promised, they had just had a picnic. Once the food and drink was consumed, he had taken hold of her hand and they had walked along the garden path, gone back into the house and watched a film. In the weeks that followed, this had happened every time he came to babysit, until at last her fear and anxiety had begun to fade.

Her tenth birthday had been the best day ever. The party had been amazing. She had been allowed to invite up to twenty friends and if that hadn't been great enough, her parents had organised a disco and strung lights around the Wendy House and garden. There had been a sleepover with six girls. Even crazy Auntie Jenny had been there, behaving in her uniquely manic way, helping her mother with the food and making her friends giggle.

Nicola remembered how she had loved the Wendy House on that day.

Then everything changed...

Chapter Ten

'I've bought Hawaiian pizza,' Bob called, as he pushed the front door closed, the whiff of oregano and cheese drifting in with him. 'I know how much you like this one,' he added, glancing up the stairs. He grinned and headed for the kitchen. Dropping the bag on the table, he pulled the pizza box out and placed it next to the bag.

Hearing Bob's voice, Nicola closed the bedtime story book she was reading to Becky. Laying it down on the bedside cabinet, she dimmed the bedside lamp and got to her feet. With only three years between them, there were times when Nicola felt much older than her sister. Unlike Becky she had outgrown reading fairy stories and playing with dolls. She leaned across the pink Barbie duvet and brushing her fingers through Becky's soft curls, placed a gentle kiss on her cheek. 'Night-night Becks, sleep tight, don't let the bugs bite,' she whispered. Standing up, she heard a soft sigh escape from her sister's lips and knew Becky was drifting into sleep.

Nicola adored her little sister and would do anything to protect her. She had never forgotten the day her mother brought Becky home from the hospital. Excited and nervous, she had sat on the sofa, her back hard against a bank of brightly coloured cushions. Her arms extended, the sleeves of her Aran jumper rolled up, she had held her breath as her mother had carefully placed baby Becky, wrapped in a shawl, into her arms. From that moment she had loved her sister. 'Night-night,' she said again in a whisper.

As Becky slipped into slumber, Nicola turned and, on tiptoes, crossed the laminate floor. Slipping through the half open door, she ran down the carpeted stairs, the mouth-watering aroma of pizza filling her nostrils. Skipping down the hall to the kitchen, it was the first time in weeks she didn't have the flutter of butterflies in her tummy or the feeling of sickness about what had happened that night weeks ago with Uncle Bob. Even her frightening dreams had lessened, to the point that some nights she slept through without them disturbing her. She giggled with glee, knowing her and Uncle Bob were friends again. He always brought her a special treat, joking to her that it was a silence present. 'If your parents had any idea what we ate when they went out, they'd have a fit; that's why it's our secret,' he would say as he unloaded the night's goodies. She loved the secrecy and loved the treats and, even though she'd not like to think it, she did enjoy being treated like she wasn't a child.

With these happy thoughts, Nicola burst into the kitchen.

'Ah! There you are,' Bob said, 'I was beginning to think you'd left home,' as he spoke, he pulled out a couple of cans of shandy. 'These are for you. I thought we needed to do something a little special to celebrate your big birthday. Ten!' He shook his head as if in disbelief. 'I can't believe you're growing up so fast,' he said, dropping the cans down on the table next to the pizza box.

'Ten is so grown up these days,' Nicola said picking up one of the cans. 'Dad made shandy for my party, but it was more lemonade than beer,' she added, reading the label.

'Sorry I couldn't make your party, Nic, but I had to work late, that's why we're celebrating tonight,' Bob said watching Nicola twist the can round in her hands.

'No worries,' she said, further scrutinizing her drink, 'These look like real ones,' she added with satisfaction, poised to pull the tab.

'Hang on,' Bob said, reaching out and taking it from her. 'I thought we'd go down to the Wendy House, like we usually do. That way it'll keep the smells of our booty out of the kitchen.'

Nicola giggled at their little plot. Since the Wendy House had been installed, every time Uncle Bob babysat they would go down there and have a little picnic. It was one of the reasons she loved the Wendy House.

'What about Becks?' she asked, watching as he dropped the two cans inside the carrier bag before picking it up.

'What about her? I take it she's asleep or you'd still be up there reading to her,' he said. 'She'll be fine, isn't she always? Anyway, we won't be long. Come on,' he said, picking up the pizza box and holding out his hand to take hers.

'I guess so,' Nicola said, taking hold of Bob's hand, then hesitating, she turned and listened. Hearing nothing but the wall clock ticking, she said, 'Okay, let's go.' As they walked out into the garden, she felt his fingers tighten round her hand.

Leaving Bob to cut the pizza into slices, Nicola wandered over to the window and looked out at the daisies that had been planted in the painted window boxes. Straight away she saw the troughs had small puddles of water laying on the surfaces and she tutted. Her sister had almost drowned the little flowers with her constant watering.

'What are you tutting at?' Bob asked, brandishing a small knife in his hand.

'Nothing,' Nicola replied, pulling herself away from the window and dragging her feet before sinking down on the sofa.

'Here, get your laughing gear round that,' Bob said, holding out the box lid containing three pieces of pizza. Nicola took hold of the box and Bob reached back to the surface top and picked up a can of shandy. He pulled the ring, it hissed loudly, the gassy liquid spilling over the top. 'Take this too,' he added.

'Wow, thanks.' Nicola said, placing the cardboard lid on her knees and the can next to her feet.

Bob pulled the ring on a beer and leant against the little breakfast bar. He watched Nicola bite into a slice of pizza. Raising his beer can, he called out, 'Cheers and happy birthday.'

Her mouth stuffed with pizza, Nicola bent to retrieve her drink. Raising her arm, she reached over and tapped her can against his. 'Cheers,' she mumbled, licking the cheesy tomato from her lips. Placing the can to her mouth she took a large gulp, then choked as the gassy liquid went down the wrong way.

'Like beer, you're supposed to sip it, not guzzle it down!' Bob laughed and in between spluttering, Nicola giggled back.

'It's just a bit fizzy,' she said, sniggering as she placed the can back down on the floor. 'This is delicious,' she added, biting into another slice.

'I'm glad you're enjoying it,' Bob said and picked up a slice from his half of the box. As he ate, he kept his eyes feasted on Nicola. Neither spoke for several moments, the only sound was their soft chewing.

'I can see you didn't enjoy that,' he smirked, reaching forward and taking the empty lid from Nicola's knee. He tossed the cardboard onto the surface top. Clasping a can of beer, he stepped forward and sat down next to her.

'Ten! I'm still trying to get my head around it,' he said, placing his arm across the back of the sofa.

Nicola looked up into Bob's face, but not before she felt the soft touch of his other hand on her thigh. A piece of pizza suddenly rose back up into her mouth, threatening to choke her. Nervously she swallowed it. As the morsel of food slithered back down to her stomach, the feeling of happiness she had felt only moments earlier turned to panic. The butterflies of weeks earlier she had thought had flown away, started to stir and flutter around in her tummy. She didn't want to think that Uncle Bob would touch her again, especially as she had more or less convinced herself he had not really done anything like she had imagined. She tried to breathe properly, telling herself not to be silly. Had they not had several picnics in the Wendy House without anything happening?

'Well?' he asked gently and this time he moved his arm from the back of the sofa and curling it around her shoulder, Bob pulled her close to him. His short-sleeved polo shirt enabled her to feel his bare arm through her top. From the corner of her eye she saw it was peppered with light-coloured hair. She wriggled in an attempt to reduce his hold on her, but his grip tightened at her movement. She could smell his aftershave, the same fragrance he had worn on *that* night. It had a lemony smell. Why hadn't she noticed it before?

'Ten! I still can't believe you're so grown up,' he repeated staring down at her, making her heart beat faster with worry. 'What do you want to be when you are fully grown up?' he asked, slowly moving his hand to the hem of her white skirt before pushing his fingers underneath and moving them up her leg.

She grabbed at his hand, 'I don't think we should do this,' she said, her breath catching in her throat. She wondered how she had managed to utter a word, because right now she felt she could hardly breathe. Gripping at his hand, she tried to push it away.

'Do what, Nic?' he said, ignoring her attempt to dislodge his hand. 'I'm not going to hurt you, but what I want to do will make you feel really nice and it will be the best birthday present you will ever have.'

Fear trickled through her veins, she couldn't think of anything he wanted to do to her that would be nice because if it was anything like before it would be disgusting. Somehow she needed to stop him. How she could do that, she had no idea, he was so strong. Her hand barely covered the top of his. With all the effort she could muster, her voice hoarse with fear, she said, 'I don't think it will.' As the words trembled from her lips, she felt the prick of tears and wondered how this had happened because she hadn't done anything to suggest that he should touch her. Of course, the last time it had been her fault, but this time she had been very careful. Unsure of how to escape, she tried to shuffle to the edge of the sofa in the hope he would let her go.

'Come on, Nic, I've been kind to you since the last time you sat on my knee. I've waited for you to come to me. I've brought you chocolates, pizzas and I've been very patient even though I know you enjoy teasing me.'

Teasing, she tried to say, but the word lodged in her throat.

'All I want is you to be nice to me and then there'll be more chocolate and anything else you want.'

'No, Uncle Bob, no! I don't want chocolates or anything. Please,' she pleaded, struggling to escape his hold.

'Okay, okay,' he said, releasing his hold on her. 'I'm not a monster. I thought we were friends with our little secret.'

Secret; so he hadn't forgotten what he did to her and she hadn't imagined it.

'You are a special girl to me and I just want to show you how very special you are. Surely it's not too much to ask that I can see just how beautiful you are? Of course if you don't want to be that special girl for me, then I can go and find another special one who might enjoy my presents.'

Nicola held her breath and nodded as if in agreement.

'Maybe I should go and see if Becky has woken up.'

Shock instantly replaced panic, 'No, no, not Becky, please no!'

'Oh, so you haven't lost your voice, I was beginning to think you'd gone mute!'

Raising both hands in the air, he added, 'Okay, calm down. I'm not going to go anywhere near Becky, she's only a child. And of course, I won't make you do something you're not happy about. You're too beautiful for that.'

He smiled at her and Nicola felt a surge of relief. 'Thank you,' she sniffed, tears slipping down her cheeks.

'Hey, no need for this,' Bob said, jumping up and wiping the tear away with his finger. 'Come on, let's clear up and then we can check that Becky is sleeping well or we can sit down here and talk about you growing up.'

On legs that now felt like jelly, Nicola moved over to the surface top where the debris of the pizza sat and tried to breathe evenly. 'There's no need to check on Becks, she's fast asleep,' she reminded him, and from the corner of her eye watched as he moved to her side.

Picking up part of the pizza box, Bob scrunched it up and pushed it into the carrier bag. 'I know she is, but what if your parents were to find out what happened before? Of course, I don't want to tell them. They're my best friends and they'll be very angry to know what kind of girl you're turning out to be.'

Nicola looked towards the door and calculated the distance. It was only a few metres. Could she reach it and run fast enough along the path to the house? Even if she ran and made it, he would follow her and no doubt catch her up. Of course she could lock him out, leave him standing in the garden and then tell her parents why he was outside. Even as these thoughts raced through her head, she knew they would never believe her. All he had to tell them was that he had brought her pizza and what was wrong with that? And she had drunk his beer - there was a lot wrong with that! Right now she felt trapped and afraid.

'Surely they don't need to know,' she mumbled.

'Of course they don't, but it's up to you Nic, you choose?'

Choose? What did he mean?

Chapter Eleven

'I've run you a warm bath,' Bob said, leaning against the bathroom door as Nicola squeezed past him. 'I'll leave you, but remember, this is our secret. You understand? Now have your bath and think of a nice present you'd like and I'll bring it the next time I babysit.'

Staring down at the cream-coloured ceramic-tiled floor, Nicola nodded, she understood fully what he meant.

'Right then, I'll be back up in twenty minutes to see you're tucked up in bed,' he reached over to place a hand on her shoulder, but Nicola stepped back.

'Okay,' Bob said, turning and leaving.

Nicola waited until the sound of his heavy footsteps thundering down the stairs could no longer be heard before she closed the bathroom door and locked it. For the first time in the last hour she felt safe. She stared at the half-filled bath, a thin cloud of steam drifted up from the hot water and she wondered if the water would sting and burn? He had hurt her badly, but as sore as she now was, she felt too numb to believe she would ever feel anything else again. The thought of touching her clothes and her body after he'd handled them added to her revulsion, yet she had to remove them and try to clean herself. It would take more than a half-filled bath of water to make her feel clean. Pulling the cotton top over her head, she dropped it on the floor, then pushed her skirt down. She almost laughed at seeing her slippers, with a sob she kicked them off, then stepped out of her skirt. With just her pants to remove, she wanted to cry out at the injustice of what had happened to her. He had removed the one item that was a private piece of her clothing and then... she closed her eyes at what he had done after that. With her eyes tightly shut, she finally slipped her pants off. Snapping her eyes open, it was then she saw the bright red marks. 'Oh no,' she whispered, panic taking a grip. What if her mother saw the blood? That could not happen and she must hide them until they could be thrown away. Picking the pants up, she screwed them into a ball as if doing this would make them invisible. Dropping them back down, she climbed into the bath and gingerly slithered down in to the water. As the water covered her damaged body, to her horror, she saw the water turn from crystal clear to a ghoulish pink tinge. Tears of despair slipped from her face and splashed into the bath. Uncle Bob had given her a choice, but it was no choice at all.

'So what have you decided?' Bob had asked, 'and if you're thinking of running to your mummy, think again, because I'll tell her it was you. It was you who insisted on drinking beer and sitting on my knee and asking to learn about what grownups do. So go ahead. In the meantime, I'll go and check on Becks.'

'Please leave Becky alone and I never asked about grownups,' a surge of anger washed over her.

'Don't be naïve, I saw the way you looked at me and how eager you were to take your clothes off and sit on my knee.'

'It wasn't like that.'

'Nic, I'm not here to argue and I'm sorry if you're upset, I only wanted to give you my birthday present. Anyway, I'll leave you to tidy away this mess,' he turned and glared at the debris of their pizza meal. 'And whilst you're doing that, I'll make sure little Becks is sleeping.' So saying, Bob had gone striding over to the door.

'Becky will be fine, you don't need to go to her,' Nicola had cried out, the anger of moments earlier draining away. Maybe all he wanted was what he'd done before and as terrible as it was, she would be able to cope. Anything to stop him going near her little sister.

Bob swung round, a triumphant smile flickering on his lips, 'I'll take that as you've decided I promise it will be the best thing that has ever happened to you.'

She didn't think it would be, but knowing there was no escape, Nicola had moved over to the sofa. She looked up at Uncle Bob, a pleading message in her eyes for him to change his mind.

'Come on Nic, it's not that bad. You're making me out to be a monster and as I said before, I'm not. I just think you are a very special girl.'

Resigned to her fate and frightened what Uncle Bob would do, Nicola sank down on the edge of the sofa.

'Now let me give you my birthday present.'

She had stiffened as firm, hot fingers touched her legs and too afraid to move or cry out, she looked on as Uncle Bob had slowly removed her skirt and then her underwear. And then...

Nicola ran her hand through the pink water; he had not done what she had thought he was going to do to her, what he did do was much, much worse and she wondered if she would ever feel normal again. Pulling the plug, she watched as the water gurgled down the drain and prayed with ever prayer she could remember that it would never happen again.

Chapter Twelve

Barbara watched as the red tail lights of Becky's Toyota disappeared around the corner and she felt the mantle of loss settle heavily on her shoulders. Family and friends had been a huge support, but she was painfully aware that they had their homes and lives to return to. Staring down the empty road, she felt alone. She took a deep breath, the cold air stung her throat as it eased its way down to her lungs. Nothing ever prepared you for losing a loved one, she reflected. The times she had comforted others, believing that her words would make a difference, but as meaningful and sincere as they had been, she now appreciated they barely touched the deep rawness of grief. So many beautiful words had been spoken since Terry's death, all said with true meaning, but she would swap every single word for him to be at her side.

The chill from the October breeze nipped at her face and she pulled her dressing gown tight around her. With heavy footsteps she made her way over the block-paved driveway towards the front door. With each laborious step Barbara stared down at the dog-tooth pattern, her gaze sweeping across the intricate design in an attempt to distract herself from the whirl of emotions that coursed through her.

The screech from a magpie flying over the garden made her raise her head and she caught the flash of its green tail. She watched it soar into the neighbour's conifer tree. Life continues, she thought, dragging her focus down to her own garden and realising it had lost its charm. In other times, she would have stopped and admired the foliage and blooms, taken in the changes the month had brought, plucked off dead heads from the late roses, or scooped up dead leaves. But today, she didn't see the beauty, nor did her nose detect the pungent fragrance from the overnight dew. Instead, all she could think about was the man she had been married to, the same man she'd had to say goodbye to yesterday. The years had slipped by so speedily, it hardly seemed possible they had been together for so long. It had been a good marriage, the usual ups and downs and, of course, the problems with Nicola. The tough times had not diminished their love, if anything, it had strengthened it. She sighed heavily, how she wished with every fibre of her body, he was still here.

Swallowing to keep the tears at bay, Barbara entered the hallway. She pushed the front door closed and hearing the familiar sound of the heavy lock engage, felt the stillness of the house envelop her. She could not recall it being so silent. It was a home that had always been filled with noise: the laughter and babble from the girls and their friends, the many sleepovers when they were young. There had been times when up to twelve children had stayed overnight. It had been deafening, chaotic and wonderful. Thankfully, the Wendy House had been an overspill, especially with Becky's friends. Nicola had always refused to sleep there... she had been difficult even back then, Barbara brooded. And, of course, there had been their grownup parties: loud music, much laughter and the heavy atmosphere from the smoking. The place had reeked of it for days, but it had made their parties famous, popular and so much fun. At the memory, Barbara inhaled deeply and although there was no trace of the pungent odour, she imagined she could still detect and taste the bitter sweet scent of grass. Not that they had indulged often; just on the odd occasion. Terry had been the party beacon. He loved nothing more than having the entire place lit up like the Blackpool illuminations and filled with friends at the weekend. Barbara took small comfort from recalling those happy days, it had been a house filled with love. Now all she could hear was a deafening silence. The smile that had curled her lips skywards at the memories began to slowly fade.

Barbara walked through to the kitchen and straight to the wide window that overlooked the garden. Taking hold of the long white rod, she twisted until the venetian blind swished open. The light from the overcast day struggled through the window, barely making a difference to the gloom of the room. She rested her elbows on the wooden surface top and gazed out of the window. Her tired eyes strayed to the dilapidated Wendy House, which like her home was silent and empty; no parties, no children, nobody.

Becky had no children and it seemed unlikely there ever would be any. Her daughter had told her that they were happy; happy in their jobs and happy in their lifestyle. Children were not on any of their lists of wants or needs. Barbara found herself regretting that. Of course, she had grandchildren, but her volatile relationship with their mother had kept her two granddaughters often at a cold distance. Thoughts of her eldest daughter sent a shiver of disappointment and regret through her body: disappointment that she had not been able to encourage Nicola to live a better life and regret that she had failed to change the path Nicola was determined to follow.

The abortion had been a turning point. Instead of bringing them closer it had created a rift that had widened. No matter how many bridges she had worked to build, none had been wide enough to span the gulf between them. Nicola had venomously insisted on blaming her for everything; the way her life had turned out and the abortion being at the top of her list.

'You made me have it,' Nicola had shrieked, after returning home from hospital.

'Then tell me how at fifteen you would bring a baby up, because you would have just been fifteen? Believe you me Nicola, bringing children up at any age is difficult. You are a child yourself.'

'I am far from being a child and I could have managed if you and dad helped me, but you wouldn't.'

'It was not a case of not wanting to,' Barbara had protested. 'We had to look at what was best for you and in the end the baby.'

'Baby? It was never a baby was it though?'

'Nicola…'

'I'll never forgive you for this. You've ruined my life. It is all your fault.'

The years had not changed Nicola's outburst. Though the words had been rearranged, but it was the same record that was played time and time again when Nicola had one of her sessions. It was wearing and the guilt of what Barbara had had to do never left her, never more so than the session that had seen Nicola march out of the house. Gazing unseeing through the window, Barbara remembered she had been preparing a casserole for dinner on that occasion and was in the middle of chopping up the vegetables when Nicola stormed into the kitchen…

'If it's not too much of an emotive question, why aren't you at work today?' Barbara asked, keeping her attention on cutting the carrots.

'What?'

Dropping the peeling knife on the chopping board, Barbara swung round. 'You'll end up losing that job if you take any more time off. Jobs are not two a penny, my girl. Have you seen the time?'

'Jobs like that are. As for the time, who cares? Anyway, I've more important things to do.'

Barbara bristled and thought about the shop assistant's job Nicola had taken after leaving school. How the supermarket kept her on with her attitude, baffled her.

'You should have stayed on at school and achieved some qualifications. That way you could be a little more choosey.'

'We can't all be like brainy Becky can we?'

'For God's sake, it's like treading on burning coals with you these days,' Barbara said, turning back to the task in hand.

'Well you won't have to worry about that from now on, I'm leaving. If you think I'm staying here any longer, you are so wrong.'

Closing her eyes as if to erase the scene that was taking place, Barbara counted to three, 'And where are you planning on going?' she called over her shoulder, afraid if she looked at her daughter she might run across the room, grab Nicola's shoulders and shake the very life out of her.

A sardonic smile twisted Nicola's lips, 'I'm moving in with Brett Morton.'

'Oh no you are not, young lady,' Barbara snapped, twisting round and facing her daughter square on, anger turning her pale face a bright shade of pink. 'Amongst many reasons, but for starters, he is far too old. He must be at least ten years older than you. And if that is not reason enough, he runs a night club.' Barbara pictured Morton, a stocky man with an arresting presence. His personality and wealth were regularly documented in the local newspaper. It appeared he liked fame. If he was not rubbing shoulders with some B-rate singer or group, he was seen with those who had made it through good or foul means. Instinct told her he was trouble.

Nicola headed towards the hall, 'I am and you can't stop me. You've no idea what it's like living here and I hate it.' She grabbed a large holdall from the floor near the front door and turned towards her mother. 'I'm leaving and nothing you say or do will keep me here. Brett loves me and I love him. Let's face it, I'm not exactly pure goods anymore.'

'Nicola wait!' Barbara called striding towards her.

'I'm going Mum, you won't stop me,' she said, her eyes flashing with anger. Pulling the door open, Nicola walked out without a backward glance.

Barbara stood on the doorstep, intuition told her to go after her and bring her back, but she knew there would be no point in chasing after her daughter. Nicola would defy her and still leave. With a mixture of anger and regret, she watched as Nicola heaved the large bag onto her shoulder.

She would be back with her tail between her legs before the week was out, of that Barbara was certain.

She had been wrong. Nicola never came back. During those early weeks she had begged her daughter to come home. Whatever had gone before, she was certain it could be sorted and they would be close again. Terry had also tried his best to encourage her back, but like her own words, his too, had fallen on deaf ears. No amount of phoning or trying to visit had helped bridge the gap. It was only when Nicola had gone into labour with her first child that she had asked for her mother. It had been unexpected, but very welcome.

Now, as Barbara wiped at her eyes from the memories she turned away from the window and strode over to the back door. She grabbed the handle and pulled open the door. Leaving the confines of the warm kitchen, she braced herself for the morning's frigid air. Still in her dressing gown, she padded down the overgrown, winding path towards the Wendy House.

The once bright yellow door now looked in a dilapidated state, the paint peeling and flaking. The damp had chewed away at the base leaving marks as if a wild animal had feasted on the timber. Barbara took in the sorry sight, saddened to see the once pretty building in such disrepair. Steadying herself, she reached down and turned the rusty key that was still lodged in the mortice lock and tugged on the door. It creaked open, swaying precariously on its rusty hinges.

The memory of laughter from the girls rang out through the passages of time. Becky had loved the place right up until she had left home, but Nicola's joy was short lived. The sound of remembered laughter faded at the knowledge that Nicola had never really enjoyed the Wendy House. There had been times when Barbara had been relieved. The thought of her eldest daughter sullying it with her rebel behaviour – drugs, smoking and sex – would have destroyed it for Becky. Oddly, it wasn't these

77

thoughts that now troubled Barbara so much as why Nicola was taking up so many of her thoughts since Terry had died. It was as if the deeds of the past needed to be raked over in the hope that in the ashes there would be a spark that would help return them to the closeness they once had. Unable to shake off her sombre mood, Barbara realised she could not face walking into the Wendy House. Gripping the door handle, she carefully pushed the door shut and turned the rusty key; it ground in the lock before it engaged.

Leaving the Wendy House as she had found it, Barbara turned her back on its decaying shell. She knew the only way to put to rest these unsettling thoughts was to visit her daughter. An involuntary shiver ran down her spine. What state would she find Nicola in when she eventually knocked on her door? The memory of seeing her in an inebriated state after the funeral flashed into her mind. Barbara headed back to the kitchen. Hopefully, a strong cup of coffee and a couple of sedatives would give her the strength she needed to talk to her daughter.

Chapter Thirteen

The music reverberated through the house. Even the walls appeared to pulse under the throb. With her knees curled up to her chest and her arms wrapped around her denim-covered legs, Nicola, now thirteen, sat in the middle of the bed and glared down at the purple duvet cover with its thin yellow stripes. A long yellow thread lay across a purple panel. Reaching out she plucked at it, fingering the cotton strand, her nerves jangling at each beat of the throbbing music. How she hated home parties. She hated them more than she hated her parents going out and leaving her and Becky with Uncle Bob. Whilst parties were great fun for them, for her it always meant one thing: the one thing she dreaded.

Unable to block out the noise and the loud voices rising from downstairs, Nicola laid her head onto her knees and, squeezing her eyes tight, sent up a prayer to any God who would listen to her. Even though she asked these invisible gods for help, she knew her voice wouldn't be heard; it hadn't been so far in the three years since *he* had done his worst to her. She didn't want to dwell on the hopeless situation and in an effort to distract herself, she teased the cotton fibre between her fingers. If the Wendy House wasn't bad enough, he now visited her in her bedroom when the parties were here. He would wait until it was in full swing, the guests having had had plenty to drink and plenty to smoke, and then he would creep into her room. She always made sure the door was closed, but it didn't deter him, he would silently open it. Of course, she knew when he was there, the dry creek of the hinges gave him away along with his dark shadow that cast an eerie image on the walls. He would creep into the room as if she should be surprised to see him. The same sickly grin staring at her as he would slip under her duvet and although he was fully clothed with his shoes on, he would expect her to be naked. If she hadn't removed her clothes, he would do it. She cringed as he either dragged them off her in a frenzy or slowly remove them, all the while smiling at her. She hated removing her clothes for him, but much worse, she loathed him doing it. He didn't do the full thing, not when there was a party going on downstairs, but he always touched her and always said the same things.

'You know, coming to your room like this is even more exciting than picnicking in the Wendy House. I know it's not just for me, but for you too. Who would dare to believe we have such a wonderful secret?' he would whisper in her ear, his hot and fetid breath breezing all over her face. What she could never understand was how her parents didn't miss him downstairs when he was in her bed. She tried to imagine the scene and wondered how they would deal with it; her naked and him fully dressed. Somehow she didn't think she would be seen as the victim.

She had spent the last three years in fear of him and hated what he did to her and how he made her feel. All she wanted to do was to find a way to stop it. She had tried saying no, but he never listened, instead he would tell her she was having fun too. No matter how much she cried, begged and pleaded it only made him do more to her. Once she had kicked him in the stomach, but what he did to her after he had pulled himself together made her so afraid that she never struck him again.

There had been other times when she had found more than an ounce of courage to thwart him, but every time she believed she would be the victor, he would shoot her confidence down in flames. Like when she had said, 'One day you'll be sorry because I'll tell my mum and when I've finished she'll believe me.'

Instead of panicking as she had expected him to, he had laughed out loud and scooped her up in his arms before sitting her on his knee, then in a serious voice he had said, 'No matter how many buckets of tears you shed, there isn't a soul on this earth who would believe you, even more so when I tell them that you came on to me. And not only do you want me to do these things to you, but you expect gifts in return.' He had then listed the catalogue of presents he had given her. 'Of course, I'll explain I've done everything in my power to stop you…' And then his voice had trailed off and he smiled, seeing the fear stamped on her face. It was always the same when she tried to thwart him.

Fear of everything he would say to her parents made Nicola tremble and her nose run. It was all lies, but how could she convince anyone of that? Then he would take hold of her hand. 'We have something very special. Why you need to cry so much defeats me, because I only ever want to love you. You know Nic, I do love you.' His words spun round in her head like a Catherine wheel. He would squeeze her hand tight whilst his other moved up her thigh. 'You're mine and I'm yours and that's how it has to be forever.' His words haunted her and all she could think was that for as long as she breathed she would never be free of him. Her life was full of shame and nothing and no one could change it. Knowing she had to keep all of this to herself was a source of constant anxiety. The image of her mother flashed into her mind. Just thinking about what her reaction would be if she knew made Nicola feel sick. All she could hear was her mother's soft voice speaking to her about boys, wanting her to know it would be a wonderful experience.

'When the time comes, it is important that it is what you want. It is your choice and if you don't want to do anything, remember there is only one word and that is "No"!' Why did her mother have to tell her such a thing? If only she knew that for her it simply wasn't true; she would never have that choice.

Sniffing loudly, Nicola used the cuff of her jumper to wipe at her face. When it had all started she had thought about running away or killing herself, but every time she thought about escaping she was reminded of what *he* would do to Becky if she was not here for him. Over the years, she had devised plan after plan in an attempt to survive through the times with him. Once he had finished, he always asked, 'If there is anything special you want me to bring next time, let me know and I'll get it for you. You deserve it.' When he uttered those words she prayed that there would not be a next time, but there always was. Most times she felt too sick to think of anything and the only thing she wanted from him was for him to stop, but that was never going to happen.

After one of his sessions in the Wendy House she had found a voice she didn't believe she'd had and before she could stop herself the words tumbled out. 'I need a new pair of trainers,' she had blurted out. Instantly, a triumphant look filled his face and as his eyes sparkled, he had hugged her.

'I think I can do that. Just tell me what size and brand, and you'll have your trainers.' A few days later he had arrived at the house with a pair of trainers, the very ones she had described to him. To make sure he wasn't asked awkward questions, he had bought Becky a pair too.

'A present for each of my princesses,' he had gushed. Her mother had taken in the scene, appreciation oozing from her. Nicola had no intention of wearing them, of course. She had told her mother they pinched her toes and rubbed at her heels, but like most things in her life, her excuse had fallen on deaf ears.

'They must have cost a fortune! I'm sure wearing them for short intervals will soon have them fitting your feet perfectly,' her mother had argued, encouraging her to put them back on with thick socks and wear them around the house. 'Nicola, you can be so ungrateful at times. You have no idea how very lucky you are. And please stop sulking,' she had admonished her. 'Your behaviour disappoints me these days,' she had added, before turning to Uncle Bob. 'You really shouldn't have bought them, especially ones so expensive.'

'I'm very fond of your girls, Barbara, and it never hurts every now and then to spoil them. Anyway, they were in the sale and you know me, can't resist a bargain,' A sly grin had filled his face as he had followed her mother through to the kitchen. As soon as they were out of sight, she had kicked the trainers off. Becky, on the other hand, had run around the lounge as if it was a race track. By mentioning the trainers Nicola had expected him to be horrified, but her impulsive moment had had the opposite effect; he had been pleased and now her mother thought he was the kindest and most generous person she had ever met, which had only fuelled his ego and his appetite for her daughter.

After the fiasco with the trainers, Nicola was conscious she needed to come up with something that would cause him to leave her alone for good. After another painful ordeal, she had decided to ask him for something seriously expensive. Maybe if she asked for too much, he would not only find it difficult to afford, but decide she wasn't worth it and would leave her alone. The night she decided to deliver her little surprise, he was pulling on his trousers and uttering those sickening words, 'Is there anything I can get you, because you only need to say?' A sickly, satisfied grin had made him look ghoulish in the tiny light of the Wendy House as he glared down at her. Somehow she had found the courage to ask for something that would shut him up for good. Feeling confident of her plan, the words flew from her mouth as if they were in a panic to get out. 'I need a new bike, but Mum says I have to wait until Christmas.'

For a few moments he had remained silent, the sickly grin slipping to be replaced with a wary regard. He neither accepted nor declined and after checking she was decently dressed, they had headed back down the garden path to the house. There was no further mention of the bike that night. A week later he brought two new ones to their home. Nothing, it seemed, was out of his range to buy. He had also had a well-rehearsed and plausible excuse for the unsolicited gifts, which he happily spilled out to her parents. 'I won them in a raffle and with no one else to give them to I instantly thought of the girls,' he had chortled. At the time Nicola had been convinced her parents would see right through him, but they hadn't. Instead of seeing a child abuser and a liar, they had placed him on a pedestal as the perfect "step-uncle" for their children. And whilst her parents could not see how devious he was, it was clear to her that she had made a mistake in asking for something so expensive. From then on it was as if he felt he had paid for what he did to her.

There were occasions when her anger would surface and she would again ask for something ridiculous, but no matter what she suggested, he always delivered. In the end she had stopped asking for anything, but it didn't stop him bringing gifts for her and Becky, her parents revelling in having such a special man doting on their children.

The party downstairs was still going strong; the thumping sound of the bass continued to throb, filling the room with its pulsating din and hammering into Nicola's thoughts. She wondered which was better, the music or her nightmare thoughts. One thing she did know was that her head was filled with so much fear that she had to do something. But what? She had ruled out running away because of her little sister, but maybe she could take Becky with her? At least she would be safe. Then, if they were found, she could tell her parents why she had run away. Even as this idea filtered through her head, she knew it would be impossible for many reasons. Becky would make too much noise, crying and pleading to go home and it was bitter cold, they would freeze to death out there. And, of course, there was no guarantee anyone would believe her when they were found, but there was one thing she could do that would be the answer to everything. The one thing that would stop all her fears, and only then would it *all* stop. She would write a letter explaining everything so that

Becky would be protected. It wouldn't matter if her parents believed her or not because she wouldn't be here.

She had at least twenty paracetamol tablets hidden in the bottom of her treasure box. Over the months she had taken one or two from the packet when she'd had her monthlies. Her mother always offered her one then. Unless the cramps were too painful, Nicola had kept the tablets and squirreled them away. She knew how many she had collected as she counted them most days. Counting them gave her hope of an eventual escape, though she had no idea how many would be sufficient to take her last breath away, but surely twenty would be more than enough?

Filled with nervous energy, Nicola jumped off the bed, swept across the room and slid open her wardrobe door. Pushing the jumpers at the front of the second shelf to one side, she grabbed hold of her treasure box, a pink plastic affair the size of a shoe box, and pulled it out.

Sitting down on the edge of the bed, she flipped the lid open and rummaged to the bottom until she felt the soft linen bag that held the tablets. Stroking the thin bag with her fingertips, she felt the pills inside. How long would it take to swallow that amount of pills and would the end be quick, she wondered. As she pondered taking her own life, the music suddenly stopped and an eerie silence filled the room. Afraid her secret stash would be seen, with urgent hands Nicola pushed the bag back down inside the box. Satisfied it was concealed, she flicked the lid shut. Panicking, she hurried across the room and stuffed the box back in its secret place. With the jumpers back in place, the box was once again concealed. Sliding the wardrobe door closed she heard the familiar creak of the floorboards on the landing, her spirits plummeted further. As if frozen to the spot, she stared at her bedroom door and watched as the handle slowly depressed, the door opened, at the same time the loud music resumed.

'Why aren't you in bed,' Barbara said, stepping into the room, a small tray in her hand. 'I knew you wouldn't be asleep so I brought you some of the smoked salmon *vol-au-vent*. And there's a few sandwiches, crisps and a can of coke too.' Barbara set the tray down on the bed.

'Mum, it's you,' Nicola said, exhaling the breath she had held as relief flooded through her. It was as much as she could do to stop herself from crying at the sight of her mother.

'You look a little pale,' Barbara said, her brow puckering with concern. 'You know you could have stayed up for a little time and enjoyed the party. It would do you good to join in a little, Nic, sometimes it's fun to be with people.'

Her mother's soft voice was so welcoming Nicola almost dropped her guard and wept. 'I'm fine, just tired,' she said and moved over to her bed.

'You're too young to be tired, my love. I see you've not got your nightie on, so come on down,' Barbara pressed, reaching her arms out to Nicola.

'Honestly, I'm happier up here. Thanks for the goodies,' she added, averting her gaze from her mother and staring at the tray.

Barbara reached across and gently stroked Nicola's face. 'Are you sure you're all right? You look like you've been crying. Come here love,' she wrapped her arms around Nicola's shoulders and pulled her towards her. 'I worry about you these days. If there is something worrying you, school or anything, you can always to talk to me. I'm your mum and I love you.'

Feeling the comforting embrace of her mother's arms, Nicola wished with all her heart that she could tell her what was happening to her, but where would she begin? The shame of it all was overwhelming. Words tumbled around in her head as she fought to find ones that might help her explain everything. Nicola opened her mouth to speak. As the first word was about to leave her lips, she looked up at her mother, but instead of seeing her loving face, her troubled eyes spied the new CD player sitting on the corner of the bedside cabinet. In an instant, she knew she couldn't say anything. How would she be able to explain all the presents? It would be impossible. What was happening to her would have to be a secret forever. She had no choice but to accept she could do nothing about Uncle Bob. With this startling revelation, she had to accept her mother could no longer save her. She wasn't worthy of anyone's love or kindness. Instead of turning into a young woman, she had turned into someone who was deceitful and ruined and carried dirty secrets around in her head, and worse, asked him for gifts in return. She shuddered at the thought that if anyone ever learnt of what was going on with Uncle Bob, it would be everlasting shame for everyone. Believing this, she bit back the words that still pushed to tumble from her lips and forced a smile. 'I'm fine, Mum, just a little bit of tummy ache,' she lied.

Barbara kissed the top of Nicola's head and held her tight against her, 'My love, you do suffer with your monthlies. Maybe it wouldn't be a bad idea to see the doctor. This day and age, there's no need for you to be in pain and down with it all.'

'No Mum, that's not necessary, it's really not that bad,' she blurted out, shrugging out of her mother's embrace. Visiting the doctor was the last thing she needed.

'What are we going to do with you, Nic? Barbara asked, shaking her head in bewilderment.

Knowing it was a rhetorical question, Nicola didn't answer. There was nothing she could say that would begin to explain.

'You were such a lively little girl until your monthlies arrived. Let's say if things don't improve, then we'll take a visit to the clinic. Okay?' Taking hold of Nicola's hand, Barbara squeezed it. 'It doesn't have to be like this,' she said.

'Yes, okay.'

'Well that's settled, but I'll be keeping an eye on you. For now, why not come down to the party? It'll cheer you up. You know most people and of course, Uncle Bob's there,' Barbara coaxed.

Just hearing his name made Nicola feel sick, 'I don't really like parties and I'd be the youngest. Honestly Mum, I'm fine,' she said, in a voice that sounded surprisingly normal, with a smile pulling at her lips. Goodness, she really was good at deceit. 'Thanks for this, though,' she pointed at the tray of food, 'it all looks scrummy,' she added, wondering how she would be able to eat any of it. She had lost her appetite lately and the thought of food, along with everything else, had her feeling sick, and on a couple of occasions she had actually thrown up.

'Okay. As long as you say you're fine then I'll leave you to it.' Barbara sighed. A frown creased her face and made her glossy lips pinch into a thin line. 'I just worry about you,' she added, heading towards the door. 'Eat your supper and I'll look in when everyone has gone. Love you, Nic,' she called over her shoulder.

'Love you too, Mum,' she called back and watched her mother leave the room, her pungent perfume lingering behind her. Nicola inhaled the fragrance and wished with every fibre of her body she had been brave enough to talk to her. At thirteen, she felt every centimetre of the distance that had grown between them. She was acutely aware that on a daily basis the gap widened and all of this was down to her. It was time to write that letter, she thought. Right now. She had to escape.

Chapter Fourteen

'I see you've got something to eat.' Bob said, his voice slicing through the heavy beat of the music. Startled, Nicola swung round and saw him advancing towards her. Raising her hand as if to stop him, her pen slipped to the floor. Tears of disappointment pooled in her eyes at the knowledge she had left it too late to write her note and take the tablets. Now what was she going to do?

She didn't miss how his pebble-grey eyes sparkled, she had seen that look many times before, and added to this, the odour that emanated from him, a pungent, bitter aura, signalled, he had been smoking. Nothing as ordinary as a cigarette, it was far more potent than a simple Benson and Hedges. Her heart lurched.

'It's been a long time,' Bob said, his words slurred as he reached out and brushed the tips of his fingers across her cheek.

Nicola flinched at his touch and didn't miss the smirk that curved his lips as he registered her reaction to him. Clenching her teeth together, she tried to hold down the knot of disgust that filled her for not being able to stop him. Pity she had dropped her pen because if she could only summon up the courage, she would thrust the point into him and hurt him like he hurt her. The thought of damaging him fuelled her imagination and she saw in her mind's eye what she would do to him if she could only be brave enough. But she wasn't brave. He was too strong for her, but one day she would do it. One way or another she would destroy him like he had destroyed her. She needed to believe this to be able to continue.

'Have you missed me? It's been a couple of weeks since we've been able to be together and I've missed you,' he said, running his hand up the side of her neck, his lecherous eyes raking over her.

Rigid, she did not move or flinch. No matter what she dreamed of doing to him, she knew that for now, it was a waste of time. At the end of the day, he would get what he wanted. Accepting, for now, that she was cornered, she just needed to stay calm and get through the next half an hour.

'I'm not hungry,' she said, ignoring his question because she had not missed him and if she never saw him again, she would not miss him.

'Well I am,' he said, turning his attention to the tray filled with food. Snatching up a *vol-au-vent*, he held it halfway between his mouth and the tray, 'In fact I'm more than hungry,' he said, then slipped the salmon-filled pastry into his mouth. With crumbs settling on his bottom lip, he shot her a look. 'It's been a long time since we had our cuddle.'

Nicola remained still and watched as he dropped down onto her bed. 'Come and sit down,' he said, 'and try to smile. There's a party going on downstairs and any minute now there's going to be one up here too.' He smirked and patted the space at his side. She recoiled as he reached out and helped himself to more of the food. Raising his eyebrows at her, he dropped it into his open mouth and devoured it.

Bile rose in Nicola's throat at the scene and she wished she had enough courage to run out of the room, race down the stairs and scream at everyone that Uncle Bob was in her bedroom, but she knew she couldn't do it, instead she remained rooted to the spot.

'I know you like little surprises and I've one or two for you tonight, but before revealing them to you, you need to relax. I can see you're as taut as a wire.' Not taking his eyes off of her, Bob wiped the back of his hand over his mouth. 'What on earth is wrong with you?' he added, exasperation replacing his calm tone. He patted the bed again. 'Please come and sit down, Nic.' He reached out his hand, 'Come on love,' he whispered, his fingers lacing around her wrist as he pulled her towards him.

Knowing there was no option, but to comply, Nicola sat down on the bed.

'You know you can talk to me about anything,' he said, not taking his eyes from her. 'You worry me sometimes, one minute you're smiling and then I get the silent treatment.' Releasing his fingers from around her wrist, he reached into the breast pocket of his polo shirt. 'You really do need to chill out more. You're too young to be so wound up,' as he spoke he pulled out a spliff. 'This'll make things appear much better,' he said, flashing it in front of her face. Pushing it between his lips, he then produced a plastic flick lighter and lit it up. Instantly, the fetid odour filtered into the air. Nicola breathed in the fumes and felt her stomach lurch, she placed her hand over her mouth in an attempt to stop herself throwing up.

Bob coughed. 'Jeez, it's a bit rich,' he spluttered. Getting to his feet, he strode over to the window. Flicking the catch, he pushed the sealed unit window open. Immediately, the throbbing music from the party overpowered the background noise that had filled the room. Oblivious of the din, Bob flapped his hand in an attempt to clear the air as he moved back to the bed. With the spliff between his lips, he squatted back down on the edge. 'Why am I getting the silent treatment? What have I done this time, apart from not visiting you?' he asked.

With no answer that would satisfy him, Nicola remained silent.

Taking hold of the spliff with his index finger and thumb, Bob took a long drag. As the drug coiled its way down to his lungs, he removed the finger of weed from his lips and offered it to Nicola. 'Here, take a drag, it'll help you relax and it might loosen your tongue.'

Nicola glared at him with loathing.

'Go on, take it.' As he spoke, he held out his hand. 'Here, take it.'

Nicola removed her hand from around her mouth. She didn't want to smoke the stuff, but it occurred to her that it might not be such a stupid idea after all. She needed to drift out of this world and if soaring high on this would help, then why not? She had smoked the stuff before and as much as she disliked it, it would have the positive effect of getting her through what he had in mind to do to her. Reaching out, she took hold of the stub and without hesitation slipped it between her lips and pulled hard. She felt a little woozy and to her delight the worry of her dilemma began to fade. She needed more of this. Greedily, she sucked on it.

'Hey, not so fast,' Bob said, grabbing what was left of it. 'Christ, what's the matter with you tonight?' But before he could say anything else, Nicola stumbled to her feet. Blinking to clear her vision, she staggered to the door and fumbling with the handle, she dragged it open. Reeling down the landing, she pushed the bathroom door open and slumped down onto her knees. Crawling on all fours, she just made it to the toilet and threw up.

The urge to howl at the injustice of it all was overpowering. Anger and self-pity churned inside her as she dragged herself to her feet. She couldn't even drug herself enough to escape from it all. It was hardly surprising she was in such a mess, she thought, steadying herself. Then, yanking on the ceramic handle, she flushed her vomit away. Watching the water spiral round the bowl, she wished she could flush herself away just as effectively. She leant on the sink unit and took in the image that reflected back at her from the mirror. She hardly recognised herself; she was pale and drawn. What had happened to the girl who had once laughed and smiled? But before she could answer her own question, Nicola heard the sleepy sound of her sister calling out in her dreams. Alarm shot through her. The last thing she needed was Becky getting out of bed to visit the bathroom and seeing her like this. Standing stock still and holding her breath, Nicola listened. Apart from the thudding of the music downstairs, there were no further sounds from her sister's bedroom. With a sense of urgency, Nicola turned on the cold tap to full pressure and rinsed her mouth, then with all the effort she could muster, she dragged herself back down the landing to her room.

Placing her hand on the door handle, she hesitated. She wanted to believe he had gone back to the party, but on pushing the door open she realised she was not that lucky. He was still there laying on top of her duvet. The tray was empty, with the exception of the can of drink. He had eaten everything. Just as well, she thought bitterly, at least there would be no need to explain why she had not been hungry. Her mother would instead be happy that everything had been eaten. Even in a dark leaden sky, it seemed there was a silver lining.

'I left the coke for you,' Bob said, sitting up as she walked in. Reaching over, he picked up the drink. 'Come here. You know, Nic Nac, you're worrying me. Have you any idea how important you are to me?' He got off the bed and padded over to the door. Wrapping his arm around her shoulder, he led her to the bed. 'Sit down,' he insisted.

Slumping onto her bed, she watched him hurry to the door and close it. *God help anyone seeing him in my room. How would he get out of that one? But doubtless he would, like he always does,* she thought bitterly. He had not only taken over her body and her mind, but he had changed her name too and started calling her Nic Nac; she hated it.

'What's wrong? It's not like you to be sick on a bit of weed.' Concern gilded his voice as he flicked her feet up onto the bed. 'Here, drink this,' he said, handing it to her. 'It's my fault, I shouldn't have given you the spliff. I could see you were a bit off colour, but I just wanted to help you relax. Come on love, tell me what's going on. I promise I'll do everything to make it right.'

Make it right? The words slammed into her brain. Turning the clock back would be a starter, but that couldn't happen. He could never make things right, it was all too late now. It was down to her to do what was right, either tell him or say nothing and take the paracetamol. The latter sounded the best solution. If she was gone, then who would care? But what if it only made her sick, like with the spliff? Then her mother would know what she had been up to and would go off at the deep end. Nicola shuddered. It seemed whichever way she jumped, she could not guarantee it would be over. Wrestling with these thoughts, she accepted the drink and placing the can to her lips took a mouthful. The bitter liquid fizzed on her tongue and she grimaced. Vomit, spliffs and Coca Cola didn't make the best of cocktails she guessed. To her surprise, she found she was thirsty and downed the entire contents. She sucked on the can to ensure she had taken the last drop then hugged the empty can to her chest. It reminded her that it wasn't so much a chest anymore, but a bust. Not only had she grown in height but her breasts had made their appearance too. At thirteen, she had more than a decent cleavage. At a glance she could easily pass for sixteen and under different circumstances she would have been proud to look older. Instead, she hated her body. She was ashamed of it. It betrayed her and yet *he* loved it. She glared at him over the top of the empty can. She could almost read his dirty mind as he took in her body. The more of a woman she appeared the more he wanted her. Even her mother added to his desire of her, insisting on buying her bras that her breasts filled perfectly, when all she wanted was to wear tops that squashed them as flat as possible. Nature was cruel in every sense, as now her breasts were not only large, but sore.

'Give me that,' he said, reaching over and plucking the can from her hand. Startled, she glared at him. She was frightened and confused and paradoxically had to admit he was the only person she could talk to. He was the only person who shared the secret. Knowing this created a pain that made her wince. Afraid of what she had to do, she tried to forget it and picked at a scab on the side of her elbow. It hurt, but it was nothing like the real pain that she lived and slept with.

'I've never known you be sick before,' he said again. 'I was hoping we could have done something a little more tonight, make it a first in your bed, seeing as how everyone

94

else downstairs is having a good time, but finding you like this, I can't. The last thing I want to do is hurt you.'

Confused by his sudden thoughtfulness, Nicola stared at him. He was smiling at her as if kindness was all he was about, but he wasn't, not when he expected her to do things with him. She had never dared think that looking and feeling sick would stop him. Maybe she should tell him after all, and then she would never have to feel his body against hers ever again. Thinking that this could be the answer, she felt her heartbeat quicken. Even the pain in her head seemed to lessen at what she saw as her way out of it all. Of course, there would be a point when she would have to tell her parents, but she could lie to them, she was good at deception these days. As if a light had been switched on, she saw everything tumble into place. Her prayers had been answered after all. Convinced she had the solution to her worst nightmare, she opened her mouth to speak, but was silenced at the knock on the door.

The door flew open. 'Oh sorry, I need the bathroom,' a middle-aged man said, dressed as if he had stepped out of the sixties, and as suddenly as the door had opened is closed.

Turning, she laughed out loud at the sight of Uncle Bob sprawled out on the floor at the other side of bed.

'Hell, that was close,' he said, his face pale.

Not close enough, Nicola thought. Maybe the hippie should have carried on walking in. That way, Uncle Bob would have had some serious explaining to do.

'I don't know why you're laughing,' he said, squatting on the edge of the bed. 'I'll wait for him to get back downstairs and then I'll get back to the party. I'll make it up to you the next time in the Wendy House.'

'I don't think so,' she said.

'What are you talking about?' Bob retorted. 'He didn't see me, we're safe. God, my heart almost jumped out of my body.'

'I know, but...' she faltered, thinking what she needed to say, she rearranged the words, but no matter how she re-ordered them, they didn't sound right.

A silence followed.

'Nicola, look at me. I'm not an ogre, I'm the man who loves you and what we do is a sign of that.' As Bob spoke, he took hold of Nicola's hand and cupped it in his. Gently, he stroked the soft skin with his fingers and traced the sprinkling of freckles on the back. 'Your hands are cold.'

She wanted to snatch her hand back, it was cold; she was cold. Had he no idea what fear felt like, she wondered. Even the short intrusion hadn't left him shocked, he still planned what he wanted to do to her. She looked into his face and for the first time in years she saw the soft eyes that she had once innocently looked into; the ones she had thought held kindness before it had been overridden by his appetite for her.

As if her mouth had taken over her thoughts she found herself saying, 'I'm scared. There's a lot to be frightened of....' The words slowly eased out from her trembling lips and as her voice filled the small gap between her tongue and lips, she didn't miss the hint of panic as his features tensed and the brightness in his eyes dimmed.

'You've told someone about us?' Bob's voice was flat.

She flinched, *he's only thinking about himself*, she thought. 'No, it's much worse than that,' she said.

Chapter Fifteen

Nicola walked out of the ladies toilets from the ground floor of the shopping centre. She had swapped her school blouse for a blue knitted top. The white blouse, now stuffed into her bag, shared the cramped space with her exercise books. A mixture of anger and fear mingled with all the lies she had told that morning. Resigned to her fate, she shrugged her bright green backpack onto her shoulders and at the same time a blast of cool air from the centre's ventilation system made her shiver. She was unsure if it was the icy air or the numbing fear that had her trembling, but she reached down and zipped up her jacket. Surreptitiously, she glanced around and seeing no one, she bowed her head and scurried through the cavernous centre, oblivious of the three floors of brightly lit shops and the domed-glass ceiling that reflected the morning light.

Nearing the exit, Nicola raised her head and turned her gaze to the large shop window on her left. A young girl reflected back at her. Her willowy frame was dressed in black, well-fitted trousers, a smart zip-up jacket and fashionable shoes. With her hair tied back at the nape of her neck, to her shock, she looked normal. The paralysing fear she felt was not betrayed in her reflection. Her physical form was the same, but it was what was inside that was damaged and no amount of peering into glass windows would reveal the fragments of destruction. The fear and anxiety that had lived with her over the last few weeks felt like a second skin and yet it was invisible. Even her mother appeared not to have noticed anything different, she still saw her daughter as moody and awkward, even argumentative, but she didn't see she was pregnant. Part of Nicola was relieved, but a tiny particle of her wished someone had noticed and asked questions, maybe then she might have told them what was happening to her. *Now I never will*, she thought, hurrying towards the sliding doors that led out into the town and King's Way.

As she approached the tall glass doors, they automatically swished open. It was then she saw *him* standing in the middle of the wide, paved concourse that flanked the shopping centre, his back to the traffic. Dressed in a smart two-piece suit, white shirt and maroon tie, he blended into the morning rush like any respectable citizen; like all the other suited men and women, faces drawn with the purposes of the day, hurrying to their offices. Except that unlike the others, he wasn't dashing to an office meeting. Instead he was taking a thirteen-year-old girl for an abortion, masquerading as the uncle instead of the father of the unborn child.

Nicola didn't miss the wide smile that filled his face when he spotted her walking out into the dull, overcast day. He raised his hand and waved to her. Instinctively she raised her hand and waved back. How could she do that? It was as if everything they were doing was normal. It wasn't, it was all wrong and illegal. Anger and loathing gripped her, making her cheeks burn, knowing she had no control over her life. She stuffed her hands deep into her jacket pockets and bit down hard on her bottom lip. It was going to be a frightening day and she had no idea how she was going to get through. She should be crying, but she was too numb to even weep. She despised him for what he had done and hated him for turning her into a dirty, ruined, deceitful person. Nobody in the world would want her now and if she were honest, she didn't think she would want anyone touching her again. He had done enough of that to last her a lifetime and what she was going to have to go through today was of nightmare proportions. She loathed him enough to want to hurt him badly and one day she would, she had to keep reminding herself of this. No matter what it took or how long, she would find the energy to destroy him. It was this anger that fuelled her, giving her the impetus to get out of bed and through each day. After today's ordeal was over she was determined he was going to pay for what he was putting her through. It wasn't just him she hated, she hated everyone, especially her parents. In her mind Nicola felt they should have some idea of what was happening to her. Surely it was obvious something wasn't right? Sinking her teeth further into her bottom lip she immediately tasted the metallic bitterness of blood. Sucking on it, she wondered if they knew, but were turning a blind eye, or even allowing it? If that was the case, it would make sense why they didn't appear to notice the real change in her. Even as she argued these thoughts, she had to tell herself it had to be nonsense. Her mother never stopped harping on about boys and what could happen if she dared to try out sex. It was during one of those serious, grownup talks that Nicola had been torn between bursting into tears or laughing in her mother's face and telling her that she knew all about sex and a lot more besides. No matter what Nicola thought and believed, of one thing she was certain: no one would believe that Uncle Bob was a child molester, though at thirteen, would she be still be classified as a child in the same way? It was only last month at school that Andrea Meadows had been called into the Head's office for flirting with the new teacher. It seemed he had made a complaint about being harassed and had been believed. Nicola was sure she wouldn't be; after all, he was a grownup and she and Andrea were just schoolgirls.

'Are you okay?' Bob asked, his voice driving into her thoughts and startling her as he stopped in front of her.

Keeping her hands in her pockets, she glowered at him, 'What do you think?'

Bob ignored her and wrapping his arm around her shoulders he pulled her close to him. 'Nicola, this is not a good day for either of us. Believe it or not, I'm feeling just as upset as you are, maybe worse.'

Nicola wondered how he could possibly feel worse; she was the one who was going to have her insides ripped out. Just thinking about what the day would bring, she felt tears sting at the back of her eyes. Not wanting to blink in order to keep her anxiety in check, she took a deep breath and let it slowly shudder down into her trembling body. Weeping and making a scene in the street would get her nowhere. Instead, she chewed down on her bottom lip and tried not to think of why she was not at school, but being taken to a private clinic to have her pregnancy terminated.

'Nicola, you have no idea how sorry I am it's worked out like this. Nothing prepared me for this to happen,' he said, adding pressure to his squeeze as if it would make a difference to how she felt.

Did he think *she* had been prepared? Nicola wanted to scream at him. He should have known; he was the grownup after all. She was just a child.

'And because of the dire day ahead for both of us,' he went on, 'I'm going to ignore your petulance and put it down to what we have to do. I have not let you down, I promised I would deal with it and I have. Now, have you remembered how we're going to go about this?' he said, ushering her towards his car.

How could she possibly forget? Today was the same as any other day - *everything* to do with him, and more lies. Letting her backpack slip from her shoulder, she managed to dislodge his arm from around her. Free from his grip, she glanced at his face and was delighted to see beads of perspiration on his top lip and forehead. He was as frightened as she was. Knowing this made her feel better. 'Of course I know what we're doing,' she replied at last. Deep down inside, she did not want to go through with the abortion or play silly charades, but she did not want to be pregnant either.

He had arranged everything from the appointment at the private clinic to the false identities; she was going as Laura Speedwell, niece of Ted (Edward) Wilkins. He had explained that her family would be destroyed if they knew about her condition. They were wealthy and very influential. She had laughed in his face when he had told her of his little charade. Her family would most certainly be destroyed if they knew... wealthy, influential, or otherwise.

Standing on the edge of the kerb, her arms folded over her chest, Nicola looked on as he unlocked the passenger door. 'Give me your bag,' he said, extending his hand. She hesitated and then, unfolding her arms, passed the bag over to him.

'I'll pop it in the boot,' he said, as he pulled at the door handle and held the door open. 'Your car, m'lady,' he mocked, raising his right eyebrow as he took a small bow. Despite herself, Nicola found her lips curving into a smile and as he straightened up she stared at his face. Under different circumstances she would accept he was good looking. Her friends thought he was gorgeous and when they had seen him during sleepovers they talked about him as if he was a film star. 'Oh my, to have someone like that visiting our house,' Beth would cry every time she spied him. Little did Beth know he was a wolf in sheep's clothing, though knowing how Beth was turning out these days, she probably would find his attention of interest. The sleepovers were no more; she did not want friends staying and finding her crying at night into her pillow. *'Gorgeous,'* she muttered the word under her breath. Beth had no idea!

Her smile slipping, Nicola placed her hand on top of the door and slid into the cream leather seat. Sitting upright and tense, she pulled at the seat belt, leaving *him* to push the door closed. Unblinking, she glared through the windscreen and heard the boot squeak open as he placed her bag inside. Seconds later his hurried steps followed as he strode round the car to the driver's door. Buckling up, she wondered how many girls were driven to a clinic where a catalogue of lies had been told about them as arrangements were put in place to dispose of their unwanted child. *Unwanted child.* She formed the words with her lips, but no sound came out only a frightened gasp of air. It still had not sunk in that inside her was a child, all she could think was that what was inside her was a mess, an unwanted mess *he* had put there.

A bitter smile twisted her lips as she recalled the night she had told him she was pregnant. She had missed two periods. Not that she had needed a test to tell her when her body screamed something was not right, but she had got a test nonetheless. It had been the night her parent's party had been in full swing and he was slightly high after smoking pot, but not high enough to absorb the shock. After blurting out her condition, Nicola had shown him the pregnancy test. 'Check this out if you don't believe me,' she had yelled. He had held out his hand and to her amusement she had seen it shake. Just noting the tremor had sent a jolt of elation racing through her and if that hadn't been enough, the look on his face had been priceless. It was as if she had held a grenade with the pin pulled out as she had flashed the results in front of him. For a brief moment she had felt the power between them shift and she was the one in control. She had actually told him something that made him recoil in shock instead of him telling her to do things that shocked her. At that moment her panic had switched from terror and fear to a deep anger; anger that festered inside every part of her body and her head. Swiftly recovering from the shock, he had jumped off the bed and grabbed her arms, shaking her violently. 'You'd better not be playing a game, lady, because if you are you'll pay,' he seethed. A mixture of anger and fear had blazed in his eyes and large drops of spittle flew out of his mouth as he spat the words out. She had wanted to laugh at him, but the moment of elation and the feeling of having one over him evaporated as speedily as it had arrived.

'Believe me, I'm pregnant,' she had whispered, her voice breaking up with the effort to speak as he held his tight grip on her arms. Then, as if everything she had said registered, he had suddenly grasped the enormity of the situation and had pulled her to him. He had hugged her tightly and as much as she hated him touching her, a sense of relief had temporarily taken over from the fear and revulsion; relief to have told someone.

'You don't need to worry, I'll organise everything. You won't suffer,' he had assured her, his voice strained and lacking the usual conviction of his words. It was not until later, when she had recalled what he had said, that she had scoffed at his use of the word "suffer". He had made her suffer for years. Now she was not only to suffer further, but be stripped of any dignity she might have had left.

She would never have imagined she could be so clever at hiding her condition. This morning she had headed out of the door as if it was just another normal day at school. How she hated herself.

'How are you feeling?' he asked, jolting her from her thoughts as he started the engine. Indicating, he pulled out into the traffic. Nicola ignored him, the fear of what lay ahead paralysing ever fibre in her body. Would it be painful? Would she be sick? Would she be able to get back in the car? Would anyone find out? There were so many questions and she had no answers, only the fear that held its grip around her. In an attempt to try and still her mind, she stared out of the passenger window. It was not long before the city was replaced by fields and all she could think was that they were travelling to a hiding place to get rid of her shame.

'I take it I'm having the silent treatment again,' he said, glancing at her.

'I've got nothing to say. Nothing that you'd like to hear,' she said, twisting round and staring at his profile.

'I understand you're frightened, but you needn't be. I can promise you it's the best clinic and has cost me a fortune to get you in there.'

Do you expect me to say thank you? she sneered under her breath.

'Sometimes you forget that I do care about you. Surely you understand that?' he said, his gaze back on the road. 'Come on Nic, it's not all bad and I've got a great present for you when it's over.' He reached over to take her hand, but she snatched it away. She was about to tuck it in her pocket when he suddenly grabbed hold. 'Your hand's still cold,' he said softly as if their drive out was to some Theme Park rather than an abortion clinic. 'Come on, let's be friends. I've not let you down, have I?'

Hearing his gentle voice and feeling the warmth from his hand, confused feelings once again flooded through her. What he had subjected her to over the years hadn't been right, but now she was in this terrible mess he wasn't letting her down, he was looking after her. To be friends was the last thing she wanted, but who else could she turn to? There was no one who would understand. The reality of it all was that there was only him to understand, and of course he did. Maybe just for today she could make an effort until it was all over.

Ninety minutes later, Bob nudged the nose of the car between two towering red-brick pillars where tall black wrought iron gates stood open. The sight of a highly polished engraved brass plate fixed to one of the pillars announced they had arrived at Burley House. The tyres scrunched loudly on the gravelled drive as Bob steered the car past wide flowerbeds and a large blue cedar tree. A sharp turn in the drive gave Nicola a full view of the sand-coloured, double-fronted building with its two floors and dormer windows set into the steep, angled slate roof. She exhaled a long breath, relieved he had not brought her to some backstreet hole in the wall. Burley House could not be more of a contrast to what she had feared he was taking her to. The building in front of her looked far too splendid to be an abortion clinic. Despite its beauty, she still felt sick and dirty.

'Here we are,' he announced, as if they were visiting friends.

'Yes,' she mumbled and wondered for the umpteenth time if she was capable of going through with it.

'I told you it was the best and you can see it is. Inside it's totally modern and staffed with medical professionals,' he reassured. 'You don't need to worry that anyone will know anything about the real you or me. Like everything, it's all been sorted. Come on, let's get it over with,' he said, leaning over and patting her knee.

Get it over with, she thought; that summed it up.

Stepping out of the car, Bob scurried to the boot and pulled out Nicola's bag. 'Come on,' he said, appearing at the passenger door.

Seeing him peering down at her, she pulled on the handle, but found she had lost the strength to open the door. Close to tears she needed to pull herself together. She had no choice. She had to go through with it. What else could she do?

'You'll be just fine,' he said, pulling the door open. Even in her state of high anxiety, she heard his voice lacked conviction.

'Do you think so?' she asked, realising he was as frightened as she was.

'I know so,' he replied, helping her out of the car and pushing the passenger door shut. Holding her bag, he placed his hand on the small of her back and guided her towards the short flight of steps that led up to the entrance. They both walked in silence.

Chapter Sixteen

'Mr Wilkins and Miss Speedwell?' a tall willowy woman in a white top and trousers swished towards them as they approached the reception desk.

At the sight of the woman, Bob squeezed Nicola's hand. 'Okay, don't worry. I'll deal with this,' he said in a low voice.

Nicola felt his grip and heard his reassuring words, aware that as much as she hated him, she needed him today. Taking in the confident woman striding towards them, she felt tears prick the back of her eyes and she willed them not to spill out, because if she started to cry she might not be able to stop.

'Do come through,' the woman beckoned turning and heading towards an area where four chairs were placed round a small, square low table. 'Please, take a seat,' she pointed at the chairs.

Nicola wasn't sure she wanted to sit, if she was honest she didn't want to be here at all. As if knowing her thoughts, the woman added, 'You'll be more comfortable sitting.'

Reluctantly, Nicola dropped down on the chair next to Bob.

The woman seated herself opposite and crossed her legs, the smile remaining as if their visit was a normal daily event. 'I just need to ask a few questions before we begin,' she said, leaning forward, 'Laura, please confirm your date of birth and your full name.'

'Twentieth of July nineteen-ninety-one Nicola— '

'Laura Nicola Speedwell,' Bob interrupted. 'Sometimes she's called Nic, but her Christian name is Laura and, of course, she is sixteen.'

Nicola stared at Bob. Everything was so unreal even the name he had just given wasn't hers and her date of birth was just as false. At thirteen her life was complicated, and she needed to be careful, because if she made a mistake she could be in serious trouble.

The woman's voice broke into her fears. 'I see. Laura, are you happy me calling you Laura?'

Nicola nodded and answered several more questions. She really did not care what they called her, she just wanted it all over with.

'Right that is it, thank you. Now if you would stay here a few moments longer, Mr Shepherd will be along to take you to your room and explain what will happen today.

Nicola remained silent, she didn't want to know the details. The least she knew the better she would be. She stared at Uncle Bob and to her surprise saw he looked pale. She hadn't missed how quiet he had been throughout the questions, maybe he was frightened too. She hoped he was.

'Hello, I'm Mr Shepherd,' a dark-suited, tall man appeared at Nicola's side. He clutched a buff folder under his arm and as formal as he looked, Nicola did not miss the softness in his eyes. 'I believe we have a little procedure to perform today,' he said, in a soft voice, extending his hand to shake hers. Automatically she held hers out and he shook it gently. 'There's nothing to worry about, I promise you it will be over before you've had time to think about it,' he said, his tone confident. 'So let me show you to your room, then we can get things moving.'

Nicola stood up.

'Good, now would you like your uncle to be with you? I suggest he should be, you will be glad of someone to talk to. I'm afraid these things can take a little time.'

The thought of *him* being there alarmed her and she was about to shake her head, but as she looked into Uncle Bob's face, she caught a glimpse of fear in his eyes and changed her mind. 'Yes, thank you,' she replied. Maybe if he saw what she had to go through, then after today he would leave her alone.

'I don't think…' Bob stammered.

'Perfect. That's settled, then please both of you follow me.'

Nicola didn't miss Bob's stutter. If only she wasn't so afraid she would smile.

Five hours later, Bob opened the passenger door and waited as Nicola climbed into the seat. Settling into the leather upholstery, to her surprise she felt nothing. No pain, no emotion, simply nothing. If she had died in that clinic she would not have felt any different because she was already dead inside.

'You don't look too bad,' he said, taking in her sombre expression. 'You can smile now, it's all over.'

Glaring up at him, she managed a weak smile and hoped with every fibre of her ruined body that it really was all over. Never did she want to go through anything like that again.

'It seemed pretty straightforward and unless anything goes a little wrong, which of course it won't, then we don't need to come back,' Bob said, his voice pitched higher than normal. He squeezed her shoulder, then pushed the door shut and walked round to the driver's door. Slipping into his seat, he turned the key in the ignition and the engine roared into life. 'So, how do you feel?'

A sneer curved at her lips as she tried to form a response. No words could begin to convey what had happened to her mentally during the whole shameful experience. He had sat at her side as she had curled up in pain, looking on and at times rubbing her back. Eventually, the shame of why she was in that sterile room oozed out of her. He had no idea how she felt and she was sure no one would ever understand. 'Okay,' she mumbled.

'Well done. I am so proud of you,' he said, a satisfied smile turning his earlier worried expression to one of relief. Gripping the steering wheel, he let the car roll forward. 'I said I'd sort it and I did. Only the very best for my princess.'

The best? Did he think paying for anonymity, with a pack of lies, in an expensive clinic was some kind of luxury day out for her? He had no idea how humiliating it had been nor how dirty and ashamed she felt, and as they left the grounds of Burley House, she not only left the clinic behind, but a very big part of her too.

Chapter Seventeen

With a mouthful of strong black coffee, Barbara swallowed down two mild sedatives. Since Terry's death she had been wound up like a coiled spring and visiting Nicola, she knew, would do nothing to ease her emotional state. She drained the last drop of coffee and placed the mug into the stainless steel sink. No sooner had she let go of it when the silence of the house was shattered with the ringing of the doorbell, jangling her tattered nerves further. She let out a weary sigh, the last thing she needed was a visitor. With laboured steps she headed to the door.

'Sorry to call unannounced,' Bob said, gripping his walking sticks, 'but I just wanted to see if you were all right,' he added, concern creasing his brow.

At the sight of her friend, Barbara's face lit up, the memories of the last half an hour receding.

'I'm so pleased to see you,' she said, knowing Bob would understand how she was feeling. She stepped aside to let him pass. 'I've just had a coffee, but I could do with another. And no doubt you could do with one.'

Bob nodded, 'Thanks Barbara. That would be just the job. I'm perished,' he said, leaning forward and brushing his cheek against hers.

'Thank you,' she said feeling his cold face. It wasn't just a thank you for the warm peck, but for all the years they had been good friends. Even now, in her darkest hour, he sensed she needed someone to talk to.

'You go sit yourself down in the lounge and I'll make a fresh pot and don't forget to turn on the gas fire and get yourself warm,' she added.

'I will,' he smiled and shuffled through to the lounge.

Pushing the front door closed, Barbara watched his laboured steps and tried not to picture the man he had been before the accident. Before that terrible day, he had been lean, fit and full of life, unlike the man she gazed at today. Years of inertia had turned his muscle-toned body to flab and his breathing to short gasps. The twill fabric of his trousers and jacket stretched tightly over his rotund belly and the face she had once thought of as handsome was now jowly and pained. Taking in the shadow of the man she had known for years, Barbara felt the weight of those years press down on her tired shoulders. There had been so much to deal with and come to terms with.

The crumbling years, as she had come to think of them, had started with the abortion. Even now, it still pained her to think about it. And, although it was a shameful time, looking back she saw that her daughter had changed long before then. Barbara could still pinpoint the moment when Nicola had morphed from a chatty, giggly girl to a moody pouting one; it had been just after her tenth birthday, the day her daughter had started her periods. The waxy odour from blowing out the cake candles had barely dissipated when Nicola announced that she was bleeding. A wave of sadness had swept over Barbara, knowing that her little girl, at ten, had the body of a woman and yet she was barely out of ankle socks. Shocked at nature's early arrival into Nicola's life, they had fussed around her, giving in to her moody behaviour in the hope she would eventually grow out of it. She didn't. In the end it became a way of life, but the abortion, when she was fourteen, was the real turning point. Even thinking about it still manged to bring her out in a sweat, beads of perspiration forming on her brow. She wiped the back of her hand across her forehead recalling how Nicola had been rushed into hospital, her life hanging by a thread. Barbara had thought the abortion was a nightmare, but the risk of losing her daughter had torn her apart. Mercifully, the medical staff had pulled Nicola through, but if she had thought the emergency would bring them close again, she could not have been more mistaken; Nicola distanced herself further. The pregnancy might have been terminated, but the wound left behind turned into a running sore that would not heal.

Even today, that sore was still weeping and she had no idea what was needed to soothe it. There was no sticking plaster that had been invented to heal this open wound.

Steam pumped from the kettle as it clicked off, pulling Barbara back to the task at hand. In her emotional state she really shouldn't be venturing down that well-worn road, it would do nothing to ease her mind. She made two mugs of coffee and placed them onto a tray.

Pushing the lounge door open, the sound of Bob coughing greeted her. It didn't sound good, she thought as he shuffled in the chair in an attempt to make himself comfortable. Her heart squeezed at how he struggled. Even after all these years the accident was still a mystery to her. She could no more imagine him running out into a busy road than see herself piloting a jumbo jet, yet the driver had been adamant to the police and a witness had confirmed his statement. Bob insisted he had no idea what had happened and had no recollection. Nine years later and he still refused to talk about it. It was as if he needed to erase the day that had changed his life forever. His recovery had been slow. After weeks in hospital he had spent more weeks in rehabilitation, but no amount of care would bring back the old Bob. He had arrived home in a wheelchair with sticks to aid his walking; a far cry from the swagger that had been his signature walk. It was clear to everyone that Bob would never swagger or walk properly again. They had helped him adjust. Becky had been amazing, helping him to come to terms with his disability. It was hardly surprising she had gone on to train as a doctor. Sadly, the same could not be said for Nicola, who at every opportunity made life difficult. Yet, thought Barbara, throughout the trauma, disappointment and upset, there had always been Terry, her rock; the man who had been there to listen and understand. She would never have got through these last few years had he not been there to try and make some sense of it all. And now he was gone.

Taking in the shadow of the old Bob, Barbara knew he did not deserve to have been crushed; he was a good, honest man. 'Are you warm enough?' she asked.

'Just about,' he said, eyeing the fire.

'I'll turn it up more,' she said, heading over to the fireplace and adjusting the knob. The flames greedily licked at the ceramic logs.

'Thanks Barbara, I seem to be permanently frozen these days,' he said, a thin smile parting his blue lips. 'Anyway, enough about my moans, how are you?' He reached his hand towards her.

She took hold of it, noting that it felt warmer. She was pleased he had come to the house, she hadn't relished the idea of going to see Nicola, even though she felt an obligation to find out how she was doing. In an attempt to ignore the guilt that she felt for preferring to sit with Bob rather than battle with her daughter, she said. 'I'm doing as well as you'd expect.' Even now, with his own sadness at losing Terry, he was here for her. That was Bob, always thinking of others. After Nicola's abortion, he had been marvellous too, showering the girls with gifts in an attempt to help Nicola over her terrible ordeal. She remembered he had bought them tickets to the cinema, had even given them each a new mobile phone, and much more. Now here he was, knowing she would be alone once Becky had left, checking she was okay. Squeezing his hand, she said, 'You know me too well. I'm exhausted and wondering how I'll come to terms with the fact that Terry will never come home again.'

Barbara's emotions were too close to the surface and she took a quick breath, she didn't want to break down in front of Bob, though he would understand. 'You know, I'm not sure I'll ever get over losing him. We had our ups and downs, but we were a solid couple,' she said. 'Funny, you know...' she pulled her hand back and laced her fingers together, 'so many thoughts have been going through my mind since Terry died. I've been thinking about the parties we had. They were fun times.' A smile travelled from her lips and lit up her eyes as she remembered those heady times. 'But it wasn't just the parties was it, Bob?' She didn't wait for him to respond, 'We had so many great times. Do you remember teaching the girls to swim? Terry was like a brick in water, he always used to sink.' Barbara even managed a chuckle at the memory. Still smiling, she added, 'And of course there was the Wendy House, all the covert work you and Terry did to build it.'

'They were good times, Barbara.' Bob stared down at his legs as he spoke. She did not miss what that signified; those wonderful days were before his accident, before their world had changed.

'Strange how when sadness strikes, the past tends to come into sharp focus,' she said, determined to try and lift her spirits with the happy events of the past.

'It does and they were good times,' Bob repeated, 'we certainly had some laughs. As for the Wendy House, it saddens me to see it fallen to bits.'

'Strange you should say that. This morning, I went down and unlocked the door, but I couldn't bring myself to go in. It's very dilapidated now.' The smile of earlier slipped away at the thought of the Wendy House.

'As you know,' Bob said, I offered in the past to have a go at bringing it back to its former glory, but Terry said it was a waste of time as Nicola wouldn't let her children play in it. I'm afraid these old pins wouldn't let me now, sadly,' he sighed.

'I know,' Barbara said, hurt that her grandchildren were not allowed to play there. She shook her head at the futility of talking about it. 'I don't know what's going on with that girl, but she's been filling my thoughts these last few days. I know she can be difficult, but I believe her father's death has hit her hard. Despite her negative attitude, Nicola is sensitive.' Lifting her mug to her lips, she took a sip. 'Nicola and Terry were once very close, you know. She was the apple of his eye and I believe she still was, right through to the day he died. He loved her beyond words and it was that love and wanting the very best for her that hurt him so deeply. He wasn't just disappointed in her, but in himself for not being able to do anything to steer her to a better life. The abortion, the drugs and then leaving home at seventeen, only to find herself pregnant again at such an early age almost destroyed him.'

Placing her mug down on the tray, she felt tears welling in her throat. 'He had such high hopes for her, Bob. She used to excel at school, you know. On two occasions she even took the title of top of the class.' Voicing the positives of Nicola for the first time in years, Barbara felt the familiar prickle of pride. *How could it have all gone so wrong*, she wondered. 'We were convinced she'd make all the grades and go to university. We even dared to dream it might be Cambridge. Back then, we believed, her life was mapped out; a road to success and happiness. How wrong could we have been?'

She stared across the room, her tired eyes settling on Nicola's first school photograph on the wall. The smiling face of her eldest at five, one of her front teeth missing and her fringe flicked up, stared back at her. Barbara felt a stab of pain at the beauty and innocence of that photograph. Who would have thought what lay ahead after the camera shutter had clicked, capturing that moment forever. If only it was possible to turn the clock back and start again with her babies. Dragging her gaze away from the photograph, she carried on. 'Instead, Nicola decided school was a waste of time.'

Barbara suddenly stopped speaking. She was doing it again, thinking and talking about Nicola. What was wrong with her? Leaning forward, as if the action of movement would halt her thoughts, she shook her head. 'I'm sorry Bob, of course you know all this and I'm prattling on. You didn't come round for me to drag up the past.'

'You don't need to say sorry to me. If talking about Nic makes you feel better, then I'm all ears. I know how upset Terry was with the way she'd turned out, but from what he often said to me, he never really gave up on her. I know she tested you both, had it been a different couple she would have broken you.'

Barbara nodded, maybe, she thought, but you never give up on your children, though sometimes you have to step back and draw breath.

As Bob rested his mug on the chair arm, Barbara saw how worn out he looked. She had been so wrapped up in her own worries and sorrow that she had not taken into account the closeness of the two friends. Bob had been like a brother to Terry and he would be mourning just as much as all of them. These days she had turned into a selfish woman, ignoring the pain of others whilst wallowing in her own self-pity. She was about to apologise for her thoughtlessness when Bob slowly pushed himself to his feet.

'Let me take your mug,' she said reaching over and dropping it on the tray next to her own.

'Thanks, these days I need both hands,' he chortled and hung on to the chair arm. With cautious steps he shuffled across the short gap and perched himself on the arm of Barbara's chair. He placed his arm around her shoulders and leaning down, he kissed the top of her head. 'I'm here to listen to anything you want to talk about, Barbara. I'm here to help if you'll let me. We are old friends,' he said.

Reaching up, she patted his hand, it felt clammy. She looked up into his face and saw tiny beads of perspiration forming on his top lip. 'Are you okay? You look like you could be coming down with something.'

'I'm fine, just tired and trying to come to terms with Terry's death,' he replied, hanging onto Barbara's hand.

'I know, and all I've done since you've arrived is harp on about Nicola. Right now we should be looking at the happy times, especially those we spent with that very special man who made life so much brighter,' she said, and this time the tears she had kept under control spilled out. She bowed her head at her open display of emotion. Her guilt at not visiting her daughter melted away. She could do that another day, a day when she would feel stronger and more able to cope with her. For now she needed the companionship of her old friend and the memories of the good times.

Chapter Eighteen

The automatic doors of the supermarket swished open. Laden with carrier bags, Nicola struggled through and was greeted by an overcast sky where watery sunshine peeked through a veil of clouds. Shrugging at her overzealous shopping spree, she peered down the road towards the bus stop, instantly her heart slammed against her rib cage. 'No!' she cried.

It was *him*! He was peering through the window of a computer shop, his hands stuffed in his pockets.

She glared at him and as if knowing he was being watched, he turned round. Nicola gripped her bags tight and tucked herself behind an elderly couple. Blending in with other shoppers she kept her focus on the bus stop and tried to hold her breath as if to help make her appear invisible.

From her peripheral vision, she spied a long stone bench and without warning, the elderly man stopped and plonked himself down, his laboured breathing loud enough for Nicola to hear; his partner joined him. Nicola groaned at the loss of cover. With the bus stop barely metres away, she kept her eyes cast down and hurried towards it.

'Nic, Nic, it's me,' he called. Nicola froze and stopped in her tracks. Alarm flooded through her. He called out her name again. This time his voice sounded closer. 'Oh God,' she cried and spun round, fleeing back towards the supermarket. Needing to know how close he was, she glanced over her shoulder and to her horror, saw he was gaining on her. *No, please no*, she silently screamed. Darting her gaze from left to right, she spotted a small cobbled side street and knowing it would take her back to the main road, she dived down it. Her arms aching with the bags of shopping, she kept up her pace and quickly reached the end. Slowing down, she felt as if her lungs were on fire with the exertion. Gasping out loudly, she looked down at her bags and to her dismay, saw she had lost several packages. It didn't matter, all she could think about was how to get away from *him*, get to the bus stop and get home.

'Are you okay, love?' A worried voice sliced into Nicola's panic. She spun round and came face to face with a heavy middle-aged woman blocking her path. 'You look like you've got the Devil on your heels,' the woman said, reaching over and touching Nicola's arm. 'Let me help you.' She bent down with ease and picked up a packet of biscuits that had fallen onto the cobbles.

'Thank you, I'm fine,' Nicola replied, her breath coming in short bursts as she reached out and took the packet from the woman's chubby hands.

'You shouldn't be running around with such heavy bags in your condition,' the woman said.

'I thought I was going to miss the bus,' Nicola lied, as she stuffed the item back into one of her carrier bags and looked down the street. Scanning the length of the narrow road, she saw there was no one else other than her and the woman. She had shaken *him* off. Relief flooded through her making her feel light-headed. It had been weeks since she had last seen him to speak to. Although he had been a few metres away from her today, she had not missed his evil smile when he spied her, the one that said he knew every intimate detail about her. She shuddered with disgust. Why was he here now after all these weeks? Once she had moved in with Brett, she had convinced herself *he* was gone from her life.

The last time he had touched her was the week before she had packed her bag and run out of the family home. She could still feel the pain and humiliation of what he had done. He had not gone to the house, instead he had been waiting outside the supermarket where she had worked.

'Get in the car, Nic, I'll give you a lift home,' he had called through the open window.

'No, I'm fine I'll get the bus.' She had been in his car enough times to know the outcome.

'Just get in,' he had insisted, leaning over and pushing the passenger door open, stopping her from walking down the pavement.

Not wanting to get in the car, yet afraid of what he might do if she refused, Nicola had sidled in. Predictably, he had not driven her straight home, but out of town to a quiet lane, where he had stopped the car.

'What do you want?' she had asked, as if she didn't know.

'I want to know why you are seeing that tow rag, Morton.'

'It's got nothing to do with you,' she had snapped.

'It's everything to do with me. For starters he's not good enough to lick your shoes, he's a user and you'll end up getting hurt.'

'You don't know him like I do,' she had flung back.

'I do, but more importantly, you're mine and always will be. We've been partners for years and I'm going to remind you what we do best together.'

Before she could stop him he had pushed the lever and the seat fell back leaving her prostrate. Seeing she was scared, he had laughed and jumped on top of her. He had been in a mean and particularly demanding mood and had taken her three times, hardly stopping to draw breath, or so it seemed to her. All she could think of was the baby. She had learned only recently she was carrying Brett's child. Having already had to lose two babies through abortions, she did not want to lose the one she was having with Brett. She had not struggled, she had just let him have what he had wanted and hoped he would eventually be satisfied and let her go.

'Are you sure you're all right?' the woman asked, breaking into her painful thoughts. Startled, Nicola stared at her. 'Yes, yes, I'm fine, she said, 'but I need to hurry my bus is due any minute.' Nicola's face flushed as she pushed away the memory of what he had done to her the last time.

'Okay, then I'll be on my way. You take care now,' the woman said, patting Nicola's arm before turning away.

'Yes, I will,' Nicola said in a voice that sounded reassuring. 'Thanks for your help.'

Gripping her bags tightly, Nicola felt her unborn baby shift in her belly. It startled her. She was almost twenty weeks into her pregnancy and mindful she should not be carrying this amount of shopping, or running like someone demented through the back streets. Neither would have been necessary had she not seen *him*. If only she could drive, then she could avoid walking the streets to bus stops, running the risk of another encounter. Brett had promised her a car as soon as the baby was born. Just thinking about Brett made her feel calmer. Nicola turned, her arms aching she headed back to the main street.

Seeing the bus stop ahead, she was about to lengthen her stride when a woman carrying a brief case nudged into her and almost knocked her over. 'Sorry,' the woman shouted, not stopping. Steadying herself, Nicola looked up and found herself staring straight into his eyes.

Chapter Nineteen

He peered into her face, his eyes bright, glaring at her, 'Nic,' he said reaching out his hand to grab her arm. 'I just want to talk to you.'

Nicola stared at him. 'No,' she gasped as he moved closure and before he could take hold of her, she spun round and headed in the opposite direction. Pushing her way through the crowds, she felt the calmness of moments earlier evaporating.

'Nic, wait!' Bob cried out, his footsteps gaining on her.

'Oh God,' she mumbled, gripped by fear. A sour taste filled her mouth as bile rose in her throat. She must not stop to be sick, she told herself, her heart slamming against her chest. She edged towards the kerb, her carrier bags, bumping into anyone in her way slowing her down. With rapid eye movement, she checked the traffic and to her relief saw a gap between a double decker bus and a dark blue car. Calculating she could make it across the road between the two vehicles, she dashed out in front of the car. No sooner had her feet landed on the tarmac, when a driver blasted his horn making her almost leap out of her skin and drop her shopping. Hanging on to her bags, she ignored the irritated driver and quickened her step. Reaching the safety of the other side of the road, she paused and took a deep breath. Taking the bus was no longer possible. Nothing would drag her back to the other side of the road; a taxi was the only option to get her away from *him* and home. Spying the taxi rank only metres away, she dragged herself to the waiting cars.

'Where to, love?' the driver asked, pulling open the rear door. She was about to give directions when an ear-splitting screech of tyres and a hail of blaring horns filled the air, followed by a sickening thud. A brief hush held everything in suspension, before the screaming and rush of footsteps replaced the sudden stillness. Nicola swung round, but all she could see were stationary cars, their doors flung open and a small crowd leaning over a body that lay in the middle of the road.

'Come on love,' the taxi driver called, appearing at her side, 'let me get your shopping in the boot. There's nothing you can do here. Just tell me where I need to get you.'

As the taxi sped away, all Nicola could think about was the person lying in the middle of the road. She did not dare to hope that it might be *him*.

The taxi journey home took no more than ten minutes, but Nicola felt it was taking hours. Sitting in the back, she struggled to breathe and tried to calm down. Even as she took slow, deep breaths all she could think of was *him* calling after her. With her mind racing, she didn't see the emergency vehicles race past in the opposite direction, or hear their ear splintering sirens as they sped to the accident scene. All Nicola saw in her mind's eye was the small group of people staring down onto the dirty tarmac. It couldn't be him, could it? she asked herself again. But then reasoned he was very likely still looking for her, searching through the crowds. No way would he have run into the road, no way! It just happened that he had called out when she had sprinted across the road to get out of his way. Just thinking about the accident had her fighting a panic attack. She tried to slow her breathing, but even inhaling she was losing control.

'Are you all right back there?' the taxi driver shouted, peering into the rear view mirror.

Unable to respond, Nicola managed a nod. She was anything but all right, but stopping the car would only delay getting to the safety of home. She attempted once again to slow her breathing, this time she felt a small measure of success.

'Hang in there, love, I'll have you home in a minute.' As he spoke, she felt the car accelerate. 'Hang in there,' he repeated.

To Nicola's relief, Rainsworth Court loomed ahead and although her breathing was laboured she felt her attack begin to subside.

At the sign that announced the name of the prestigious building, the driver pulled over to the kerb and brought the car to a halt outside the entrance. Turning in his seat, he peered over his shoulder. 'All right?'

Nicola nodded. She would be, once she was inside her apartment.

The driver smiled. She saw the relief in his eyes. 'Nice place you've got,' he said, taking in the luxury apartment block that dominated the top of the hill, with commanding views of the town.

Nicola did not respond. Never before had she been so appreciative of living in such an affluent and safe place. The entry system and the door commissionaire, she had scoffed at when she had first arrived, were now a welcome sight.

'Here, let me help you out,' the driver said, jumping out of his seat and pulling open the rear passenger door. Extending his hand, 'Here, take this,' he said with a sheepish smile.

Reluctantly Nicola took hold and as he assisted her out of the car, she didn't miss how he ogled the smoked glass windows and large balconies. She could almost read his mind as he added two and two together and came up with his own answer as to why a young girl in the family way and with bags of shopping, lived in one of the most prestigious parts of town. 'You hang on there a mo while I get your bags,' and with unnecessary haste, he strode back to his car. Nervously, she looked around afraid that *he* might have followed her. She couldn't see anyone, but she was convinced he wouldn't easily give up looking for her.

'Come on love, let's get you ensconced inside,' the driver called, a bag in each hand. Glad to be home, Nicola headed to the entrance, the driver keeping pace with her. Too afraid to look further, she kept her head down.

'Hope you'll soon be feeling better,' he said placing the bags down at the door.

'Thanks.' She fumbled in her handbag, pulled out two ten pound notes and pushed them into his hand.

He stared down at the money, 'That's way too much,' he said.

'It's fine. Keep the change,' she said, keen to get into the sanctuary of the apartment block.

'Right then, thank you and you take care,' he said, his smile wide as he stuffed the notes into the breast pocket of his jacket. 'Thanks again,' he called, hurrying back to his car.

'It's you, Miss Knight,' the commissionaire called in a nonplussed tone, pulling open the entrance door as he gazed down at her, his six foot frame resplendent in a dark blue uniform. Touching the side of his cap as if in mock salute, he added, 'I saw a taxi pull up and just needed to check before I opened the door,' he said, in a voice that Nicola was certain held sarcasm. He knew nothing about her, but he had made assumptions and not good ones, his attitude towards her verging on tolerance. She disliked him, though right now she did not care. All she wanted was to be safe and hide behind the façade of Brett's apartment.

'Let me take these bags,' he said, his hand shot out and scooped up her shopping.

'Thank you,' she said, though she wasn't fooled by his politeness. She had never failed to miss his disapproving looks, as if she was living in Rainsworth Court under false pretences.

With the commissionaire behind her, she hurried down the brightly lit corridor, its thick, plush carpet muffling their footsteps, and headed straight to number three. Fishing in her pocket, she pulled out a set of keys, unlocked the door and stepped inside. Instantly, a high-pitched ear-splitting wail filled the area.

'The alarm, Miss Knight, the alarm!' the commissionaire barked above the din.

'Yes, yes,' she cried, turning to the alarm pad, her hand trembling, but she couldn't remember the code.

'Miss Knight,' the commissionaire hissed, his exasperation evident.

'Oh my God, what is it?' she cried, her head was in such a muddle she couldn't think straight. Placing her fingers on the key pad, thankfully the number came to her and, she punched it in. A silence descended. With the tranquillity of Rainsworth Court restored, she took her bags from the commissionaire.

'Now you're in, I'll say good evening, Miss Knight.'

Nicola watched him march briskly back down the corridor. 'Thank you,' she muttered, embarrassed at forgetting about the alarm, but seeing *him* in town had terrified her. Moving in with Brett, she had believed she was safe, but after this afternoon it was clear she wasn't. *Why now*, she wondered, closing the door. She just hoped he had not followed her and was just waiting for the right opportunity to ring the doorbell. She must not think about it, it was just too much and Brett would be home soon. Right now she needed to calm herself and look normal, she didn't want Brett seeing her like this. He had no idea about her past; he had never asked and she didn't want him to know. He knew she wasn't a virgin, of course, but it hadn't bothered him, he had accepted her as she was. What Bob Wakefield had done to her was something she must keep a secret, if not she would be alone forever. Alone and with a baby.

To distract her from further thoughts of what had happened that afternoon, Nicola pushed the shopping into the fridge and cupboards, then shrugged off her coat and draped it over one of the breakfast bar stools. She smiled for the first time in hours. Brett's apartment was enormous. There was so much space she felt lost when she was there alone. Even the kitchen had more cupboards than she knew how to fill. Today's spree to the supermarket had barely made a dent in the enormous fridge. It was hard to believe he had lived here alone in this cavernous place before she had moved in.

She had met the confident Brett Morton not long after her second abortion. He had been in the "Dark Prince's Night Club". That particular night she had been out with Debs, a girl from school who was three years older than her, though neither knew each other back at school. Debs had left education as soon as she could and now worked behind the bar at the club. She was tall and with a bosom that made Dolly Parton look flat-chested. Debs knew how to show off her assets in all their glory. Nicola had met her new friend after she had be taken to the club by a bloke she had become friendly with, who supplied her with anything that would take the pain and fear out of her head. She hated having to use the stuff she acquired on the streets, but at times she had needed to keep the demons away as well as try to control her need to harm herself. Her arms were a mess, pitted with marks and ugly white scars.

That night in the club, Brett's eyes had met hers and she had been mesmerised. Debs had seen the exchange and had grabbed her arm. 'Keep away, he's trouble and you're far too young anyway,' she had warned. Nicola had heard what Debs had said, but minutes later the tall, well-dressed Brett had made his way over to where she was standing. Her first reaction was to flee. It was one thing to admire from a safe distance, but to have someone's hot breath close had her breaking out in a sweat.

'Aren't you going to introduce us?' Brett asked, his eyes watching Debs' bosom heave up and down.

'She's too young for you,' Debs snorted, a salacious grin parting her ruby lips.

'I'm old enough, if you don't mind,' Nicola had found herself answering.

'In that case, this young lady needs protecting from people like you,' Brett retorted, holding out his hand to Nicola. 'Let me introduce myself,' he had said, his voice surprisingly cultured as he had cast his piercing eyes over her. 'I'm Brett Morton and you are the prettiest thing that's walked through these doors in a long time.' He took hold of her hand, lowered his head and gently placed a soft kiss on the back of it. Standing up straight, still holding her hand, he had said, 'And you are?'

Nicola laughed. He certainly was a show boy and having had a little booster before leaving to go out that night, she was well relaxed. 'Nicola Knight,' she had replied, emitting the air of a confident, streetwise young woman, not a frightened and abused girl who, until that moment, had hated men.

'Well, it looks like you've found your knight in shining armour,' Brett quipped. 'Now let me get you something suitable to drink.'

Before Nicola or Debs could make any comment, Brett had insisted on a bottle of champagne. That night he had seen her home. In the club carpark, he had asked if he could have sex with her. She had never been asked before and at first wasn't sure how to answer. If she said no, would he force her? If she said yes, would it be okay? Instead of answering, she had giggled. He really was a gentleman. 'I don't know,' she had eventually said.

'Well let me give you a taster of what I can do for you,' he had suggested.

She hadn't stopped him. Nauseated and gripped by fear she had stiffened, but Brett had carried on and in the end had made the moment beautiful. It was the first time in her long experience of physical intimacy with a man that she had found it could be enjoyable. She had returned to the club the following night, champagne had flowed again and in the back office, they had done it all over again. She would never have believed that sex could be so good. Brett Morton had shown her how two people could have fun without her being hurt.

Weeks later, she had found herself pregnant, but more than being pregnant she was in love. Brett treated her as someone special: he spoilt her and she loved the attention he paid her. And although she went home most nights, she spent many nights in his bed. For the first time in years she felt safe and did not mind his insatiable appetite every time they were together.

'I'm pregnant,' she had told him flatly after a heavy session.

'I'm more of a man than I thought,' he had replied, taking her again. 'If you think you can cope with my demands, you can move in,' he had added, grabbing her wrist and pulling her on top of him.

Filled with happiness and eager to get away from *him* and her parents' home, she had moved in the next day. Her parents had been livid, even more so when they learned who she was leaving home for.

'He's no good for you,' her mother had screamed, 'he spends much of his time being talked about in the papers. He's got his fingers in every pie known to man and most of what he gets up to is questionable. God, Nicola, why are you so determined to destroy your life? You have everything going for you and yet you throw it away like rotting rubbish,' her mother had added, in a voice that verged on hysteria.

'He's a good man. He cares about me and more importantly, he loves me.' Nicola had stopped herself from saying anything about her pregnancy. It was on the tip of her tongue, but whilst her mother knew nothing about the first abortion, she had organised the second one. The fact that her mother had made her go through with it meant Nicola was not going to risk her knowing about this pregnancy with Brett. So she had bit down hard on her bottom lip and held all the words of anger in check. Escape was what she needed: Brett Morton offered her the opportunity to be away from them all. He loved her enough to give her a future and she was going to grasp it with both hands. 'I'm going to live with him, end of!' she had screamed back.

Within the hour she was on the other side of town, ensconced in Brett Morton's apartment. It was not only a love nest, but a refuge with an entry video system and more mod cons that she had ever seen. Importantly, it was safe and well away from *him*. And although it wasn't quite the dream she had been expecting, her life was better than it had been. No more was she molested by a family friend, a so-called uncle who made her do things she didn't want to; things she hated. Now she had sex with someone who loved her and if he wanted it then so did she.

Lost in happier thoughts, she almost leapt out of her skin when the phone rang out. She froze and felt the blood drain from her face. Was it *him*? Had he after all followed her back and somehow managed to get hold of her telephone number? 'Please no,' she cried. How could he do this? Oblivious of her state of terror, the phone continued to ring out. As if welded to the spot, Nicola ignored it and waited for the voice mail to take over. A further four rings tormented her before Brett's voice sang out from the recorded message, apologising for not being able to take the call. Then, 'Hello Honey, it's me…'

At the sound of Brett's 'real' voice, Nicola almost tripped over her own feet in her haste to grab the phone. 'I'm here Brett, just got back from shopping,' she trilled, in the hope it masked her inner turmoil.

'I'm sorry, but I'm not going to make it home tonight. Something urgent as come up and I need to stay in town.' Nicola felt her legs weaken at the thought of Brett not coming home. She would be alone in the apartment. What if *he* was out there, watching? As much as fear gripped her, she managed to control her voice.

'Oh no,' she said, her voice flat. 'I was planning on making your favourite meal.' It was a lie; she was in no fit state to think about cooking or food.

'No worries, I'll be home tomorrow and you can cook it then,' Brett said, adding, 'take care and don't go rushing around. I need all your energy for me.'

She almost choked on his last words. 'You know me, I only do slow these days,' she said, her heart sinking further down to her boots at the prospect of being home alone.

Nicola replaced the receiver. Fear raced through her veins and she felt an urgent need to take something to calm her down. Looking round the kitchen she spied the kettle and almost laughed out loud. A cup of tea would not help. She needed something that would blot him out, she told herself and at the same time her eyes feasted on the small wine rack. She disliked red wine, but apart from a couple of bottles of expensive champagne, there was nothing else to drink. For a man with so much wealth, Brett's drinks cabinet didn't exist, all he had was a table top wine rack filled with four bottles of plonk. She hesitated for a brief moment, not sure she should be drinking while she was pregnant, but quickly reasoned she'd had a terrible shock and argued that if she stayed in this state much longer she could lose the baby. With no one to share her torment or comfort her, she reached over to the wine rack and pulled out a bottle of red wine. Opening a tall cupboard, she plucked out a large glass. Searching in a drawer, she found what she was looking for and with no finesse or understanding on how to open quality wine, she ripped the foil away and, after a battle, pulled the cork out. A small sliver of cork remained in the bottle neck. Tutting, Nicola poked at the piece with the tip of the opener and pushed it inside, then poured a generous amount into a large glass. She lifted it to her lips, and without ceremony, glugged down half its contents. Gripping the stem of the glass, she cringed at the unpleasant taste, grabbed hold of the bottle, and with the glass in her other hand, padded through to the lounge.

Plonking the bottle on the coffee table, she switched on the TV. Immediately the screen filled with scenes of a protest as a news reporter, muffled up in scarf and heavy overcoat, spoke into a furry covered microphone. Half listening to the monotone voice of the presenter, Nicola downed the remaining contents of her glass. She hated television. Seeing decent-looking men on the box always reminded her of that very first night with *him*. The "dishy doctor" had been the start of it all for her, and all because she had thought *he* looked like the actor on TV. And now, after she had left home and moved in with a decent man, *he* still managed to stalk her. She hated herself and she hated *him* and she had no idea how to stop him.

Nicola looked down at her empty glass and grimaced, this was not the answer, but what was? Not knowing what else to do to drive her demons away, she reached over for the bottle and emptied the contents into her glass. The wine and lack of food fuelled her imagination and she began to believe *he* would turn up at Rainsworth Court. Despite the place being like a fortress and even though she reasoned he couldn't get in, she could not get past the fact that he had been calling out her name and chasing her. She already thought she could hear him hammering on her door, demanding to see her.

Frightened, she clicked off the TV and with the wine glass in her hand, shambled through to the bedroom. Placing the glass on the bedside cabinet, she pulled off her clothes and let them drop to the floor. She stepped over them and slipped on her fluffy pyjamas before crawling into bed. No sooner had she laid her head on the pillow when the feeling of nausea enveloped her, the mixture of wine and panic playing havoc with her stomach. Not relishing the thought of getting out of bed, Nicola tugged at the duvet and buried herself underneath it. She closed her eyes, but try as she might, sleep would not take her away from it all.

'Why, why, why?' she repeated. In a state of agitation, she rolled out of bed and went in search of her handbag. Finding it in the hall, she carried it back to the bedroom. Rooting through it she found what she needed: a packet of sleeping pills. 'Sorry baby,' she cried, 'but we'll not make it if I don't stop all this rubbish from going round in my head. Taking two pills from the packet, she promptly swallowed them with the last dregs of her red wine and struggled back into bed. She needed to sleep and blot out the world for a few hours. A few minutes later Nicola felt the weight of her eyelids beginning to close her eyes. When she could no longer open them she smiled, thankful that sleep was about to take her away from it all.

Chapter Twenty

The ringing slowly drifted into Nicola's subconscious bringing her half awake. She rolled over, pulling the thick duvet over her head. All she wanted was to sleep and block out her world.

The ringing continued.

Nicola groaned with grogginess and struggled to surface from a deep, drug-induced sleep. With an effort she flicked her eyelids open. The sudden brightness of the room scorched her retinas. She snapped them shut. 'Oh my God,' she moaned and pushed the duvet back. The cool air washed over her bare arms and she shivered. Pushing herself up onto her pillows, she winced at the pain in her head. The noise continued unabated. As it penetrated through to her brain, she tried to work out where it was coming from. She had not set the alarm clock and the burglar alarm was not armed; it never was when Brett was away. She was too afraid it would go off if she had one of her nightmares and ended up running round the apartment in her need to escape.

'Stop, stop!' she bleated, reaching out and knocking over the alarm clock. It crashed to the floor, but the noise persisted, drilling into her pounding head. Thinking it would never stop she covered her ears with her hands. Silence suddenly filled the room. Nicola snapped her eyes open and lowered her hands. With all the effort she could muster, she tried to focus on the heavily papered walls covered in large black and white flowers, but everything appeared to pitch and sway as if she was sitting in a rowing boat on a rough sea. She grabbed the edge of the duvet to steady herself and blinked rapidly. Slow seconds passed before her focus returned and her mind began to clear. As the memory of what she had taken the previous evening filled her head, shame washed over her and she clutched at her stomach. She had swallowed down a cocktail of wine and sleeping pills. What damage might she have done to her baby? What had she been thinking?

The ringing noise started again. 'The phone,' she hissed through dry, cracked lips. Reaching towards the bedside cabinet, she grabbed the handset and punched the green button. 'Hello,' she croaked.

'Good God, where have you been? Trying to talk to you is like trying to contact the dead. I've been ringing for hours,' Barbara shrilled down the phone.

Nicola winced at the sound of her mother's high-pitched voice. She had no idea what time it was and wondered if it mattered. Any time would be too early to wake up if she had to see *him* again.

'I'm ringing to let you know I'll be with you in about half an hour. It's important that I see you.' Before Nicola could utter a word of protest, her mother cut the call.

'Half an hour!' Nicola winced, the pain in her head reminding her of last night's overdose. What could be so urgent that her mother needed to come to Rainsworth Court? Her mother would rather swing from a trapeze than drive across town to visit her in Brett's home. She dropped the phone down on the duvet. The last thing she needed right now was her mother marching in and reading the riot act again. Feeling sick, Nicola flopped down on the soft pillows and burst into tears. All she wanted to do was curl up into a tight ball and stay in bed feeling sorry for herself, but it was never going to happen with her mother racing across town. Nicola knew that if she didn't pull herself together she would have to explain why she felt so ill. Resigned to the impending untimely visit, she wiped the back of her hand across her nose and wondered what she would say if her mother was to see her like this? *Oh Mum, I've been chased across town by Uncle Bob!* Or should she just blurt out she was pregnant, yet again? Nicola flinched at the thought of uttering either of these excuses to her mother. Knowing she was left with no choice but to shower, get dressed and try to look normal, whatever that was, she dragged herself out of bed.

Tripping over her clothes that lay crumpled on the floor, she shuffled into the bathroom, the nightmare of yesterday still playing like a film trailer on replay. Standing in the large shower cubicle, the hot water raining down on her taut, aching body, she groaned as the pressure from the jets pummelled on her skin.

Nicola was in no doubt that she would have to put on an act of normality to avoid a barrage of questions. What worried her now was why her mother was racing across town to see her? Had she come to drag her home? She had made no secret of her dislike of Brett and disapproval of her daughter living with him. 'Oh God,' Nicola cried. If only she didn't feel so ill, she would be able to cope with the confrontation she was certain was imminent. As the hot water hammered onto her, the tension eased in her muscles and her body began to relax. If only the water jets could do the same for all the frightening thoughts in her head, then maybe she could be like any normal seventeen-year-old, she laughed, because she would never be a normal seventeen-year-old or any normal person again.

Turning the shower off, Nicola plucked a large white towel from the heated rail and wrapped it around her body. 'Brett,' she whispered, Just thinking about Brett and the baby made her feel loved. There had been no talk of getting rid of the baby or Brett telling her he didn't want anything more to do with her, Brett accepted his responsibility. She loved him so much. It was an emotion she never thought she would feel for a man after what *he* had done to her. Though if she had to think about it, Brett was rather mysterious, apart from him living here in Rainsworth Court and owning a nightclub, she knew nothing else about him. He worked very strange hours; staying away from home, often, several nights a week, but this hadn't stopped her falling in love. Mystery or no mystery she was more than fortunate to have someone so gorgeous who loved and wanted her. She didn't really care what he did or where he went, he loved her and that was more than enough.

Letting the feeling of his love flow through her Nicola padded over to the wash basin. She stared into the large mirror and the shock of her reflection pushed thoughts of Brett away. A pale face covered in red blotches glared back at her. Two dark circles shadowed her eyes, making her look like a panda. She looked more like an old woman living on the streets than a seventeen-year-old in love. This would not do, she groaned, her mother must not see her looking like this. The worry of why she was on her way to Rainsworth Court to see her brought a pained expression to Nicola's tired face. Something had to be wrong. Then, as if a switch had been flicked, she instantly understood what had happened and why her mother had insisted it was important. It had to be about *him*.

Nicola groaned; yesterday she had ignored him and run away and it was clear he was mad with her and out for revenge. Had he told her mother how she had led him on? No doubt pleading his innocence as he begged for forgiveness? She shivered as these thoughts gained momentum. Not only had she run away from him yesterday, but weeks ago she had run away from him to live with Brett. Bob had been furious when he had learnt of this. Now he was making his final stand: if he could not have her, he was making sure no one else would. In her hungover state Nicola convinced herself he had told her mother what they had done, making her out to be some kind of sex mad adolescent who would not take no for an answer. He would get away with it of course, and she would be blamed for everything. It was clear he intended to teach her a lesson even at risk to himself.

Nicola pressed the heels of her hands into her eyes in an attempt to push back the pain that throbbed there and try to erase what was brewing. How could she face her mother? How was she going to explain Bob Wakefield was lying; that he had molested and forced her since she was a child? No matter how much pain she suffered, she had to find a way to tell her mother the truth and convince her *he* was the evil one.

Nicola was close to falling apart after yesterday, what had she to lose by being honest?

Chapter Twenty-One

'Hello Mum, come in,' Nicola said, her voice concealing her inner turmoil as she hung on to the door handle.

'Nicola, I can't believe it,' Barbara said, looking at her daughter.

'Mum...' Nicola faltered, a lump rising in her throat, all the words she had put together during the last half an hour slipped out of her head.

'It's such a trek across town these days, what with all the new one-way systems,' Barbara moaned, undoing the buttons on her dark woollen jacket. 'The only saving grace is the ample parking here,' she grumbled, as she brushed past her daughter.

'I've made coffee,' Nicola stuttered, closing the door and following her mother, wondering what the one-way system had to do with her visit.

'Believe you me I need it and you will too after what I've got to say,' Barbara said, slipping onto one of the white leather chairs placed round the octagonal smoked-glass table in the kitchen.

Her mother had only been to Rainsworth Court twice before, but she had not forgotten where the kitchen was. She marched through as if she owned the place, thought Nicola, annoyed. Taking hold of the coffee jug, she attempted to fill one of the coffee mugs, but her hand shook so violently she had to place the mug back down on the surface top. From the corner of her eyes she could see her mother staring at her. Why was she looking at her like that? Was she checking to see if there were any signs of what she was about to explode over? Perhaps she should speak first and tell her that she wasn't to blame and that she never once had wanted *him* to touch her and she hated having to have the abortions. Could she say all that without her mother interrupting?

'Mum, before you start, can I tell you about me first…'

'What?' Barbara cut in. 'Nicola, I haven't driven all this way for you to talk about yourself. We are not going down the *me* road. I am here because I have sad news that affects us all.' Barbara's voice faltered as she dug into her jacket pocket and pulled out a tissue. Dabbing at her eyes, she glared at Nicola.

Stung at the put down and feeling her spirits plummet further, Nicola ignored the coffee and dropped down onto a chair next to her mother.

'You might think you're grown up Nicola, but you are still a child. And as much as I'm appalled at what you're doing, I'm not here today to say my piece. You know how we feel, your father and I. Today, I am here to tell you something I know will be deeply upsetting, hence why I battled across town to talk to you in person. These things can't easily be spoken about on the phone.'

Her mother's words echoed inside her head and Nicola was filled with a renewed dread as she waited for the axe to fall about her secret. Right now she wasn't sure she was strong enough to cope with it, her head throbbed and her stomach was rebellious. She should never have mixed the alcohol and sleeping tablets. She had failed to escape from it all and was now paying a high price for still being alive.

'What's that in your hair,' Barbara suddenly said, reaching over and plucking at a strand of hair. She frowned at what she held between her thumb and forefinger. 'Blood…'

'It's from a spot on my scalp,' Nicola, burst out, wondering what her mother was playing at, maybe she should tell her she had caused her scalp to bleed by scratching at it until it hurt and bled. Of course it bled, but it had helped her to cope as she waited for her mother to arrive. If she piped up right now it would stop all this cat and mouse game. She needed desperately to get it over with.

Oblivious of her daughter's distress, Barbara reached over and took hold of her hand.

'Mum…'

'My love, I'm afraid there's been an accident,' Barbara said, ignoring Nicola's interruption, 'Uncle Bob has been badly hurt. He was knocked down by a car in the middle of town yesterday afternoon.'

'Really?' Nicola blurted out. Feeling the colour drain from her face she wondered if she was about to faint. This was not what she had been expecting and she swayed, reeling from the blow of her mother's words.

'Nicola, you've gone as white as a sheet,' Barbara cried. Jumping to her feet she immediately wrapped her arms around her daughter, pulling her close. 'I'm sorry darling, I knew it would be a shock,' she soothed, rocking Nicola gently against her whilst kissing the top of her head as she brushed the spiky hair aside.

With her earlier worries forgotten, all Nicola could hear was the screeching of tyres, the blaring of horns and the silence that followed before the shouting filled the void. It was *him*, it *was* him! Oh my God! Did they know it was her who had lured him across the road, knowing the traffic was heavy? But she hadn't lured him, had she? He must have followed her. Was he dying? Oh God, she was to blame. Disbelief at what had happened choked her and any words she might have dared to utter lodged in her throat. She looked up at her mother's face and saw for the first time since Barbara had arrived that it was drawn and her eyes were puffy from weeping. Nicola took in her mother's sadness and saw tears trickle down her cheeks. It was heart-breaking. She had not seen her mother weep since that dark day when she had been rushed to A&E after her second abortion. And yet here her mother was, weeping like a child over a man whom over the years Nicola had wished dead more times than she could count. She felt a deep sadness, not for being responsible for the accident, which she undoubtedly was, but for witnessing her mother's utter distress.

'Mum…'

'It's all right love, thankfully they say he's going to live,' Barbara sniffed, stroking Nicola's cheek, 'but we have to wait to see how the operation went,' she added, still holding Nicola close. 'Dad and I went last night after the call from the hospital. They told us his legs were crushed, but the doctors are hopeful. They can do so much these days,' Barbara said, her voice rising with emotion. 'He's in the best hands,' she added, releasing her hold on Nicola.

'What happened?' Nicola found herself asking, worried he might have told her parents why he was in town or worse, that it was her he was following. Had he mentioned her name? What was a nightmare before yesterday was nothing compared to this. Could she be arrested for attempted murder? After all, hadn't she deliberately gauged the closing gap in the traffic and dived through it knowing he was behind her? Had she guessed he would follow her into the road? She was no longer sure, it was all a blur and the more she tried to remember, the more blurred it became.

'He's not able to speak at the moment so we don't know much. All we've been told is that he was in a road accident. Evidently, as soon as the ambulance arrived at the hospital he was taken straight to theatre. It seems he'll have to be on a ventilator for a while.'

Nicola didn't miss the worry in her mother's voice and she desperately wanted to feel something, if only relief he couldn't get near her, but all she felt was numb.

'Why don't you come back home with me for the day? When Dad and I go to the hospital later you can come with us,' Barbara suggested, taking in the shocked expression that filled Nicola's face. 'I'm sure it will do him good to know we are all there for him,' she encouraged.

Nicola silently balked at such a preposterous idea, she could not be there for *him*, not now, not ever. Even more so when he would eventually speak and tell everyone it was her who had tried to kill him, deliberately leading him on. If only he had not run after her. How had it all come to this? All she had been doing was shopping. Now more than ever, no one would believe her about what he had done to her. She screwed her eyes up tight and winced. What was going to happen to her now?

'Nicola, are you all right?' her mother asked, concerned.

'I'm fine. It's the shock,' she managed to say, at the same time trying to work out how she could stop her mother insisting she go to the hospital to see *him*. She simply couldn't do it. My God, what was she to do? Not only could she not go to the hospital, but spending time at her parents' was not what she needed either. For a start, they might see she was pregnant and right now she did not want them to know. They would be horrified. She could already hear her mother ranting about how young she was. Would they demand she have another abortion? Was she strong enough to resist them if they did? Could things get any worse?

'No Mum, I don't need to come back home, I'll be fine here. When he's feeling better maybe I could go and see him then,' she said and hoped she sounded normal. Years of lying had turned her into a good actor, though her stomach churned with the worry of it all. Would that man ever be out of her life and her nightmares?

'I'm not happy leaving you here with such news, please come home love,' Barbara said, frowning as she took in her daughter's pale face. 'You're in shock and leaving you alone is not an option I am comfortable with.'

'No Mum, honestly I'm fine. Brett will be back later and I'd like to be here when he gets in,' Nicola said, while thinking, *if she thinks I'm in shock now, wait 'til I have to see* him*! What will she think then?*

'This is a family emergency and let's be honest you've hardly known this Morton fellow five minutes,' Barbara pressed, her lips pulling into a thin line.

Nicola sniffed, it hadn't taken her mother long to swing from compassion to having a dig at her, she thought, trying to ignore the snide remark about Brett. How could she go to the hospital and stand at *his* bedside knowing it was she who had put him there?

Struggling to her feet, Barbara looked down at her daughter. 'Come on love, why don't you and I go to the hospital now and then I'll drive you back here afterwards. You can come home at the weekend to see your dad. Right now, your Uncle Bob needs us,' Barbara insisted, taking hold of her daughter's hand and squeezing it to convey what she expected.

Unable to see a way out of going with her mother, Nicola pulled herself up from the chair. She did not know how to say no and mean it.

'It can't be too much to ask,' Barbara continued when her daughter remained silent. 'He's been a true uncle to you, Nicola, as much if not more than any real one could have been. It's at times like this we have to be united as a family. I hate hospitals too, but we'll have each other for support. Go get your coat and we'll be on our way.'

A part of Nicola thought it would be a solution. If he had anything to say to her, he would surely be guarded in front of her mother and it might give her an opportunity to find out what he had told anyone else about what had happened to cause the accident. Her mother had said he wasn't able to talk, but what did she *really* know about him? Nothing! Nicola wondered what her mother would have to say if she knew what had actually taken place yesterday afternoon. As yet she didn't, but there was every likelihood she soon would. There was no doubt it was a hopeless situation as far as Nicola was concerned. 'What about Becky?' she asked, attempting to create a temporary diversion.

Buttoning up her jacket, Barbara looked up, 'She's at school of course, working hard on her lessons. Naturally she's upset, and like you, she worships Uncle Bob.' She shook her head, 'We will be taking her tonight when your dad and I visit. So do we have we a deal, Nicola?'

'Deal?'

'Yes, you come to the hospital and I'll bring you back here. If that's what it takes to have you see him, then I'll happily do that. Please Nicola,' Barbara pleaded.

What choice did she have? None, Nicola told herself. 'If that is what you want,' she said, feeling utterly defeated, 'but I'll need to go to the loo first.'

'No rush, whenever you're ready,' Barbara said, sounding triumphant.

Heading to the bedroom, Nicola grabbed her handbag and scrabbled through the contents until she found the little packet. For an emergency she kept a small supply of pills. Last night was one and today was another. Slipping her finger in the end of the packet, she pulled out a tiny white pill and without hesitation popped it into her mouth and swallowed it down. She tried not to think about what she was doing, she was starkly aware she should not be pill popping, but knew she would never get through the hospital doors if she didn't have some help.

Chapter Twenty-Two

Locked in her thoughts, Nicola pushed her fist into her mouth and stared through the passenger window. She needed to try and distract the feeling of nausea that threatened to overwhelm her. Why couldn't he have just let her cross the road without following? As if her life hadn't been hard enough through him, here she was frightened out of her wits, on her way to hospital to see him. Why did everything revolve around *him*? These days she felt as if she were the only member in an exclusive club of abuse and fear. She pinched her lips together tightly in a bid to arrest anything from coming out of her mouth. Even the weather didn't have the decency to pour down in sympathy with her; instead there were white, fluffy clouds scudding along a sapphire blue sky and like her behaviour, it was deceptive. She was frozen inside and the weather was freezing outside. They had a lot in common, they were both window dressing.

'Do you think you've got something to tell me Nicola?' Barbara quizzed, glancing in her direction.

Nicola swung round, startled. Removing her hand from her mouth, she wiped the spittle away. What did her mother think she had to tell her? It was cat and mouse time again! Had she known all along what had happened yesterday afternoon and lured her into a trap where there was no escape and where she could deal with her? Was this the reason she had insisted on taking her to the hospital? Trying not to panic, all Nicola could think of was that she was not to blame for the accident. How could she be? It was not her fault he had chosen to run after her.

'Well?' Barbara asked, her tone demanding a response.

Unsure how to answer, Nicola remained silent, then wondered if she should acknowledge she knew what had happened yesterday afternoon, explaining it was an accident. But then her mother would insist on details: why was Bob running after her and why didn't she stop and wait for him? The questions would be endless and she knew that any answers to these would provoke more questions, and then where would it end? Everything would come out and her mother would know her daughter was nothing but a dirty tramp.

As Nicola toyed with what to say, her mother snapped, 'You're pregnant, aren't you? Nicola, please tell me I'm wrong,' Barbara pleaded, her voice rising as she checked her rear view mirror.

Shaken by her mother's statement, Nicola had no idea what she had done or said to advertise her condition. Then she remembered, the woman in the alley she had bumped into when running away from him had said something about her condition. Until then she had no idea she was showing still believing she was slim and beneath her loose fitting T-shirt she was hardly showing yet. 'What makes you say that?' Nicola asked, her voice shaking, wondering what her mother was thinking and not missing the sly look she gave her. If ever she had felt trapped, she did now. How was she going to deal with this too? She quietly groaned. Then it occurred to her that talking about the baby might swing the emphasis away from her mother going on about *him* in the hospital. Feigning surprise, she responded. 'Yes, but only just and Brett is thrilled. He loves me Mum, he really does and we're a serious couple. You have nothing to worry about; he's there for me and will be there for the baby.' She couldn't stop the words tumbling out. It was as if all her anxieties were keen to escape, along with the need to justify her pregnancy and lifestyle to her mother.

'Nicola, you're too young! What is it with you that you need to rush into adulthood and now motherhood?' Tapping her fingers on the steering wheel to display her disappointment, Barbara continued. 'Have you not learnt *anything* from what you went through a couple of years ago? Good grief, Nicola, this is the last thing we all need right now.'

What did she mean right now? It was right for her and as far as she could see, it had nothing to do with what her mother needed. Nicola seethed.

'How far gone are you?'

'Not that far,' she said petulantly and wondered why her mother was always so dominant. She couldn't even be pregnant without getting the third degree. Could her mother not see she was now living away from home and with a decent man?

'How far, Nicola?' Barbara insisted.

'But how do you know?' Nicola asked breathing in.

'I'm your mother and you forget I've seen that look before.'

What look would that be, Nicola wondered. Whatever it was, her mother had not noticed it the first time when she'd been thirteen. Not wanting to go any further with this, she answered her mother's earlier question. 'Twenty weeks.'

'Oh, Nicola, where did we go wrong with you?' Barbara said, her tone sharp with distress.

Where indeed? Nicola silently screamed. Here she was, against her better judgement, being driven to *his* bedside, close to a mental melt down and all her mother could do was castigate her for not being the dream daughter she had wanted. *Why do I never learn?* It was always the same whenever she was in the company of her mother.

'What about your job?' Barbara asked, oblivious to Nicola's increasing tension.

When would the questions end? Nicola wondered. She had not mentioned that she had left her job as shelf-stacker, after moving in with Brett. He had told her he didn't want her working now she was pregnant, not that she could tell her mother that.

'I'm on sick leave at the moment,' she lied.

Barbara tutted, 'And there's your younger sister working her socks off to achieve good grades at school. I'm beginning to think you were swapped at birth,' she said, slowing down as a set of traffic lights loomed ahead. 'Look at the length of this queue, the lights can't be working properly,' Barbara moaned, again tapping the tips of her fingers on the steering wheel with irritation.

If the lights never changed, it wouldn't bother her, Nicola thought, that way they would never get to the hospital. Just thinking about how close they were to *him* had her breaking out into a sweat. She pushed the button on the door arm and the window slid open. The frigid air whipped at her face.

'It's all part of it,' Barbara snapped, as the icy air mixed with the warmth from the car heater. 'I hope you're taking care and seeing the doctor. Goodness, Nicola, I can't believe you've allowed this to happen. Are you sure you want it? What is it with you? You are too young for all this behaviour, when I was your age we thought about sex, we didn't rush into it like there's no tomorrow.'

'Yes, I'm sure,' Nicola snapped. She closed the window and wished she'd had the courage to put her foot down and insisted on staying in the apartment.

'Looks like we are on our way,' Barbara said, exasperation dripping from every word as she nudged the car forward to keep up with the car in front. 'Thinking about it, maybe it wasn't such a good idea taking you to see Uncle Bob. It's not such a great a place at best, but even more so if you're pregnant; far too many germs flying around!'

'I'm happy to go home, I do feel unwell,' Nicola burst out, not daring to believe her mother would turn the car around.

Barbara stole a glance at her. 'You do look pale,' she agreed, 'but then you did when I arrived. At seventeen, you cause me more worry now than ever you did as a baby.' Barbara took in the traffic travelling in the opposite direction, 'I'd turn round but with this traffic and the fact we're so close to the hospital, I think it best we carry on.' Reaching out with her left hand, she patted Nicola's knee. 'For now I'll not harp on about your condition, we've enough on our minds at the moment. Let's just concentrate on getting to Uncle Bob. He'll be over the moon to see you. And, of course, it will be your way of looking out for him like he's always done for you. Just think of all those treats he gave you after the abortion to make you feel worthy again.'

Oh, he did all that and more, Nicola thought, wanting to scream. *And if you knew just how he treated me you would not be ranting on about how marvellous he is and how he loves us. You've no idea!* Anger gripped her, but not as much as the fear of seeing *him* did.

Barbara managed to squeeze her car into a narrow space at the furthest point from the hospital entrance. 'And they have the audacity to charge for parking. We are miles away from the hospital,' she said, feeding the parking machine with pound coins.

With the ticket placed on the windscreen, Barbara slipped Nicola's hand into the crook of her arm. 'Come on, let's see how he's doing,' she said, negotiating round parked cars and heading towards the hospital entrance.

With each step, Nicola felt her fear grow.

'He's in Rowan ward. Well, it's not a ward as such, he has his own room. He needs it with all the machines and special nursing,' Barbara said, as they walked through the wide entrance and headed off down a corridor to their left. The pale yellow walls and paintings of local landscapes were a blur to Nicola's eyes. All that was framed in her mind was a body lying in the road; a crowd gathering round. Reaching the end of the long corridor, her anxiety had built to such a level she was sure her legs were about to give way and she would end up sprawled on the disinfected floor.

'Are you okay?' Barbara asked, slowing her pace.

'Fine, I think, it feels like my legs want to cramp,' she lied. Lying was almost as natural as breathing these days, she thought, without a hint of guilt.

'Well, we're in the right place for help, let me call a nurse over,' Barbara insisted. Spying a uniformed woman ahead she raised her hand to attract the nurse's attention.

'No Mum, honestly I'm all right, please let's not make a fuss,' Nicola hissed.

'Are you sure? It's not a problem getting a nurse to look you over while we're here.'

'I promise, I'm fine,' Nicola said, wishing the floor would open up and swallow her because she wasn't sure how she was going to walk into *his* room. Oh, why had she allowed her mother to bully her? At seventeen, she was more grown up than most, though in her mother's eyes she was still a child and she was still expected to do as she was told, especially in situations like this.

Without warning, Barbara stopped and turning to her daughter placed her arm around Nicola's shoulders, a concerned look forming creases across her forehead. 'We might have our differences these days, darling, but you never stop worrying me and I can see you're not a hundred percent.' Barbara nodded as if to emphasise her unease. 'And like I promised, once we've seen how he's doing, I'll take you home. I can see it was a mistake to bring you here. I should have left it until he was awake and speaking.'

A raft of emotions shot through Nicola at her mother's concern. It took all the strength she had left not to break down and cry. 'Thank you,' she said, her voice catching in her throat on a ball of emotion. All she had ever wanted was for her mother to approve of her like she did Becky, not always find fault and disappointment.

'Come on then, let's see how he's doing,' Barbara said, a smile softening her features as she took hold of Nicola's hand. 'Here we are.'

They stopped outside a pale green door. Nicola's gaze locked on the window to the left. Cream-coloured vertical blinds were snapped shut leaving no hope of a glimpse inside. She swallowed hard, but there was no moisture in her mouth. It was as dry as a desert.

Her mother pushed down on the handle and nudged the door open. Instantly, a low buzz of machines filled the silence between mother and daughter. Barbara made her way into the room and tiptoed to the side of the bed.

Nicola stood motionless in the corridor. She did not think she could enter the room. She wanted to flee, yet she felt rooted to the spot.

'Come on in,' Barbara said in a whisper, 'and close the door.'

Nicola still did not move, she just stared at the end of the bed.

'It's okay,' Barbara said, walking back to her. 'You're shocked. It's a normal reaction.' She ushered her into the room, then gently pushed the door closed.

There was nothing normal about her reaction, Nicola thought. Her heart was thumping so hard in her chest she was convinced its loud beat would be heard above the machines. She sucked in her lips and holding her breath, crept towards the bed. Her gaze didn't miss the monitors with their thin wires that stretched across the bedcovers and were clipped in place on *his* fingertips. He was alive. Of course he was. She wasn't sure if she was pleased or disappointed; pleased because she wouldn't be arrested for manslaughter and disappointed that he would continue to create a paralysing fear in her.

Her mother smiled down at his sleeping features then turned her attention to a chair to her right. 'Come and sit down,' Barbara murmured.

Ignoring the chair, Nicola edged closer to the bed. As she reached her mother's side, Bob's eyes snapped open and he glared up at her, the shadow of a grin parting his lips.

Chapter Twenty-Three

After four months of nightmares that oscillated between screeching car tyres, car horns blaring and Uncle Bob snapping his eyes open and glaring at her, Nicola could not take in what her mother had casually told her on the phone.

'Nicola, at last we have some good news,' Barbara trilled, 'Uncle Bob is leaving hospital and coming to live with us until he can cope on his own.'

'No!' Nicola cried.

'I beg your pardon,' Barbara called down the phone.

'Surely he can go home now after all the help he's had?'

'If only it was that easy, but he's weak and living alone is no place for someone who depends on sticks to walk.'

Nicola could never have imagined a worse situation, she was about to give birth and no way could she take her newborn to the house with him there.

'I suppose it'll be just a couple of days and then he'll go back home,' she said, in the hope that would be the case.

'I somehow don't think so. He needs support and, of course, he's looking forward to seeing you. It's been a long while, Nicola, since you took time to visit him and you only went then because your father insisted.'

Oh my God no, Nicola thought. *Him* being at her parents' was the last thing she wanted. Over the last couple of months she had managed to avoid seeing him, telling her mother she wasn't well. To her surprise, Barbara had believed her and had not made a fuss. But now, with this latest development, Nicola knew she would have to work out how to stay clear of him. It would not be easy. So far he had mentioned nothing to her parents about the accident. 'They don't need to know what happened,' he had told her the last time she had seen him, 'but if you ever say anything about what we've been doing all these years, I'll have you arrested for attempted murder.'

She had shrugged her shoulders in an attempt to appear unconcerned, he had no proof she had even been there, but as if reading her mind, he had added, 'Don't think I won't be able to prove it, because I can and will. I'm only letting you off now because I don't want to see my best friend's first grandchild orphaned.'

Nicola felt sure he couldn't prove anything, but then again, past experience reminded her how devious and clever he could be, nothing would surprise her of what he was capable. At the end of the day, it would be her word against all his lies, and like all the years before, he had her corned. She was a seventeen-year-old adolescent; he was an adult. Who would anyone believe? Knowing all of this, how was she ever going to be able to go home with her new baby?

'Nicola are you still there?' her mother called down the phone.

'Yes, Mum, I'm still here,' she replied and wished she wasn't just on the other side of town, but on the other side of the world.

'You sound tired, Nicola. I hope you are resting enough?'

'I am tired *and* resting enough. In fact I'm fat and tired.'

'That is only to be expected, but never mind, it will soon be over. Now, have you got everything ready? If not, I'll battle with the traffic and come over.'

Nicola did not miss her mother's lack of enthusiasm to drive over. She was thankful for that, she didn't want her mother fussing, it would only end up with her being reminded how young she was and how she would regret rushing into motherhood. 'Yes. everything's fine. Brett helped me get my bag ready. He's good to me Mum and he's just as excited about the baby as me.'

Nicola heard a sharp intake of breath from the other end of the line. 'He should be,' her mother snapped. Anyway, love, I'm here if you need me, so please pick up the phone and call. I'll not be going far now I've got Uncle Bob to take care of. I'll call again tomorrow to see how you are. Take care, bye for now.'

'Thanks, bye Mum.'

Dropping the phone on the kitchen table, Nicola fumed. How could they do that? How could they let *him* live there? Opening the fridge door she pulled out a ready meal; chicken casserole. Nudging the door closed with her elbow, she stared down at the picture on the packet. It had appeared appetising when she had bought it, but her mother's call had robbed her of any desire to eat.

'I'm home, Nic,' Brett called out, breezing through the door and drawing her attention away from her latest nightmare.

'It's me,' he called again, as he strode towards her. Turning towards him, she registered the smile on his face and a large bunch of flowers in his hands. Just seeing his handsome face, her tension eased and thoughts of *him*, trickled away.

'You're back,' she cried, a beaming smile masking her tired look.

'Yes, your master is home,' Brett chuckled, 'didn't I say I would be today?' he added, thrusting the flowers into her arms and dropping a hot wet kiss on her lips.

Nicola caught the faint whiff of alcohol on his breath. 'I've missed you,' she said, 'you've been gone days,' she added, clutching the fragrant blooms and trying to keep hold of the microwave dinner as she watched him shrug out of his coat. Draping it over one of the kitchen chairs, he glared at her for complaining.

'Brett...'

'You're right, it's been days and I need to shower and change and only then will I be decent to spend a little time with you,' he said, winking at her.

'But...

'I'll answer all your buts in a minute, for now I'll leave you to put the flowers in water and hopefully make me a bite to eat.' He stared down at the packet she clutched and pulled a face, then added with a lascivious grin, 'I'm starving.' He pinched her cheek, conveying the kind of hunger he was referring too.

She didn't want to eat anything. In fact, she didn't want to do the other either, but she knew she would have no option. Brett was insatiable when he had been away. Thankfully, once he'd had what he wanted, whatever food she served up he'd be happy to wolf down as if he had not eaten for days.

Disappointed, she dropped the microwavable meal down onto the surface top along with the flowers, and rubbed at her back. Today it ached beyond words. Reluctant to take any more pain relief — she felt guilty enough having to resort to sleeping pills when Brett was away — she took a deep breath in an effort help ease the pain. Nicola leant against the work top; she was bone tired and could not remember when she'd had a full night's sleep without nightmares. Since the accident she hated closing her eyes. It was as if the back of her eyelids were TV screens and what had taken place that afternoon played over and over again as if to torment her. After that harrowing afternoon and the days that followed her visit to the hospital, her dreams had been filled with *him* chasing her, always down long dark streets that ended with the heart-stopping thud of him bouncing off the bonnet of a car before he was thrown to the ground. It was the same dream, the same scene and the same screams every time. Even Brett had grown tired of her nocturnal behaviour and had once almost suffocated her as he had placed a pillow over her face in an attempt to silence her. She had not told him about the accident, it would be too complicated. How she hated needing to sleep. Once she had managed to avoid sleeping for three days and nights. Even after such sleep deprivation she had not slept properly without a supply of sleeping tablets. If only she didn't have to close her eyes, but even she knew she had to sleep at some point. The sleeping pills helped.

Placing her hands on her large belly, Nicola groaned at her size. Pill popping was not good for the baby, but then, not sleeping was not good either; it was a no win situation. Everything had changed after the accident, she was constantly on edge. Nicola gripped the edge of the surface top to steady herself. If only Brett didn't need to be away so often for work, life would settle down for her. She still wondered where he went and what he did to earn the vast amount needed for his extravagant lifestyle. She could not begin to imagine how he managed it all by just running a night club. Her parents were of the opinion he was up to no good. *"No one could have all he has without breaking the law and mixing with undesirables,"* her mother crowed on a regular basis. What puzzled Nicola was her parents' inability to see how happy Brett made her. He hadn't abandoned her when he had found out about the baby, he had been the perfect boyfriend; he had taken her in his arms, hugged her tight and brought her to his home, the actions of a caring and loving man.

Hearing a noise, Nicola glanced up and saw Brett heading towards her, dressed only in his boxer shorts. She eyed up his toned, sexy body and her angry thoughts melted away as the butterflies fluttered in her tummy, replacing the grip of dread. She loved this man. A smile of delight filled her face. Even the pain in her back appeared easier. She was so happy to have him home.

'Come here,' Brett said, grabbing her arm. 'I've been away three days and I've come home to a sulking fat woman who...' he glanced over her shoulder, 'is about to cook me a microwave dinner.' He smirked. 'So I'll take it that it's my duty to provide the starters.'

Nicola giggled. No matter how tired she felt or how big and ugly she must look, he never stopped wanting to make love to her. Thankfully, she did not mind. If it made Brett happy, what was there to make a fuss about? He could be rough with her at times, but she always put it down to his impatience to have her; he simply got carried away with his enthusiasm to love her. None of it troubled her. Having sex with Brett was far removed from what *he* had done to her. At least when Brett grabbed her she wanted it with him and sometimes she even enjoyed it. There was no fear, no feeling of disgust, no revulsion at what she was forced to endure.

'I've just got your dinner out of the fridge,' she said, as he pulled her towards him. Instantly, Brett's hot breath caressed her cheeks as he kissed her hard on the lips.

He pulled back enough to look into her eyes. 'Let's not waste time,' he said, his breath coming in short bursts. He pushed her against the kitchen unit and, with remarkable ease, spun her round to face away from him. As she stared down at the bunch of flowers on the work top, Brett, with practised deftness, dragged her trousers and pants down. 'I've missed you,' he moaned. Pushing her legs apart, he thrust into her.

Nicola gasped as her swollen belly pushed against the surface top. It wasn't long before she heard him sigh with satisfaction. Still pinned against the unit, she felt him enter her again, his urgency no less. It was all over in minutes. Nicola felt the relief of his weight off her back as he moved away and adjusted his boxer shorts. Without a word, he strode across the kitchen, then stopping as if he'd forgotten something, he called over his shoulder, 'I'm off to get dressed. We'll eat when I get back and then we can sort out dessert,' he said, smirking at her.

Nicola watched Brett strutting out of the kitchen like the cat that had got the cream and wondered if he realised how close she was to giving birth. He had not asked how she felt or how the baby was doing. It didn't matter, the important thing was he loved her and he always came home after whatever his business had been about. She couldn't deny him what he wanted and needed, not when he had given her this wonderful home, and right now sex had stopped her thinking about what her mother had told her.

Pushing the unwanted thoughts to the back of her mind, Nicola bent over in an attempt to reach down. It was impossible and she giggled at the stupidity of even considering it. Her belly protruded far enough that she had long lost sight of her toes, so what made her think she could reach her trousers? Still chuckling at her state of undress, she shuffled over to one of the kitchen chairs. Plonking down, she reached over her enormous belly and was about to pull up her trousers when she took in the sight of her knickers. They were hideous; a good imitation of a parachute. Nicola sniggered at how Brett had managed to pull them down so swiftly. If only she could get them back up as easily, she thought, as she dragged them on. Struggling to her feet, she felt a sharp pain rip through her side and, reaching out, she grabbed hold of the back of the chair to steady herself. She took several short, sharp breaths and with her free hand rubbed at her side, the pain subsided. The baby had kicked hard against her.

'Phew that one hurt,' she hissed. Her baby girl was due any time and if Brett carried on like he had just done, she just might pop out any minute. Nicola groaned, staring down at the unwashed kitchen floor. She had not had the energy to mop it, but she would tomorrow, she sighed. Wincing, she pulled herself up straight and tried not to think about giving birth. The abortions had been bad enough, what pain would she have to go through to give birth to a fully formed baby? It wasn't just giving birth that played on her mind, she worried about coping and being a good mother. Brett simply shrugged his shoulders when she mentioned it. 'It's natural with you girls, you'll be fine,' he had muttered, at the same time he had run his hands over her swollen breasts. He was probably right, she would cope if she had to. The same could not be said for her family. She was under no illusions about what they thought of her situation and they made no bones about telling her. Even her few friends had melted away, either to work or college, none of them interested in her any more. The only words she heard these days were, "You're too young to get yourself caught out like this," or, "Why did you let it happen?"

Sometimes what they said was crude and blunt, but she did not want to think about those people with their dirty opinions and loud mouths, she had enough going on in her head as it was. Sex with Brett wasn't dirty, it was beautiful, and he loved her. She had lost two chances at being a mother, this time she was going to be a good mother; the best. Her heart skipped a beat at how things had turned out for her with Brett. 'Chelsea,' she whispered to her baby, 'I can't wait to see you.' With these thoughts, Nicola felt a surge of happiness engulf her. The sound of Brett whistling, added to her bliss, he was as happy as she was.

Filled with euphoria, Nicola waddled over to the surface top and picked up the chicken dish. Reading the instructions, she smiled, it was simple: pierce the plastic lid, slip into the microwave, select high and cook for ten minutes. She studied the picture of a steaming pot of casserole, but no way could she eat any of it. She felt nauseous, her mother's news still in the forefront of her mind. With a sharp knife, she stabbed at the thin film on the lid and pushed the plastic tray into the microwave. With the timer set to ten minutes, she left Brett's dinner to cook.

Finding a vase in the cupboard under the sink, Nicola filled it with water and dropped the flowers in. With no idea how to arrangement them, she left them as they had landed. Sniffing in the fragrance, she picked up the vase and placed it in the middle of the table. They looked pretty, she thought, not used to receiving flowers. With the table set for one, Nicola pulled out a large can of beer from the fridge for Brett.

'Smells good,' he said breezing into the kitchen and heading straight over to her.

'I hope it tastes as good,' she said as he gently nudged her against the fridge. She fell against the cabinet and felt the door swish closed. Brett wrapped his arms around her shoulders.

'I hope you're for dessert,' he said, nuzzling his mouth into her neck. 'Pudding club tart!' he added, laughing.

Nicola ignored the discomfort of the baby moving and groaned. Brett wanted more sex and although she had missed him she was weary. Hearing the microwave ping, she managed to wrestle her way out of his hold. 'Let's get your dinner onto the table first and then you can consider afters,' she forced a chuckle.

'That's my girl,' Brett said, grabbing the can of beer from her hand before moving over to the table, his gaze never leaving her.

That night Nicola lost count of how many times he took her before he fell into a sated sleep. She was so uncomfortable, she didn't know whether to lie down or sit up. The baby was restless too, no doubt protesting at all the activity in such close proximity. Just as she managed to drift off, the alarm rang out. Surely it couldn't be morning already? To her dismay, Brett turned over and once again made love to her. For the first time Nicola wished she had the strength to push him away. Hadn't she already done enough? What was it with men?

'Now my little dumpling,' he sniggered, 'I have to go away again this morning, but I'll be back tomorrow night. I've not had enough of you yet.'

'Surely you'll not be staying away, the baby might come today,' Nicola cried, struggling to sit up.

'I'll do my best,' Brett replied, swinging his legs from under the duvet. 'I admit I'll be glad when it's here, it's not easy getting round you the size you are now,' he added, dashing to the bathroom.

Crestfallen, Nicola heard the torrent of water from the shower and tried not to think about Brett being away if she went into labour. The last thing she needed was to have to call her mother if her waters broke and she was alone. The sting of tears pricked at her eyes and the news Barbara had gleefully gushed down the phone yesterday sprung back in her mind. Would her mother be too busy looking after *him* to come to the aid of her daughter? With the back of her hand, Nicola wiped at her eyes. And how could she take baby Chelsea to meet her grandparents knowing *he* would be there? It didn't bear thinking about and yet she was unable to stop.

'I'll do my best to be back,' Brett said, making her jump as he stood naked at her side. She looked up at him and smiled.

'I'm so tempted to have you again,' he said, moving in front of her so she could see his arousal. Nicola groaned, she was too tired for any more.

Chapter Twenty-Four

'Mum,' Nicola cried and tried not to panic. 'I think the baby's coming!' Her knuckles had turned white with her grip on the phone, the pain coming in spasms.

'Have your water's broken?'

'Yes, all over the floor,' Nicola replied, her voice barely a whisper as she stared down at the puddle around her feet.

'Okay, so where's Brett when all this is going on?'

'He's not here. He's been away for a couple of days. Mum, I'm scared.'

'Good grief,' Barbara hissed, 'Right, then you'd better call an ambulance and I'll get over to the hospital. It will be much quicker than me trying to get across town to you. And, then call that partner of yours, he needs to be there too.'

Nicola grimaced. Her mother never missed a moment to have a dig at her about Brett. Though even she couldn't believe he wasn't here. She had called him several times with each call going to voice mail. On top of that, she had texted four messages and only after the last one had he replied. *I'm in a meeting, will be in touch as soon as I can. Xxx.* What was he thinking? She was about to give birth. What was he doing that was so important he couldn't come home?

'Nicola, can you hear me?' Barbara shouted down the line, 'I'm going to call the ambulance from here,' she added.

'Thank you Mum, thanks,' she cried down the phone, relieved her mum was on the case.

'Now get your bag and don't forget your mobile phone. The ambulance will be with you shortly,' Barbara said. 'I'll set off to the hospital as soon as I've called them. And please try to stay calm, they'll be with you any minute now. Don't worry, my love. I'll see you at the hospital. Take care,' she said, and ended the call.

Ten minutes later an ambulance pulled up outside Rainsworth Court. Nicola had never felt so pleased to see someone who would help her. Her pains were coming regularly and she was frightened at what was happening. More than anything she just wished Brett would call and talk to her, or at the very least, text her. Settled in the ambulance, Nicola kept checking her mobile to no avail.

'I can't do this anymore,' she said, drained. The hours had ticked by and her baby had not made an appearance. 'It hurts,' she said plaintively.

'Come on love, just try one more time,' her mother urged, feeling Nicola's grip on her hand that was sufficient enough to crush the bones.

'I can see the head,' the midwife called, jubilation in her voice. 'Here it comes,' she cried as Nicola screamed out a final heave and the baby finally slipped into the world. Within seconds the gusty cry of the newborn filled the room.

'It's a girl,' the midwife confirmed, wrapping the baby in a white towel. 'Six pounds five ounces,' she said.

Exhausted, Nicola held out her arms and took hold of her little girl. 'Is that all? I thought I was giving birth to a ten-year-old it was so difficult.' She smiled and with her fingertips gently stroked the shock of dark hair that covered the baby's head. 'I'm calling her Chelsea,' Nicola said with pride, 'Hello Chelsea,' she cooed looking down at her daughter's face.

'It's a beautiful name,' Barbara said, taking in the joy that radiated from her daughter's face. 'May I?' she asked, holding out her arms.

'Thanks Mum, thanks for being here,' Nicola said, carefully handing Chelsea to her mother. As she did so, another sharp contraction seared her belly. Alarmed, she looked up at the midwife, who smiled. 'Don't worry dear, it's just the afterbirth. I'll soon have you tidied up.'

A few minutes later, Barbara, her arms still wrapped around her granddaughter, smiled down at her beautiful face. 'She gorgeous,' she said and looked up to see that Nicola had fallen asleep.

'Nic,' Brett said, standing at the end of the bed. At the sound of his voice, Nicola looked up from breast feeding Chelsea and saw he clutched a small teddy bear and a bunch of flowers. She managed a weak smile and knew she should be happy to see him, but the disappointed of him not being here for their daughter's birth filled her with sadness.

'Where have you been?' she asked taking in his dark chinos and crisp white shirt, the top button open revealing his dark-coloured chest hair.

'I'm sorry I couldn't get here any sooner, everything went wrong, but I'm here now,' he said, handing over the teddy bear.

Cradling the baby's head, she met his gaze, 'We've got our little girl,' she said as Brett stared down at her.

'She looks tiny. And how are you?'

'Sore and tired. She might look tiny to you, but it was hard work getting her out I can tell you,' she gave him a weak smile. 'Now, looking at her, it was all worth it. I've called her Chelsea like we agreed.'

'Chelsea,' Brett repeated, and moved closer to Nicola.

'Would you like to hold her?' she asked, gently detaching the baby from her breast.

Brett placed the flowers down on the cabinet next to the bed, 'Why not,' he said and stooping down picked up Chelsea and like an expert cradled her in his arms.

Nicola was taken aback at how naturally he held their daughter. She was not expecting that. 'You're a natural,' she beamed at him.

'She really is tiny,' Brett said, examining her fine features, 'and pretty like her mother,' he smiled.

'So, you've decided at last to come and see my daughter and *your* baby,' Barbara said in a sharp voice, taking in the scene as she strode towards the bed.

Brett swung round and glared at her. 'I'd have been here if I hadn't been the other side of the country,' he retorted, 'business is business no matter what's going on.'

'Well, thank God Nicola's got a mother,' Barbara snapped back, the look she threw him had him stepping back a pace. 'What I can't understand is why a man would need to be hundreds of miles away when his young partner was about to give birth. What could be more important than that?'

'As I said, Mrs Knight, business is business.'

'Mum, please don't have a go at him. He didn't know the baby would decide to come when he was away. He can't be in two places at once,' Nicola said in a placating voice, her weary gaze flitting between the two of them. 'He's here now and holding his daughter,' she added.

Manoeuvring her way to her daughter's side and avoiding Brett, Barbara asked, 'How's she doing?'

'She's fine. I believe she slept through the night. Unfortunately I was out for the count. Until the nurse woke me I didn't know a thing.'

She had slept for over twelve hours and yet still she felt tired. After being allowed to wash and freshen up, Chelsea had been placed in her arms. To Nicola's surprise breast feeding had come naturally. Chelsea, eager for her milk, had suckled her instantly and Nicola's love for her first born had surged through her as she felt the tug at her nipple.

'Breastfeeding is wonderful,' Nicola beamed at her mother.

'Enjoy it while you can. If she's anything like you were, you'll be up and down for the next few weeks,' Barbara advised, clearly doing her best to ignore Brett.

'Thanks for everything, Mum. I couldn't have done it without you. I love you.'

Tears stung at Barbara's eyes. 'I thought I'd never hear that word again from you. Thank you Nic.' Determined not to cry, Barbara added, 'I love you too and always will.' She bent down and gave Nicola a gentle hug, dropping a kiss on her forehead. 'As the baby's father is here, I'll leave you for now, but let me know if you need anything. Okay?' Barbara glanced over at Chelsea, a concerned frown darkening her face, she then turned and walked away.

'Thank you Mum, I will,' Nicola called after her.

As she left the ward, Barbara heard the note of disappointment in her voice and knew Nicola was saddened by the way she had ignored Brett. It was clear her daughter was besotted by him. As far as Barbara could see, he was a waste of space and she feared for Nicola: no good was going to come of it she was sure.

Chapter Twenty-Five

Barbara watched Bob struggle into the taxi and felt a great admiration for her old friend. He never gave up no matter how much pain he was in and although he never complained she was aware of his constant discomfort. Today, after Becky had left and Barbara had felt so alone in the empty house, Bob's unexpected arrival had lifted her out of the depression that had dropped over her like a blanket as she watched her youngest daughter drive away. He had put her first when he could have been resting at home.

As the taxi pulled away she raised her hand and waved. The smile that had filled her face for much of the day, remained, making her appear less strained. There was no doubt in her mind that Bob's visit had been a tonic. They had talked endlessly, laughing and giggling like youngsters. Lost in happy memories they had consumed two bottles of expensive wine and half a bottle of fine cognac, along with a lasagne she had taken from the freezer. As the wine and food had slipped down effortlessly, together they had dragged up forgotten memories, each adding their own version to the events. Like the time Bob had lost his keys and ended up sleeping on their sofa, she had come down in the morning to find he had moved out to the Wendy House, saying it was more comfortable on the floor there than on their old leather sofa. Bob loved the Wendy House and Barbara did not miss the fleeting look of sadness that crossed his face whenever he gazed down the garden and saw how dilapidated the play house had become. It occurred to her that she should have it restored and brought back to its former glory, if only to put back the look of pride on Bob's face. Thinking about the renovation reminded her just how much she owed him for all he had done for her and her family. Already warming to the idea of getting the Wendy House repaired, she hurried back indoors. Yes, she mused, today had been a good day spent with her old friend and for the first time in the last couple of weeks, her thoughts had not dwelt on her eldest daughter.

Padding through to the lounge she felt the silence of the house drape itself around her like a shawl and the hours of merriment slowly slipped away. Would she ever become used to an empty house? Somehow she did not think she would. As she pushed the door open to the lounge, the oppressive heat hit her. 'Goodness!' she cried out, heading straight to the gas fire and reaching down, she turned it off. Fanning her face with her hand, Barbara sighed, knowing that Bob had sat all day in his jacket as if the room was a fridge rather than a hothouse. Even with all the extra weight he carried these days, he always appeared to be cold. It hurt her to know he was far from well.

In an attempt to cool the room down, Barbara pulled open the door to the hall. Feeling the cooler air brush against her face, she found herself studying the row of photo frames that lined the centre shelf of the Ladderax unit. Reaching out, she picked up the small silver-framed photograph of Chelsea and Mya, taken four years ago. Their cherub faces smiled at her and she returned their smile as if they could see her. Studying the bonny faces of her grandchildren she felt that age-old longing to hug them. At two-and-a-half, Mya was the image of Nicola when she had been that age. If only her eldest could have stayed two-and-a-half forever then they would not have had so much pain to deal with. Moving her attention from Mya she took in Chelsea's pretty features and frowned, unable to decide who she looked like most, Nicola or Brett, her father. Even today, at nine, Barbara still would not be able to say. It was one of her little foibles; she liked to see family resemblances. It fascinated her how past generations could be seen decades later in a great-grandchild or even a great-great-grandchild; nature was marvellous. Whoever Chelsea and Mya took after in their looks, she saw nothing but beauty in her granddaughters. They were animated and intelligent and Nicola was a loving mother, but as loving as she was, her children's lives had had more than a few disruptions. Barbara frowned, it was not helped by Nicola keeping her distance, unless there was a crisis and then she would hurry home for help. There had been a few of those over the years, Barbara thought, exhaling an audible sigh that broke the silence of the house. Despite her good intentions she was doing it again, she told herself: trawling over the brittle embers of the past. Although there was the odd silver lining that brought satisfaction; one being that the children's father was no longer on the scene. She had no idea what had happened, for as with most things, Nicola told her only what she wanted her to know. All she had said was that Brett had left with no forwarding address, leaving her and the girls with the rent paid for six months on a decent semi-detached on a popular estate. At least that was something, Barbara had supposed, and as sad as it was for her granddaughters not to have their father in their lives, she could only be relieved that Nicola was rid of him. There was something that never quite added up with Morton. He was secretive and possessive and often away. He had not been there for Chelsea's birth and, once again, he had been on the other side of the country when Mya was born. What man could not be bothered to be home for the birth of his children? Of course, Nicola refused to talk about him. It pained Barbara beyond words to know that her daughter, still only in her twenties, had experienced more pain and distress in her short life than many did in a lifetime. Barbara stroked her finger down the glass as if she could feel the soft skin of her granddaughters' faces, recalling that the photograph had been taken at Chelsea's fifth birthday party. The occasion had been overshadowed with yet another drama in Nicola's life. That particular one was Morton's disappearance and Nicola's sudden move, not to a popular estate, as Barbara was later to discover, but to a small, two-up-two-down in a very questionable neighbourhood on the wrong side of town. She had never found out what had caused Morton's moonlight flit from his palatial apartment in Rainsworth Court nor why he and Nicola had split up. Not that she was surprised.

With the thoughts of Chelsea's fifth birthday party playing in her mind, Barbara placed the photograph frame back on the unit. Shuffling it into its own space, her gaze flickered across the row of photographs. Cheeky smiling faces of her own girls and her granddaughters stared up at her and now more than ever, she realised nothing was as important as spending time with her family. Whatever it took, she would work relentlessly to pave a way for herself and Nicola to be close again. Barbara shuddered at the memory of the last time she had tried, not long before that photograph had been taken. That was when she had tracked Nicola down and found her living in that dreadful place. Well *this* time she would not allow herself to be pushed aside by Nicola's behaviour. Just thinking this made Barbara feel instantly uplifted.

With a determination in her step, she headed through to the kitchen. Retrieving her mobile from the table, she clicked on the message received earlier from Becky and read it again. A warm smiled spread across her face knowing her daughter had arrived home in good time. Barbara tapped in a reply: *Take care my love. It was wonderful to see you. Love Mum xxx*

Satisfied, she pressed the send button. Tomorrow she would call Nicola and put in place all she had promised herself she needed to do.

Chapter Twenty-Six

Still reeling from the shock of leaving Rainsworth Court in a panic, Nicola could not believe that her mother was standing on her doorstep looking at her as if she was staring at a stranger. Nicola's head throbbed as if a dozen jack hammers where in there and on top of everything, she could not get hold of Brett.

'Oh my goodness, Nicola what is going on?' Barbara gasped taking in the shabby two-up-two-down. 'What are you doing here?' she cried and wrapped her arms around her daughter, 'Whatever has happened?'

Nicola heard the questions, but had no idea how to answer any one of them. In the last few days her life had been turned upside down.

'You and the girls are coming home with me,' Barbara continued, looking over Nicola's shoulder at the peeling paint on the white doorframe.

Shrugging out of her mother's embrace, Nicola pushed down a mixture of emotions that threatened to overwhelm her. 'Mum, come on in,' she said and ushered her into the narrow hall. She had not missed the shocked look on her mother's face at where she had found her living.

'Where are the girls?' Barbara enquired, as Nicola, closed the door.

'They're watching a DVD in the lounge. Please don't disturb them I've just got them settled.' She did not want to add that they were unsettled and confused with all that was happening. Letting her mother know this would lead to questions that Nicola did not want to answer, and on top of this, she was worried sick. She had no idea why they were here, where Brett was and why he would not answer her calls. Instead she forced a smile.

'Come on through to the kitchen and I'll stick the kettle on,' she said, not sure she would be able to drink a cup of tea while her stomach was in knots with worry.

'Never mind that,' Barbara said, following Nicola and taking in the sparsely fitted kitchen. 'Whatever is going on? You can't live here, love.'

Nicola just wanted to be invisible as her mother glared at the dark brown Formica worktop, then grimaced at the worn linoleum floor covering.

'What is Morton thinking?' Barbara hissed. 'No way can you and the girls stay here. Come on, let's get your bags packed and I'll take you home with me.'

'It's not that bad,' Nicola said, too afraid to admit it was the pits. 'There's no need, Mum, but thanks, we'll be okay here. We've already started to settle in,' she lied. Nothing could be further from the truth and she wished she could accept her mother's offer, but knowing *he* was a regular visitor at her old home, meant it was impossible. It was challenging enough trying to be polite to him on the few occasions she and the girls had visited. No; she needed to stay here for when Brett came back. Importantly, she had to understand what was going on and why they were no longer living in Rainsworth Court.

'Nicola, are you listening to me?' Barbara asked, 'You can't live here, it's—'

'I know, Mum,' Nicola interrupted, 'but it is only temporary. We'll be sorted very soon,' she added, praying her words sounded reassuring. She had no idea why they were living in such a terrible place and she had no idea where Brett was. At the end of the day, it seemed she knew nothing at all. It had been five days since they had been huddled out of Rainsworth Court before being unceremoniously dumped here. Brett, in a whirl of anxiety, had handed her a set of keys, pecked her on the cheek and almost run out of the house, calling over his shoulder, 'Don't worry, I'll be back soon.'

'What do you mean?' she had screamed after him as panic tightened around her like a belt that was too small.

Ignoring her cry he had jumped into his car and sped off. The girls had clung to her as if she was a lifeline. Their father had not uttered one word to Chelsea or Mya as they had watched in bewilderment.

Shocked at what had happened, Nicola had grabbed up her mobile and punched in Brett's number, but like each one of the many calls she had made since that day, he had not answered.

The next morning when she had slid back the thin curtains, she saw to her shock her old car was parked by the kerbside outside the front door. Downstairs she had found the keys on the mat, having been pushed through the letterbox. No note, just the keys. Who had brought her car here and why was she being ignored? A shiver had run the length of her spine. What was Brett involved in that had made him disappear? As she had stared down at the keys, hundreds of thoughts had filtered through her head, none making any sense. If he had been in an accident, the police would have been round to tell her. If only Brett would talk to her, tell he was fine, then everything could be sorted, but all she came up against was a wall of silence. Oddly, her mother had not been off the phone wanting to talk about Chelsea's fifth birthday party. Ironic that the very person from whom she needed to hear avoided her, whilst her mother, the last person she wanted to speak to, was full on.

'She's not having one,' she had said, anxious to get her mother off the phone and leave her mobile free for Brett.

'Why ever not?' Barbara had volleyed back. 'Every little girl loves a party.'

In the end her mother had worn her down and to her dismay, she'd then had to tell her they had moved.

'Not before time,' Barbara had enthused, 'children need a proper home with a garden. That apartment was highly unsuitable.' Then, as if her mother had detected her despondent tone, she had asked, 'What's happened, Nicola?'

Nicola had almost laughed out loud, but not with humour. It was a question she would also like an answer to. Not daring to tell the truth, she had told her mother a lie. 'It's a temporary move, Mum, just until our new house is ready.'

'You don't sound particularly excited, which tells me something is troubling you. I'll come over and we can talk about Chelsea's birthday. Now give me your new, *temporary*, address.'

'There's no need, I'm up to my eyes in packing cases and sorting what we need for now.'

'Then that's all the more reason for me to come. I can give you a hand and it will do me good to see my granddaughters. Heavens, Nicola, Chelsea is almost five and I hardly know her!'

In the end Nicola had given in and braced herself for what she knew would be an outcry from her mother.

Now, as they stood in the poky kitchen, she could not bring herself to talk about the worry that had her head aching and her mind filled with uncertainty.

'I could stand here all day until you tell me what is going on, but I know I'll be wasting my time. I'm worried about you, but if you won't let me help, please let me take the girls until you get yourself sorted?'

Nicola shook her head, unsure she could look at her mother without breaking down. Picking at a scratch mark on the back of her hand, she said, 'Thanks Mum, but they are staying with me. Anyway, I thought you'd come to talk about Chelsea's birthday party?' Maybe the party was a good idea after all, Nicola had thought, it would give her mother something else to think about and stop her insisting they move back with her.

Looking around the room, Barbara, pulled a face, 'I did, but I wasn't expecting this,' she said, glaring at the damp patch staining the bottom of the wall next to the back door.

'It's okay for now, let me make that tea and then we can talk about the party.'

Barbara, shrugged her shoulders, 'I think what we should be talking about is what's going on with you?' she said.

'Honestly, Mum, we are fine and like I said, this is temporary. We'll be out of here in a matter of weeks, sadly not in time for Chelsea's party though.'

'Well there is no way you can have a party here,' Barbara shook her head as if to reinforce her words.

'No,' Nicola agreed, she did not have the wherewithal to think about a party at the moment, nor argue with her mother. 'Maybe she could have it at yours?' Nicola hated giving in, it was the last thing she wanted, but she could not think of another way to distract her mother from giving her the third degree. And anyway, Chelsea should not lose out because of the mess they were in, it wasn't fair.

'Well of course we can have a party back home,' Barbara's face lit up.

Defeated on all fronts, Nicola tried not to think about *him* being there. Right now she did not have the capacity to take on any more worries.

'I think you've made the best decision,' Barbara said, leaving the remains of the cold tea in the bottom of her cup.

Nicola just wished she could agree, but for now it was all she could do. Her mother would organise a party, which Chelsea would more than enjoy and so would Mya.

Collecting the two cups and placing them in the sink, Nicola ran water over them, 'Thanks Mum. I'm sorry we're in a muddle just now, but it will all be sorted soon,' she said, forcing a smile, for as defeated as she felt, she didn't want her mother picking up just how desperate she was.

'I hope so, though you've not said anything about this new house?'

'I will, but later; nothing is going to plan, but before you go, please say hello to the girls, they will be sad if they miss you.'

Nicola headed towards the hall in the hope that fussing over the girls would distract her mother from the topic of a new house, because what could she tell her? Nothing! There was no new house and as far as Nicola knew, this hellhole was about as new as she was going to get at the moment. 'They would be heartbroken if they knew you'd been and gone without giving them a hug,' she added.

'And I'd be upset too,' Barbara said, tucking her handbag under her left arm. 'Thank you Nicola, but please consider coming home for a while. I've no idea what is going on, but I do know something is wrong.'

As Nicola was about to protest, her mother raised her hands as if to ward off an attack. 'I'm not going to interfere or say anything more, just take care and remember your dad and I are always here for you.'

'Thank you Mum,' Nicola said, nodding in acknowledgment and wishing she could tell her everything: Brett disappearing; Uncle Bob; the first abortion; the accident.... Like a laden yoke it all weighed heavy on her shoulders and today she was barely holding up. 'We'll be fine. You know me, tough as old boots.'

'I wouldn't go that far,' Barbara said, leaning forward and placing a kiss on her cheek. 'I'll sort the party out and you, young lady, sort out a proper place to live.'

'I will,' Nicola said, walking across the hall and through to the tiny lounge.

'Nana!' squealed Chelsea and Mya in unison above the noise of the TV.

Barbara bent down as the girls rushed into her open arms. She hugged them tight, splashing kisses on their faces and soft hair.

Ten minutes later, Nicola stood on the doorstep and watched her mother walk away. She wanted to run after her, throw her arms around her neck and cry out that they would move back home. Instead, she crossed her arms over her chest and watched her drive away, a plume of white cloud twirling from the exhaust pipe.

Chapter Twenty-Seven

Nicola pushed the door shut with more force than was necessary. The sound from the TV drifted from the lounge; at least for the moment the girls were settled. She wondered how much more she could take. Pushing her back against the wooden door she stared up at the ceiling, the cheap lightshade swung like a pendulum from the draught. The urge to reach up and punch it with her fist was overwhelming. Just thinking about hitting it, she could picture the shards raining down on her and if it wasn't for the fact that she'd have a mess to clean up she would have done so. Rubbing her knuckles as if she could feel the pain from striking something, her frustration bubbled up and almost overwhelmed her. She had failed.

Pushing herself away from the door, Nicola headed to the kitchen. She grabbed her mobile phone from the table and stared down at the screen. There was no notification of a new message or a missed call. What was he playing at? Did he not think she had enough to deal with, without having to cope with it all on her own? She needed him here to answer the many questions that were buzzing around in her head. 'Where the hell are you?' she shouted out and let the phone clatter down onto the table. Dragging a chair out, she dropped down onto it and lowering her head into her arms gave in to her misery. Salty tears spilled out from tired bloodshot eyes and rolled in rivulets down her face, soaking her hands and arms. All she could hear were those two words: *"Don't worry."* The words echoed round and round in her head. Worried! If only she was simply worried, but she was frightened too. What was to happen to them?

'Where the hell are you?' she repeated as the childish voices of the Teletubbies filtered from the lounge. Her children's world had been thrown into confusion and unfamiliarity and she had no idea how to deal with it or where to start.

Nicola raised her head and took in the tiny kitchen with its basic, imitation woodgrain kitchen units and the dark brown worktop. The washing machine had slivers of rust around the door hinge and the filter trap hung on by a thread. The free-standing cooker resembled one of those that stood outside on the pavement in the second-hand shops that littered the top end of the High Street. Staring at what was now her home, all she could see were shades of cream and brown. Another sob lodged in her throat and she swallowed hard to dislodge it. Breaking down and snivelling would not change anything; after all, she had gone through a lot worse. If only Brett would come home, or at least talk to her and explain. If she understood why, then she would be able to cope better. It was the not knowing that was driving her crazy.

Wiping her face with the back of her wet hand, Nicola rose and paced across the worn lino to the kitchen sink and back to the table. After five years of living with Brett and having two children, she was no wiser as to what he did for a living, who he did business with, or where all the money came from. He was away as much as he was home. When he was at home, sex was the first thing he wanted. In fact, she thought, sex was *all* he wanted. He expected the girls to be sent to their room so he could have his way and he was always greedy, taking her two or three times and always in a rush. She had never minded what he wanted so long as he was kind to the girls and provided a roof over their heads. And he had: a beautiful one at that. Throughout the years they had been together he had never given her a regular monthly or weekly allowance, leaving her unsure when the next amount would come. Instead, after he had been home a few days and worn her out with his expectations, he would leave a wad of cash in the drawer at the side of the bed before he left again for whatever work he did. Nicola swallowed the sob rising harshly in her throat. Her life was not turning out the way she had dreamed when she had first fallen in love with Brett Morton.

Leaving the luxury apartment had happened in a flurry of chaos and panic. Only weeks earlier they had been viewing brand new executive homes with five bedrooms, en-suites, laundry rooms, playrooms, even a snooker room and double garages. Dreaming of their move had had her planning every detail. Spending hours window shopping for all the new things that would be needed to furnish such a magnificent house. In between checking out the large stores, she had agonised over artists' drawings and room sizes, as Brett had left it up to her to decide which house best suited their lifestyle. With a head full of possible furnishings and a dream house in her sights, Nicola had been brought down to earth with a shattering bump when they were suddenly moving out of Rainsworth Court. Their precious few belongings were pushed into cardboard boxes and suitcases and before she could ask what was going on, she and the girls had been bundled into Brett's Range Rover. Forty minutes later and with no explanation, they were pushed through the front door of number forty-two Ashgrove Terrace. And whilst the previous apartment may have been unsuitable for two little children, this place was very much worse: two bedrooms, a downstairs bathroom and a back yard that stank of cat's pee, with nothing more than a crop of nettles that covered for a lawn. The front garden was a metre square of dark, damp concrete; home for the unsightly wheelie bin.

Nicola shuddered. It had been a long time since she had felt the stabbing pain of fear and with every hour Brett did not come home or answer her calls, it increased.

'Where are you?' she asked again, as if by repeating her plea an answer would be sent to her.

'Mummy, can you do the DVD again,' Chelsea called out. At hearing her daughter's voice, the sound twisted at Nicola's anxiety adding anger to her emotions. What was he playing at leaving them all like this?

'Yes, darling, of course, I'm coming.' Even to her own ears her voice sounded false.

With the DVD restarted, Nicola pressed the play button and watched as Tinky and Winky swayed lazily onto the set, arms moving up and down in a jerky fashion. Chelsea and Mya giggled, clapping their hands in excitement. She was grateful their minds were full of the colourful characters whose lives consisted of a magical garden. If only she could escape so easily. Seeing them settled again, all she could think was that she needed a drink. It wasn't the answer, but right now it might help her unjumble her thoughts. Then maybe she could try to find a clue that would help her grasp what was going on. Remembering there was a half empty bottle of white wine next to the sink, Nicola headed back to the kitchen. She unscrewed the top from the bottle and sniffed its contents. A bitter whiff of vinegary wine assailed her nostrils. She might be desperate, but not that desperate, she gagged and tipped the contents down the sink. As the stale wine glugged down the musty drain, her mind replayed the last few weeks. As if pressing an invisible rewind button, she went over and over those times in an effort to find a sliver of a clue as to where Brett was and why they were living here. Then, without conscious thought, she remembered the car he had given her. One day Brett had arrived home in a new car, another Range Rover; it was top of the range. Not long afterwards, as soon as she had passed her driving test, he had bought her a new BMW. She had loved it. Unfortunately, when she had been pregnant with Mya the car had been stolen. After that Brett had bought her a Ford Fiesta. It was second-hand. There had never been any talk about the stolen car or the insurance pay out. Strange she should remember that detail now. Thinking back, it seemed odd.

Nicola dropped the empty bottle in the flip top bin. It wasn't just the cars that now sprang to mind. When Brett was home, his mobile was constantly ringing. She could never imagine how anyone could be in such demand that their phone constantly rang out. Rinsing her hands under the cold tap to rid them of the vinegary wine, she recalled the time he had just got her pants down and was ready to do the business when his phone rang. He had jumped up and answered, but hadn't come back to finish what he had started. That was not like Brett; he was normally insatiable. But as she thought about it, Nicola realised that sex with him had not been the same of late; it was even more rushed than usual, and he seemed tense, as if he could not wait to get it done. When he wasn't pressing her against a wall or down on the floor, he was constantly listening out anxiously for his phone. But at least he wanted her and that counted for something. Didn't it?

A memory from a few weeks ago popped suddenly into her mind. The doorbell had rung, which was not something that ever happened when Brett was home. He had gone to answer it and that was the last she saw of him for three whole days. It had made Nicola acutely aware that she knew very little about the father of her girls. How did he earn his money? Was he involved in dangerous work? If so, had he been hurt? She didn't want to believe it would be anything sinister, yet what else could it be? Afraid of where her thoughts were leading, Nicola was in no doubt that Brett had changed. Not only had he eased up on his demands, coming home less and less, but when he did come home he always seemed stressed. But she loved him and as a father he was not unkind. He had never laid a finger on Chelsea and Mya, even when they tried his patience, although he blew hot and cold, one minute showering the girls with presents, the next sending them to their room because he needed peace, space and, of course, the usual. Nicola wanted to help him with whatever he was involved in, if only he would come home, sit down and talk. What had she done to deserve all of this? And what else could possibly happen?

As if in response to her questions, the doorbell rang out. The sudden sound jangled Nicola's already frayed nerves, making her jump. Swinging round at the intrusion, her arm caught a plate resting on the draining board. Unable to grab it, she watched in dismay as it smashed to the floor. 'No!' she cried, sighing heavily as she stared down at the mess. Who was at the door? Was her mother coming back to take them away from here after all? For the first time in years, Nicola hoped she was.

The bell rang out again and this time the noise persisted, as if someone held their finger on the button. 'I'm coming,' Nicola called, stepping over the broken plate before breaking into a trot down the narrow hallway.

In her urgency to stop the noise she yanked the door open with so much force it slammed back against the wall. Expecting to see her mother, Nicola was surprised to see a tall, slim, smartly dressed woman standing under the porch canopy. 'I'm looking for Brett Morton,' she stated in a matter-of-fact voice.

With her mouth open, Nicola stared at the woman, a feeling of foreboding enveloping her as she looked the stranger up and down. Even at a glance she could see the woman's clothes were expensive. Her jeans fitted her as if they had been tailored for her slim frame, and the leather jacket was not one of the cheap ones Nicola had seen hanging on the rails in the indoor market. Nor were the dark brown knee-length boots either. The woman's hair had been cut into a stylish bob and the sleek blonde strands had been highlighted. Nicola didn't need to look at her own clothes to see how shabby she appeared; her jeans and top were clean, but a long way from designer labels. Her hair, longer than it had been in years, was pulled back and held in place by a large green clip. Whoever this person was, Nicola felt at a disadvantage. 'He's not here,' she finally said.

'So he does live here then?' the woman asked.

Removing her hand from the doorjamb, Nicola stood up straight and with a presence that belied her inner turmoil, asked, 'And who are you?' As she spoke, a nervous tick twitched at the side of her left eye, betraying her false bravado.

The woman flashed a sardonic smile, revealing even white teeth. 'That's the very question I'm here to ask *you*.'

'I'm not the one knocking on strangers' doors,' Nicola retorted, 'so unless you tell me who you are and why you're asking about Brett, I'll shut the door,' she said, amazed at her sudden boldness. She waited for what seemed minutes, but the woman just glared at her in silence. Nicola was about to close the door when, to her shock, she saw a tear trickle down her visitor's face.

'Please,' the woman begged.

Recognising the distress in her voice, Nicola stood back, 'I don't know who you are or why you're standing on my doorstep, but you'd better come in.'

Stepping to one side to allow the woman to enter, Nicola felt her heart miss a beat. *What now?*

Chapter Twenty-Eight

Pulling out one of the wooden chairs and indicating the woman should sit, Nicola hastily grabbed up the brush and dustpan, swept up the pieces from the broken plate and dropped them into the bin. She tried not to read too much into this woman's visit, but it was difficult. How did she know Brett lived here? Until a few days ago Nicola had not known this place existed, yet here was an attractive woman asking after him.

'I'm sorry, this wasn't what I had planned when I rang your doorbell, but seeing how young you are was my undoing,' the woman said, wiping at her eyes with her finger tips. 'Do you know who I am?' she asked, her voice, clear and accent-free, each word enunciated as if being forced through tight lips, 'because, I know who you are.'

Glaring at her, Nicola had no idea who the woman was, but was acutely aware she was about to find out. Fear trickled like perspiration down her spine as she realised her world was about to implode.

'You're Nicola Knight and although I only learnt about you a few weeks ago, it has taken me all this time to gather the courage to seek you out. You see, I'm Brett's wife; Jill Morton.' Her eyes reflected a mixture of anger and pity as she stared at Nicola.

Nicola felt the shock waves from Jill Morton's words and fell against the surface top. She gripped the edge to steady herself and felt as if the word *wife* was being delivered to her ears in slow motion. As it collided with her eardrums, it flew into her head and ricocheted around her brain like a pinball. She closed her eyes in an effort to still the noise in her head and the dizziness that threatened to unbalance her as she struggled with the revelation. She was aware Brett wasn't all he appeared to be? But not this. No! Please no.

'That's not possible. Brett and I have been together for years,' she said, yet something deep down inside told her if anyone was mistaken it was her. There had been times when she had believed he could be playing around and when these thoughts had promised to bring her down, she had convinced herself that if he was sleeping around she would know. But if this woman really *was* his wife, then she hadn't seen the signs. She had believed him when he said he was away working. Was it all a lie? Had he in fact been going home to his wife?

Nicola could not bring herself to believe it. In denial, she snapped, 'I don't know who you are or what your game is, but you are very much mistaken and I want you now to leave.' Clearly spoken, the words came out of her mouth in staccato. The only person she wanted to talk to right now was Brett, most certainly not this woman.

Getting to her feet, Jill Morton faced Nicola, 'Believe you me I want more than anything for all of this to be a terrible mistake, but it is not. Brett has told me all about you.' Jill clutched at her bag and headed towards the door.

Nicola was caught off balance, could this really be true? It would answer many questions, such as why she could not get hold of him and why they were living here. 'Why should I believe you?' she asked Jill's retreating back. 'For all I know you are the other person in my Brett's life coming here to cause trouble.'

Jill spun round, 'Yes, I *am* the other person: his wife! Do you know where he is right now? No, of course you don't because he's not answering your calls and messages.'

'He is. He'll be home later today. You can stay and wait if you like,' Nicola barked back and wondered why she had said something so ridiculous. Was this woman really Brett's wife? Throwing her out would not answer any questions and as frightening as it was, Nicola needed answers. 'I don't know what to believe anymore,' she said, the bravado of seconds earlier evaporating. Everything in her life was unreal, yet she had shared a roof with Brett and they had two children. That was real and she wanted to believe that their living arrangements were temporary and Brett was dealing with it, but how could she when this immaculate and well-spoken woman was standing in her house and was apparently Brett's wife?

Even while Nicola tried to deny what she had heard, she knew deep down that it had to be true' It explained so much. She opened her mouth to speak, but her tongue remained still, as if too afraid that the words which would tumble out would confirm the lie she had been living.

'I'm sorry,' Jill said, 'I don't know what I wanted when I rang your doorbell. Looking at you, I'm not sure who is the most shocked.'

Nicola remained leaning against the surface top. 'I don't want to believe you are his wife, but I do want to know where he is,' she said, pointing at the chair Jill had just vacated. 'Sit down. I take it you want something. Though you can see I've nothing to offer.'

'I don't know, to be honest, I just wanted to see you and find out why.'

Nicola stared at Jill Morton for what seemed a long time, she still wanted to believe this was a mistake and the woman had knocked on the wrong door.

As if to fill the brief silence that had invaded the room, tuneless singing from Chelsea floated from the living room and broke the spell. Jill's gaze drifted to the door where the sound came from and her face paled. 'Who is that?'

'Our daughter,' Nicola said protectively, a weak smiled pulling at her lips on hearing the cheerful sound of her eldest. 'We've two daughters. Didn't you know?'

'No,' Jill said, her voice less positive than earlier.

'I thought Brett had told you everything? Seems he's been selective with the truth to you too,' Nicola retorted, wondering what else Brett had not said. Maybe this Jill was not who she said she was after all, but if not, who was she and what was her game? 'That's Chelsea singing,' she said, 'she's coming up five, and Mya will be three next birthday.' As her words crossed the short space, Nicola saw shock fill the woman's face.

'Are they Brett's?' she asked, her words barely above a whisper.

'Of course,' Nicola answered, 'who else's would they be? We've been together for over five years. We are a family.'

'I thought that too,' Jill responded, not taking her gaze off Nicola, her voice level and devoid of emotion.

'Are you saying you have children too?'

'I really shouldn't be answering your questions,' Jill said evenly, 'I should be demanding you tell me what you have been doing with my husband, but ...' she paused, looked around the kitchen and winced. 'I'll be honest, I was hoping against hope my journey had been a waste of time. I wanted to believe I had everything wrong, but your car added to my fears. That old Fiesta parked in the street was once mine.'

Any hope Nicola had of telling herself this woman could still be wrong, instantly vanished. She could guess how she had ended up with Jill Morton's old car. 'I don't suppose you run around in a black BMW?'

Speechless, Jill nodded.

Nicola stared at Brett's wife and saw that the woman who moments earlier had stood tall and bold on her doorstep, had no fight left in her. She appeared as broken as Nicola felt.

'What a mess,' Jill said, 'and yes, we have two, but we have one of each.'

Nicola did not miss the use of *we*. It stabbed at her like a knife.

'Sam is eight and Megan will be five at the weekend,' Jill continued.

Nicola felt her world crumbling. Brett had fathered another child at the same time as she was carrying

Chelsea. Unsure if she wanted to know the answer, yet feeling compelled to ask, she said, 'What date?'

'This Saturday, the eleventh,' Jill responded, a puzzled expression crossing her face. "Why?"

Nicola was not sure she could take any more. Brett's daughter with his wife had been born a day before Chelsea. She snorted in derision. Now she understood why he had not been there for Chelsea's birth. He was no doubt gowned and masked, sitting at his wife's side, holding her hand and rubbing her back. Soothing her with kind words as she pushed his daughter into the world. Of course, there would have been tears of joy at him being a father – and all the time she had been doing the same, but with her mother holding her hand and rubbing her back.

'And yours?' Jill asked, cutting into her thoughts.

'The twelfth.'

Nicola watched as Jill Morton crumpled. Any composure left had deserted her. Nicola knew exactly how she felt. 'Thinking about our relationship, I should have suspected something,' she said. 'Brett promised to be there for Chelsea, but he never came. Of course not, he must have been with you. Even he couldn't be in two places at once,' she added bitterly. 'In fact he was often away and when he did come home it was only for one thing really.'

Jill nodded, 'He always was demanding…' she said, her voice trailing away, unshed tears sparkling in her eyes.

Nicola did not say that she believed Brett loved her and that demanding sex was his way of showing how much he wanted her. Unlike *him*, the beast who had stolen her childhood. *He* had wanted her too, but she had hated him and still did. Brett was the first man she had loved and she wanted to believe he cared about her and the girls, but his silence told her everything. Instead of being a man and telling her what was happening, his wife had come to do the deed for him.

'Does Brett know you are here?'

'No.'

'How did you find out about me?'

Jill sighed, 'It was pure chance. Had it not been for the roadworks in town I probably would never have found out. An old school friend of mine moved into the area. We arranged to meet and I drove the thirty miles to meet her. I'm not that familiar with the town and when I found Burton Way and Catherine Walk cordoned off due to an accident, I was diverted along other roads; roads I was unfamiliar with. I ended up getting lost and found myself driving past Rainsworth Court. You can imagine how taken aback I was at seeing Brett entering the apartments. I pulled over and called his mobile. He answered after two rings and told me he was in Milton Keyes and wouldn't be home that night, adding he would call me as soon as he got out of his meeting. I didn't need to be Miss Marple to work out he was lying! I drove home and looked up Rainsworth Court and then phoned the commissionaire. He told me he couldn't divulge details of residents. I thanked him and put the phone down, but I wasn't finished. I dug around some more and eventually found out that Brett Morton and his partner had moved out. Strangely, there was no mention of the children. I told that snooty commissionaire I was a debt collector and needed Brett's new address. He hesitated, then to my surprise relented and gave it to me. Once in possession of the information, I wasn't sure I wanted to know about what my husband was doing behind my back, but then I argued I needed to know because he was away so often. Now I know where he was during his nights away.'

And so do I, Nicola thought, and had it not been for the roadworks, Brett would probably never have been found out. Right now she wished he hadn't been, then she could have remained in blissful ignorance. Now that she knew, she had no idea what was going to happen to her and the girls.

'I take it Brett is home with you because I've not seen him since we moved here,' Nicola said, the sense of abandonment draping over her like a second skin.

'He is now. The children and I spent time at my parents' house. I needed space and time to think after what I'd learned. I told him I knew about you and Rainsworth Court. Naturally, he denied it. For the week I was away he never ceased begging me to return, admitting there had been someone else but that it meant nothing.

Nicola gasped, Jill's words cutting her like a knife. Unable to speak, she stared in torment at Brett's wife.

'I must add,' Jill went on, 'he never mentioned the girls. In the end I eventually agreed to return on my terms, which were to give you up and promise to be home every evening.' Jill's words were delivered in a voice that reflected her utter distress. 'I'm sorry, because I have no idea what the future holds. It is far more complicated than I could have ever imagined.'

If only it *was* complicated, Nicola thought, beginning to understand Brett's panic to be out of Rainsworth Court. As far as she could see it was quite simple: she had been taken for a ride; used and abused. It was the story of her life. But, learning all of this did not help as she tried to take in the enormity of the situation. Whatever happened from now on, their lives would never be the same again and it was certain she would not be the winner.

'Mummy?' Chelsea burst through the door, Mya close at her heels. 'It's finished.' Seeing a stranger, Chelsea stopped in her tracks.

'Come here darlings,' Nicola called, holding out her hand. 'This lady is a friend of Daddy's. You can come and say hello.'

From the open door, both girls muttered a shy hello before turning and running back to the living room.

'Oh my goodness!' Jill squealed, covering her mouth with her hand. 'The older one is so like Brett. What are we going to do?' she cried, looking at Nicola. Reaching across the table, Jill sought Nicola's hand and held it tight.

Confused and frightened, Nicola felt this woman's pain and for a moment believed Jill Morton felt hers too. 'I don't know, do you?'

Brett's wife shook her head. 'No, I'm afraid not.' Nicola had never felt so alone. What would become of them?

Chapter Twenty-Nine

'Can I come in?'

Nicola felt her breath catch in her throat as she stared up at Brett. It had been less than an hour since his wife had walked out of the door he was standing in front of. She was still reeling from the shock of Jill's visit and although they had parted amicably, it was clear to Nicola that Brett's wife was not going to give him up.

'What are you doing here?' she asked, trying to stay calm. 'I've been calling you for the last five days and now suddenly you appear.'

Brett shrugged, 'I know Jill's been here,' he said, speaking in a matter-of-fact tone. 'I followed her and have been waiting until she left. We need to talk.'

Talk? she wanted to scream. Had she not been trying to do just that since they had been bundled out of Rainsworth Court? She glared at him and felt a sliver of satisfaction at his loss of weight since she had seen him last. His designer jeans no longer hugged his taut thighs and his jacket sagged across his broad shoulders. Hopefully, he had been suffering too and she wondered what he saw as he stared back at her. Did he see a young woman, alone, worried and out of her depth? Or was he seeing the seventeen-year-old who had let him use her? The same young girl, now twenty-three and the mother of his children, who believed he loved them all.

Speechless, she stared up at him and as numb as she felt, she was filled with anger, humiliation, hatred and even love. What an explosive combination, she thought. She had run into Brett's arms to escape *him* only to find she had been used again. Why did men want to abuse her? She had never knowingly encouraged their behaviour. Though Brett was not an abuser in that respect, more of a greedy and demanding over-sexed man. Her daughters had not been born out of abuse, but from love, at least as far as she was concerned. As for Brett, she was under no illusion now that the girls meant anything to him, they were mere by-products from the fruits of his loins. He had shown little interest when she had believed he was her partner, so it was highly unlikely he was going to turn into the perfect daddy to them now. Just thinking about her two little girls made Nicola's heart constrict with love for them and anger for their father.

She took in his pathetic appearance and wanted to yell at him to go away and never come near her again, but fear still paralysed her when it came to standing up to people. The things that had been done to her would have had many girls on medication for years, if not for all their lives. If only she'd had the courage to stand up to *him* then perhaps she would have sussed Brett out a long time ago and her life, at twenty-three, would not read like a catalogue of disasters. Aware a panic attack was building, Nicola tried to control her breathing and stay calm. She hated and feared the attacks and unless she could get it under control she would end up being sick, shaking and very likely fainting. She had been surprised she'd not had an attack with Jill's revelations, thankful she had not shown herself up by being melodramatic with a panic attack. Needing to breathe steadily, she fumbled in the front pocket of her jeans and pulled out her puffer. Placing it to her mouth, she inhaled and felt the rush of relief as the tension slowly eased. Over the years she had managed to deal with the attacks and for most of the time succeeded in concealing them. If it was necessary to use her puffer in front of others, she had used the excuse of having asthma. Her panic attacks were another one of her secrets.

'You'd better come in,' Nicola said in a hushed tone. Her breathing laboured, she stood to one side. As he made his way past he brushed against her, the usual frisson that fizzled through her body when he touched her was missing, this time replaced with a sense of anxiety.

'I know what you're thinking,' he said, filling the small space of the hallway.

Nicola scowled at his bulk and wished she had the courage to tell him she wanted him to leave, to go back to his wife and children, but she could hardly breathe, let alone draw enough breath to utter a word. She wasn't brave, she was worried and frightened; worried how she would cope and frightened about what he would want from her. He had never been violent, though when he was tense he wanted sex. That was the last thing she wanted him to have from her now.

'She's no doubt told you that we're a happily married couple,' he said, striding into the kitchen. Nicola heard him snort as he glanced around the small room.

Not inviting him to sit, she answered him. 'Jill told me you'd been married for ten years and have two children; your youngest is the same age as Chelsea. I wanted to believe it was untrue, but I know it can't be.' Nicola didn't miss the pain that crossed his face at the mention of his wife's name.

'So why, Brett?'

'Why what?' he asked, turning to look at her.

'Why me?'

He grinned, a lecherous glint in his eyes. 'She's not that fond of it, not like you. She might have many qualities... she's beautiful, educated, even sophisticated for someone like me, but the sex? Let's just say she's not very adventurous. Lays herself down on the bed and, well...' Brett trailed off, a grin on his face. 'You were up for it anywhere, anytime. You're a bloke's dream.'

Shocked at his words, Nicola felt the past racing to catch up with her. Her panic attack threatened to bring her down. Fearing she would lose control, she leaned her back against the surface top for support and drawing her breath in she willed herself to stay calm. What was it with men? She had believed Brett loved her and wanted her, but he was no different to *him*. The only difference was she had been allowed to keep her babies. She wondered if she would ever know real love and be treated with respect. Maybe her body was fit for only one thing. 'I take it you're leaving us?' Even as she asked she wanted to hear him say "no".

Brett dropped down onto the chair his wife had vacated earlier. 'Come and sit down and let's talk about how we go forward, eh?'

Knowing there was nowhere to escape, Nicola perched on the chair opposite. She held her puffer in a tight grip and kept her eyes down, staring at her hands.

'I'm not going to hurt you, I've never hurt you. That's not my style, but now you know what the score is I'm happy to carry on as we did before and I'll continue to provide a roof over your heads as long as you keep me happy. Of course, Jill never needs to know, but if she finds out, then she'll have to decide what she wants.' As Brett spoke, he took in the grim room. 'We could do much better than this,' he said, shaking his head. 'I had to get us out of Rainsworth Court and as time was tight, this was all I could get.'

Tempted as she was to ask why, right now she did not want to know the details. It didn't take a genius to work out it was to do with his wife.

'What happened to your plan of having a big house? Or was that another one of your lies?' she asked.

Brett stared at her, the lewd glint in his eyes replaced with disappointment. 'No it wasn't. It was as much my dream as yours, but I'd lost a great deal on some business I was doing and I needed to sort things out fast. On top of that, Jill had found out about you.'

She listened to his excuses. He might have had misfortune in his business, yet she would bet Jill and the children still lived in their home. From what Jill had told her during their moment of solidarity and openness, it was a large place in a very expensive area. As tempted as she was to ask if Jill had been pushed out of her home, she let the question dangle on the tip of her tongue and remained silent.

'So what do you think?' Brett asked. Smiling at Nicola he took hold of her hand and pulled it hard enough to make her stand. Once on her feet he tugged and before she could steady herself she was on his knee.

She could feel the heat from his body through her jeans as his fingers gently stroked her thigh. Nicola shuddered, the panic attack receding and being replaced with disgust. What choice did she have? How could she keep a roof over her girls' heads? She needed time to find a way, but until then she had to submit. Glaring at his hand, she tried not to let the nausea of earlier rise up and choke her. She loathed herself for what she was about to allow. How did she always end up being the one boxed in and the one that had to live a lie? Would this kind of life for her ever end?

Not waiting for her answer, Brett unzipped Nicola's jeans, and before she could do anything about it he pushed his hand inside.

'The girls are in the sitting room, they could run in,' she protested.

'They won't. And if they do, they know Daddy likes to cuddle Mummy when he comes home.' He pulled at her jeans with his other hand. 'I knew you'd see what we have is a good deal,' Brett said, as he took what he wanted.

Closing her eyes tight, Nicola tried to still the memories of the past and prayed she would one day find a way to live without having to be humiliated and used.

Chapter Thirty

Lost in so many painful memories, cramp brought Nicola back to her senses to find she was still sitting on the floor in the en-suite. Yesterday she had got drunk and created a scene at her dad's funeral. Her mother would never forgive her.

She unclasped her arms from around her knees and rubbed at her legs to ease the cramp. Her skin was damp from all the spilled tears. How long had she sat here? She had no idea and right now she didn't care. Seeing *him* at the funeral so close to her mother was unbelievable, but hearing him talk about her father and how marvellous he was, how close they were and how he felt he was part of the family; a family he loved as if they were true family, was sickening. He had no right to be there let alone speak. The farce of it all had virtually tipped her over the edge. What she couldn't get her head around was why her mother couldn't see who he really was. After all these years, she still saw *him* as special. Why?

Staring down at the pitiful white blotches and craters that peppered the inside of her arms, Nicola dragged the tips of her fingers over the pitted skin. Disgust filled her at what she had done. Only now did she regret destroying her body, but at the time it had been the only way she had been able to cope. Cutting and slashing at her skin was the release she had needed when she had lacked the courage to take her own life. On more than one occasion she had gone so far as to pop the pills into her mouth, but as she had added more and more, she had ended up gagging and choking on the bitter taste before finally spluttering them out across the floor. Not able to find the wherewithal to truly escape she had found herself slicing into her skin like a demented killer, eager to release the pressure of wanting to die. A sharp knife or nail scissors were easy enough to conceal and when her desperation gripped to the point of strangulation, she would grab hold of one or both and jab and cut away at her arms. In her frenzy she felt no pain. Its absence had her cutting until the blood oozed and ran down her arms. Only then did she stop. It was afterwards, when the pressure eased in her mind and she felt able to cope again, that the pain seared through her body at her reckless behaviour. She would grit her teeth and tell herself she would never do it again, but of course she did. Then she would pick at the scabs until the sores wept. The stinging of the sores balanced out the lack of pain when she cut herself. At last she had been punished for not being able to cope with it all and stop *him* from touching her.

Nicola fingered the scars, a reminder of what had happened in that Wendy House. She was ashamed of her arms and would only wear three-quarter length or long sleeves. Her mother thought she was odd and made no bones about telling her. *'Nicola, why don't you take that top off? The sun's cracking the flags! Goodness, what is the matter with you?'* she would snap at her. If only she knew why, Nicola thought with anger. If only she could see what *he* had done, but instead her mother continued to wear rose-tinted contact lenses and saw a decent man, who had been callously struck down leaving him sick and helpless.

Lowering her head Nicola pressed her lips on to the scars and wondered how a mother could not know what was happening right under her nose. There must have been *something*; a tell-tale sign. Or had she been so brilliant at deceit and concealing? Now she was a mother herself she was convinced she would know if anything was wrong with either one of her girls. Admittedly she watched them like a hawk in the knowledge that she knew all the signs of abuse and evasion and would recognise them for what they were. Her mind might be on the wrong tracks most of the time, but she had worked to build a relationship with her girls so they could talk to her about everything. She was not just their mummy, but their best friend; someone they could confide in and trust. Nicola never wanted that to change. She had attempted to hide, as best she could, her own anxieties, trying to keep from them the bitter disappointments and fears of her own life, making their lives as normal as she could. Brett had deceived her, used her, humiliated her, but he had never touched the girls. Sex with Brett had been normal greedy lust, not perversion. He had never wanted to know about her past, even the state of her arms he had never mentioned. Brett's interest had been only for the parts of her body that offered pleasure, not revulsion. And like *him,* in the end he had left her with no choice but to submit. Emotional blackmail was silent and cruel and because she had needed to keep a roof over their heads and food on the table she had gone along with Brett's suggestion. It meant he had what he wanted whenever he wanted it. After the visit from his wife four years ago, she had prayed that Jill Morton would find out, but if she had, she never came back to see her. Nicola had wanted her to, but it had not just been Jill Morton who had washed her hands of her. So had Brett in the end. After an all-night session where he had taken all he had wanted, leaving her exhausted, he had announced that he was bored and was moving on. Without a backward glance, he had walked out of their lives leaving two broken-hearted little girls. To Chelsea and Mya he was Daddy, not the abuser of their mother.

A few weeks after he had left, Nicola had learnt that he and Jill were divorcing. Brett, it seemed, was going abroad; not for work, but running away with yet another woman; someone else's wife, and with the tax man and a few unsavoury organisations snapping at his heels. Until that moment, she had thought there was no justice in the world. In the end, leaving her had been the best thing he had done for her in all the years he had been in her life. She wiped the back of her hands across her face and pulled herself up from the floor. As if too weak to hold her, her legs buckled and she found herself down on her bottom. Determined to get to her feet, she leaned against the tiled walls and pushed herself up. The past would not let go, the nightmares persisted and the panic attacks of the last week had unnerved her. At twenty-seven, she had travelled down more dark roads than many, now it was time to sort things out. She owed it to herself, she owed it to her beautiful girls and, just as importantly, she owed it to the new man in her life.

Chapter Thirty-One

With her head filled with how to deal with *him*, Nicola did not hear the door slide open or the sound of soft footsteps cross the tiled floor.

'Hello,' Tony murmured placing his hand on her arm.

Startled, Nicola stared up at him.

'Sorry, I didn't want to disturb you, I felt you needed a little time to sort out whichever demons where troubling you.' Tony took in Nicola's tearstained face. 'Oh sweetheart,' he cried, wrapping his arms around her shaking body. 'Nothing is ever that bad,' he added, stroking her damp, tangled hair. 'I'm here to listen and help if you'll let me. I love you for all you are and all you've coped with and come through.' Tony hugged her tight and kissed the top of her head. His handsome face, etched with pain.

Nicola felt the warmth from Tony's body as she nestled in his tight embrace. The caring and loving words slipped so naturally from his lips and she knew he meant them. She had never loved anyone like she loved Tony. She had once believed she loved Brett, but she knew now that all she had achieved was running from one abuser straight into the arms of another. Men, it seemed, only wanted one thing from her and she had given it to Brett willingly in her haste to escape forced, painful and shameful sex. Tony's love was a different kind of love; he had shown her what love really felt like. Since meeting him, for the first time in her life she felt truly safe. But as safe as she felt, she was painfully aware that she did not deserve him and she never stopped wondering why he loved her and wanted to share his life with her. Even sex was different. She was allowed to say "no" and Tony accepted this. Neither of her abusers had ever understood the word "no". Both had ignored her protests and taken what they wanted. Nicola often wondered if controlling her was what their thrill was truly about. Yet being able to say "no" had its own difficulties. Pleasing Tony was uppermost in her mind; saying "no" left her feeling guilty and selfish to the point she would instantly change her mind and agree; except Tony was different. *'If you don't want to make love, then nor do I,'* he would say holding her close to him. *'We have a whole life to enjoy each other, there's no need to rush.'* She didn't understand how he could accept this, but he did. It seemed he loved her as if she was perfect.

'Come on, let's get you back into bed and I'll make you a cuppa. Tomorrow we can talk and see what can be done to help you. I love you so much Nic. I don't like to see you this way.'

Once snuggled under the duvet, listening to the sound of Tony's footsteps thundering down the stairs to the kitchen, Nicola felt as if he had been in her life forever, yet it was only eleven months since they had met. It had been pure coincidence, just before Christmas, the day of Chelsea's school play; a day when a heavy frost hung over everything like a net curtain. Her daughter had been given the honour of a leading part. The school had been ambitious and instead of the traditional Nativity Play, they had staged a collection of short musicals from three popular films: *Mary Poppins; The Sound of Music,* and *Bed Knobs and Broomsticks*. To Chelsea's great excitement, she had been asked to play the part of Jane Banks in *Mary Poppins*.

With the heating on low in the school hall, Nicola and Mya, still in their coats, had settled down in the third row from the front and watched as Chelsea took to the small, makeshift stage. Holding her breath in wonderment, goose bumps washing over every inch of her skin, Nicola had listened as her eldest daughter's voice filled the small assembly hall and without missing a beat she sang, "The Perfect Nanny". At the end of Chelsea's breathtaking performance, Nicola was sure she must be the proudest parent in the room as, applauding loudly, she leapt to her feet. Eventually, sitting back down, lost in admiration, she had basked in a glow of pride. It had taken Mya's voice to bring her back to the play.

'Mummy, do you know Taylor, the boy sitting next to me? He's in my class.'

Glancing at her daughter, Nicola had placed her index finger on her lips, 'Shush.'

'But his mum died last year,' Mya whispered, ignoring her warning.

Looking towards the little boy Nicola saw the handsome man sitting next to him was smiling at her.

'Hello,' he said quietly. 'Your daughter tells me it was her sister singing up there. You must be very proud.'

Beaming at him, she had nodded and mouthed, 'Yes, I am very proud.' She had felt ten feet tall that day.

The next group of singers had started up then and Nicola, her gaze riveted on the stage, had sat in silence throughout the rest of the show. After the applause had died down and all the children had taken a final bow, Taylor's father had leaned over, 'By the way, I'm Tony.' He had extended his hand and reaching out she had taken it and returned his smile.

'Pleased to meet you, I'm Nicola, Mum to this little one too,' she had said, giving Mya a gentle squeeze. Their eyes had met briefly and she had seen sadness there. Before she could utter another word, Chelsea had pushed her way through to where they were sitting, her face flushed with success. 'Oh Mum, I was so nervous,' Chelsea had cried.

Nicola had got to her feet and hugged her little girl. 'You were wonderful.' She had said, feeling Chelsea shivering. 'Come on, let's get you home.'

'It's freezing out there,' Tony had remarked as they all shuffled out of the assembly hall, buttoning up their coats and wrapping scarves around their necks.

'It's not much warmer in here,' she replied, feeling unaccountably nervous and shy.

He had rubbed his hands together, 'You're right and I know the perfect place where we can quickly warm up. This place does super large mugs of hot chocolate swimming with marshmallows.'

The girls' eyes had lit up, both begging her to say "yes".

In the warmth of the coffee shop they had settled round a large circular table, the three children shuffling on the chairs before deciding that Taylor should sit between Chelsea and Mya.

'Kids, what are they like?' Tony had smirked, raising his eyes to the ceiling before placing his order with the slim young girl who marched between the tables, pen and pad in hand.

Nicola's nervousness had slipped away, Tony's easy going manner making her feel strangely comfortable. It dawned on her that this was the first time she had experienced the adult company of a *real* man; one who wanted nothing from her, and it felt good.

'Here they come,' Tony called out above the din from the three children. 'Quiet please or I'll have to take all the marshmallows away.' And as if someone had frozen the children's tongues, there was an immediate silence. A large tray holding five mugs of steaming hot chocolate topped with foamy marshmallows was placed in the centre of the table. Leaving the three kids to enjoy their hot drinks, Tony had talked to her about how he had lost his wife to cancer eighteen months earlier. 'It was so aggressive we hardly had time to think about how ill Sandy was. In less than three months from feeling poorly we had lost her.'

The sadness Nicola had detected earlier in Tony's eyes manifested itself again and for the first time her own problems paled in comparison to losing someone you loved.

'How about you?' he had asked as she had tried to understand how his exuberant nature had not been extinguished with grief, or was he, like her, good at hiding raw feelings?

What a question! How could she even begin to talk about her life, they would be here for months, and even if she *could* confide dealing with her shame to a total stranger, how would it sound compared to dealing with bereavement? Trying to work out an appropriate response, she found herself gazing at him, taking in his features, and caught him doing the same to her. Nicola liked what she saw. If only her life had been simple then the question would not be testing her to answer. In the end she had replied, 'Single mother. The girls' father did a runner eighteen months ago. It seems he now lives abroad, but with no forwarding address, I really have no idea where he is.' She had shrugged her shoulders and smiled as if to convey it was normal these days, but it had been a struggle after Brett left. The only decent thing he had managed to do for them was to pay the rent for six months on the three-bedroomed semi they still lived in. Unfortunately, the bastard had left no other funds for them to live on and not wanting to go cap in hand to her parents and risk another lecture on the waste of space Brett was, Nicola had got off her backside and gone job hunting. It had been soul-destroying with more rejections that she could paper the walls with. One day, at her wits end, she had quite by chance confided in one of the mothers as they stood together outside the school gates waiting for their children. A week later, the school secretary had called her over and asked her to go to the admin office.

Filled with her usual trepidation, Nicola had dragged her heels as she made her way along the labyrinth of corridors to the office, trying to work out what the girls had done, or worse, if she had missed some small fee needed for a school trip or something that needed a contribution, which would be embarrassing as she had no money. But as it turned out, she had been asked if she would be interested in an administration job. Unable to believe what she was hearing, she had stared open-mouthed at the office manager and nodded, speechless. She must have looked pathetic, but thankfully, it hadn't deterred the manager and after all the necessary checks, Nicola had started a job at Meadow Green School. Weeks later she learned that the cousin of the mother in whom she had confided lived in the same road as her and the girls, and had put in a good word. The mother had duly mentioned Nicola's predicament to the school secretary, who had in turn spoken to the office manager.

With no idea that she was visible to her neighbours, it had come as a shock to Nicola to discover she had been talked about, but it didn't matter. She had thanked her saviour with a bunch of flowers bought with her first month's salary. It was the best thing that had happened to her in years. She found she was neither stupid nor thick, but was a quick learner and had an ability to retain even the most trivial of facts. She loved the job and now, having been there for over sixteen months she had a new self-confidence. For the first time in her life Nicola had begun to think she could do most things if she put her mind to it. Even her down days were fewer.

'It's tough being on your own at times,' Tony had said, slicing into her ruminations as he dunked his last marshmallow in his hot chocolate.

'Yes, it can be,' she had said, bringing herself back to their conversation, 'though the real down side of being a one parent family is that your own parents think they have the right to press gang you for Christmas day!' She had smirked as if to make light of being a one parent family. 'Though if I'm brutally honest, it's not me they want to see, but their grandchildren.'

'Snap, it's the same for us. Though I think in my case it's down to pity about the fact that I'm a widowed father. Taylor is more than spoilt by the family when we are there.' He had shrugged his shoulders, then leant over and ruffled his son's blond hair. 'I don't mind, he's worth it.'

Now, reflecting on that first meeting with Tony, Nicola smiled. It had been strange and wonderful in equal measures. There she was, just days before Christmas, sitting in a noisy café talking to a total stranger about having to spend time with her parents!

The first Christmas after Brett left she had spent the festive season at her parents' and it had been a huge strain. *He* had been there, as if he had more rights than she did, cornering her when no one was looking, reminding her how he loved her and that at the end of the day she was his. *'We share too many secrets to be free from each other,'* he had said, grabbing hold of her hand and filling her with fear and loathing. Unaware as always of what Uncle Bob was up to, her mother had harped on endlessly about Brett. Nicola could not wait to get away. Since then she had been dreading spending another Christmas with her parents knowing *he* would be there like always.

Before she could stop herself, she had found herself saying to Tony, 'You can both come to ours on Boxing Day if you like; the kids seem to get on.'

She had watched as he shifted in his seat and she had bitten down on her lip with embarrassment. 'Sorry, I'm so out of order, I shouldn't have said that, we hardly know each other,' she had added, wanting the ground to open up and swallow her along with her stupidity. Feeling ridiculous, she had reached out and pulled Mya to her. 'Come on girls, it's time to go so get your coats on.' Ignoring their protests and with her car keys in her hand, she had got to her feet and turned away.

'Can I say yes?' Tony had said sheepishly. He had stood up and turning back she found herself looking into his face. 'I said, can I say yes,' he repeated, adding after a brief pause, 'I mean, yes *please*?'

Catching her breath, she had not missed Taylor giggling with her girls. 'Right… yes, of course… yes, I'd like that,' she had stuttered sounding suddenly like a moron and wondering what had possessed her to invite him. But thank goodness she had.

Tony and Taylor had arrived mid-morning on the twenty-sixth. She would never forget that Boxing Day, it had been the beginning of their friendship, a whirlwind romance that had turned into something special. For the first time in her life Nicola felt at ease with someone of the opposite sex. Tony did not expect anything from her and was just as happy to sit and talk or watch the children play as he was to make love to her. Over the months, they had shared with each other many aspects of their lives. Tony was open about Sandy and his love for her. Nicola had talked about Brett, but had found it impossible to talk about *him*.

Then one night, after one of her worst nightmares in years followed by a breathtaking panic attack that had lasted two hours, she had opened up about *him*.

Until that night, Nicola had never told a soul and yet in the early hours of that Friday morning she had revealed some of the most painful things she'd had to endure. She told Tony about the first time *he* had touched her, the first time *he* had taken her and the terrible years that followed. She had talked about the Wendy House; the two abortions; the feeling of worthlessness and shame, finally ending with the accident. It seemed that once she had started she could not stop. It was as if the dam she had built to hold everything in tight and safe had begun to rupture and the more she talked the wider the fracture grew until the dam collapsed and everything spilled out. As the light from the dawn of a new day crept through the curtains of their bedroom window, exhausted and spent she had finally stopped talking.

There had followed a long silence between them, as if neither knew what to say. A million thoughts had raced through her mind and all returning to the same conclusion: Tony would run as far away as possible from her. Why had she told him, *why*? As her fear mounted to an explosive point, she had raised her head and cried out, 'Please Tony, say something.'

Like the crack from a whip her words had snapped at the silence. Unmoving he had continued to stare down at her, tears dripping off his chin. Nervously, she had searched his weeping eyes and to her horror had seen raw pain in their depths, making her wish she could take back every word she had spoken. The silence had lengthened and just when she had begun to accept their relationship was over, Tony had spoken.

'I love you Nic…' he had said, his breath catching in his throat, 'but, I can't take it all in.'

'You don't have to, please forget I said anything, *please*.'

'How can I forget? I just don't know how you came through it.'

'Does that mean you believe me?' she had said.

'Believe you? Yes, of course. Why wouldn't I?' he had sobbed.

In a swift movement he had taken her in his arms and with tears cascading down his face, had held her in a vice-like hug as if afraid to let her go. When he had eventually unfolded his arms Nicola had felt as if a huge weight had been removed from her whole being. She felt so unburdened that she would not have been surprised had she been able to float, rising above everything until she was up with the clouds. But the feeling of release lasted only a few moments and as it evaporated it had left her feeling dirty and ashamed.

'What must you think of me?' she had wept, moving away from him, wanting to melt away into the last remnants of the night shadows before daylight spilled finally into the room.

'No!' Tony cried, pulling her back to him, his voice catching in his throat, his pain palpable. 'No,' he repeated, fat, heavy tears slipping from his face, soaking into her nightdress and through to her skin.

As wretchedness washed over her Nicola had wondered why she had been so selfish. Why now of all times did she feel the need to share her darkest secret and talk about the very thing that had destroyed her past? At last she had found a wonderful man and here she was ruining it all with her shameful behaviour. What was wrong with her?

'It's all too much,' she had cried, trying to pull away from him, but he had held her firm. With no idea of what to say or how to extricate herself from his hold, she had stayed rigid. Nothing had prepared her for his reaction of open emotion. Was he shocked or disgusted with her? She hadn't dared to ask.

Eventually he had released his grip. ''My God, Nic, I love you more than ever,' he had said. Then he had planted kisses on her face, her head, her neck as if he had needed to reassure her of his feelings. Several more minutes passed before Tony had managed to utter another word without breaking down. This time he had held her at arm's length.

Afraid to touch him or look at him, Nicola had peered down at her bare feet, 'I'm sorry. I shouldn't have told you any of this. I've never told anyone before, not Brett or my parents. I'm so ashamed that I didn't stop him, but he said if I didn't let him do what he wanted he'd do it to my little sister instead, and if I told anyone they'd never believe me and I'd be punished for lying. Please forget about it Tony. It doesn't matter anymore,' she had pleaded, certain she had lost him.

'I can't forget and I never will. How could anyone do that to a child?' he had said, his voice taut with anger.

Knowing she had unleashed a horror, she had begged, 'Tony, you must keep all of this to yourself. You have no idea what he will do, what will happen to me and my children. He's clever, very clever and he'll say it's not true and that I caused his accident. I'd be arrested for attempted murder. They would take my girls away from me. Please Tony, please, I should never had said anything. I'm sorry.' Her fear had reached new heights and she was close to passing out with panic.

'For God's sake, Nicola, you were ten years old!' Tony's face was a picture of utter misery. 'I love you, Nicola Knight. I can't get enough of you. You have to accept I can't imagine anyone doing or wanting to do such things to a child. I'm heartbroken it happened to you, but I can't agree with you remaining silent. There is no way the incident you have described could be seen as anything but an accident. It isn't as if you pushed him into the road, he was following you. It was not your fault, Nicola, he brought it on himself and no court in the land would think otherwise. Something has to be done to bring that odious bastard to justice and I'm here to help you whenever you are ready. I love you little lady, more than you will ever know.'

Eventually, after several weeks had passed, Nicola had gradually accepted that despite her disgusting revelations, Tony still loved her. Almost, it seemed he loved her even more because of them. Now, as Nicola lay under the duvet, her eyelids heavy, she knew she owed it to Tony to find the courage to seek help. Maybe it was time to call Uncle Bob's bluff and get in first with her version of events. After all, she just might be believed. Tony believed her. With this knowledge, she gave in to her exhaustion and allowed her eyelids to slide shut. A contented sigh slipped between her lips; sleep was closing in at last. She did not hear Tony coming back with her cup of tea, nor was she aware of his smile as he quietly placed it on the bedside cupboard and tiptoed from the room.

Chapter Thirty-Two

Barbara felt she'd had the best night's sleep in weeks and although today was going to be a challenge, she felt strong enough to be able to cope. Now, with her jacket buttoned up, she twisted the thermostat knob on the central heating down a couple of degrees. Satisfied the house would be comfortable for her return she grabbed her handbag from the hall chair and slipping it under her arm, she pulled her car keys out of her pocket and headed out into the cold morning. Suddenly she found herself smiling. It had been a long time since she had felt positive about facing her daughter. They still had a long way to go before she could feel at ease with Nicola, but things had improved since the girls' father had left then in the lurch. How her daughter had got herself mixed up with him in the first place still baffled her, but now was not the time to rake over the whys and wherefores of Brett Morton. Her priority at the moment was to work on building bridges between herself and Nicola. She recognised she had been harsh with her daughter over the years; both of them managed to bring out the worse in each other. She also accepted she needed to show a little more compassion, too. They were all grieving and Terry would have wanted them united, not constantly at each other's throats.

Barbara shivered as the cold air pinched at her face. There was a light covering of frost on the car windows. It had just turned ten o'clock and the sky was a sapphire blue, but the sun had yet to travel round the roof tops before there would be a slow thaw in the garden.

Five minutes later the car windows were clear and, with her hands feeling like blocks of ice, she reversed out of her drive. It wasn't the easiest of journeys to Nicola's as she had to navigate through the centre of town, which at any time of the day suffered from congestion. God only knew what the planning officers were busy spending their days on, but it never appeared to be on traffic management, she thought, moaning loudly after negotiating the first of many roundabouts along her route. Resigned to a stressful drive, she wondered what her daughter's mood would be like today. Maybe she should have called Nicola first to check it was convenient for her to come over, then decided that if Nicola knew she was planning a visit, she would likely tell her not to bother. They had not parted on the best of terms after the funeral and all she wanted was to make amends. Find a way to heal their smarting wounds.

After sitting in lines of stationary cars at temporary traffic lights and following poor signs for diversions due to road works, Barbara arrived at her daughter's home.

She gazed over at the nineteen-seventies semi-detached house and to her delight, saw Mya waving at her through the lounge picture-window. Her mood lightened at the sight of her granddaughter and she waved back, thankful someone was pleased to see her. Still waving, she headed down the short path, but before she could reach the front door, it burst open. Mya and Taylor, calling out to her, jumped up and down with excitement on the threshold.

'Hello Nana,' both cried in unison.

'Hello lovelies,' she said, bending down and taking them both into her arms. The fresh fragrance of vanilla soap filled her nostrils as she hugged them close. Taylor, although not her grandson, seemed to think she was his Nana too and clung to her as tightly as Mya did. Secretly she revelled in being called "Nana" and suddenly she felt very proud of Nicola for taking on someone else's child. There were hidden depths to her eldest.

Taking hold of Mya's and Taylor's hands, she ushered them inside glad to feel the warmth from the central heating.

'Mum's in the shower,' Mya piped up, gripping hold of Barbara's hand and leading her through to the lounge.

'Hello, Mrs Knight, this is a surprise,' Tony said, appearing in the lounge doorway. He clutched a tea towel, a worried smile filling his face. 'Nicola never said anything about you coming over, is everything okay?'

'Yes, everything is fine, I just thought I'd surprise her,' she said, taking in the dark circles shadowing Tony's eyes and the way his shoulders slumped. The man looked bone weary. None of this she had noticed at the funeral. She knew little about him, though on the occasions they had met she had seen a kind and confident young man. Today all she saw was exhaustion and tension. She didn't want to think that Nicola and Tony were experiencing problems, her daughter could be difficult, but she didn't want her hurt or unhappy.

'Is everything okay with you all?' she asked.

Tony nodded, 'We are all good, but sad for Nic losing her father. I know what it feels like to lose someone close.'

Of course he did, she reminded herself and regretted driving over without phoning first. 'I am sorry. I should have called to check it was okay for me to visit, but, I'll be honest, I was afraid if I did, Nicola would find a reason for me not to come and I really would like to talk to her.'

Tony reached over and placed his hand on her shoulder, 'You don't have to make an appointment to see your own daughter, Mrs Knight, you are always welcome here,' he said with a genuine smile. 'Please make yourself comfortable and I'll put the kettle on.' He motioned for her to sit on one of the sofas. 'Nic's having a shower, she had a bad night last night.'

Barbara was about to ask what he meant when Tony turned and spoke to Mya. 'Go and find Chelsea and tell her Nana's here.' Without a backward glance, Mya ran out of the room as if someone had fired the starting gun at a race. Taylor followed closely at her heels. The thundering of their feet drifted into the room as the two raced up the stairs. A pang of sadness washed over Barbara at how little she knew of Nicola's new relationship. 'They seem to get on well together,' she said lamely, deciding not to ask about Nicola's bad night for now.

'Yes, they do,' he said, heading back to the kitchen.

Barbara slipped out of her jacket and laid it on the sofa arm then, ignoring Tony's offer to sit down, she followed him through to the kitchen. He appeared relaxed and from what she had seen and sensed in the few moments since she had arrived, the house felt like a happy home, so different from the last one when Nicola had been living with the girls' father. She just hoped she was right and that it was indeed a happy home. She took a deep breath, aware she had a lot of making up to do and feeling a sense of shame that things had reached the point where she felt a stranger in her daughter's house. Realising this, Barbara strengthened her resolve to find a way for them to be close again.

'Here she is,' Tony said, beaming as Chelsea breezed into the kitchen.

'Hello Nan,' Chelsea said, keeping her hands behind her back as if to hide something.

Grateful of the distraction from her painful thoughts, Barbara reached out, 'Hello darling, you look like you've got something you're hiding.'

Bringing her arms to the front, Chelsea proudly held up a knitting needle with a ragged knitting square dangling from several loose stiches, a ball of blue wool was speared on the other needle. 'Look Nan, 'I'm learning to knit,' Chelsea squealed, waving the knitted square as if it was a prized procession. 'Nana Penny's been teaching me and I've already knitted a square. Look,' she cried pushing her work of art in front of Barbara's face.

Barbara bobbed down, took hold of the woollen piece and carefully examined it, reminded again of what was happening in her grandchildren's life and that she was not a part of it. She was determined to remedy this state of affairs for which she was as much to blame as Nicola. 'You are clever, Chelsea. That is really very good. Maybe next time you come to visit me we can find a few coloured balls of wool for you. I think I might still have a book on knitted toys. In fact I'm sure I have.' Barbara wasn't too sure were the book might be, but she would certainly make certain there was one in the house for Chelsea's next visit.

'Wow! That would be great, thanks Nan,' Chelsea said, taking back her knitting and without hesitation wrapping her arms around Barbara's neck. 'You're so cool, Nan,' she cried before standing up and hugging her knitting.

Lost for words, Barbara nodded at her granddaughter, she could not remember ever being told she was cool, but from Chelsea's animated expression it was spoken as a form of endearment and she found herself liking it very much. All of a sudden she felt old and out of touch with everyone. Maybe after all, her visit would not be a waste of time. Maybe the bridges she had come to build were not so much needing construction as a nip and tuck. She fervently hoped so.

'My mother believes everyone should learn to knit,' Tony said, pouring water into a large teapot. 'Even Taylor has a pair of knitting needles. And, yes, she taught me too, but I was never any good at it.' A slow smirk crossed his face. It hid the tiredness and had him appearing like a mischievous young boy.

'Have you any sisters?'

'No, hence why Mum wasted her time teaching her only son to knit and sew, thankfully she drew the line at wanting me to play with dolls.' Tony laughed; it was an infectious chuckle and Barbara found herself chortling. At the same time she felt a stab of jealously that a woman who was a stranger to her and no relation to her grandchildren was teaching her granddaughter to knit. She was missing out on so much.

'Okay Chelsea, put your knitting away and go and find your shoes and coat,' Tony said. 'When Mummy comes down, we four are going out.' He turned back to finish making the tea and added, 'We're leaving Nana and Mum at home.'

'Hmm,' Chelsea said, flashing a look at Barbara as she wound the lose strands of wool over her needles. 'Can't I stay with Nan, you know it's really cold outside?'

'Nope, but if you all behave we can stop and have hot chocolate in the park.'

'Cool,' Chelsea cried.

'We'll see, scoot!' he ordered, smiling as Chelsea raced out of the kitchen as if afraid the café would sell out of hot chocolate before they got there.

'You've probably noticed, but *cool* is Chelsea's word of the moment,' he chuckled, handing a mug of milky tea to Barbara.

She had and was thankful it was "cool" and nothing else, like the words she had heard some children come out with these days.

'The kids seem to think there's only one speed at the moment and that's to run everywhere. I'm tired just watching them,' Tony said, picking up the second mug and carrying it over to the table. 'I don't want to be talking out of turn, but I'm pleased you've come to visit. You and Nicola need to make your peace. Things need sorting because she's not in the best place at the moment.'

Barbara frowned, when wasn't her daughter in *the best place?* In the few minutes she had been in the house she had begun to warm to Tony, but his implied criticism on what was needed to be done galled her.

'I've no idea what Nicola has been telling you, but sadly my daughter is at times a troubled soul,' she said, keeping her voice even and wondering what Nicola had said to Tony. She glared at him as if it would reveal what he was referring to because no doubt Nicola would have portrayed her in a very poor light if she had told him about the abortion. It had nothing to do with him and she hoped he was not sitting in judgement. It was a period in their lives that had brought its fair share of misery and that was one of the reasons she was here. What she did not want was to be told she needed to make peace with her daughter. Was he judging her when he had no idea of the real circumstances? *Stop it Barbara*! she castigated herself, she was here to offer an olive branch, not to fell the tree. In an attempt to extinguish her annoyance, she looked around the modern kitchen, relieved it was a far cry from the two-bedroomed dilapidated place Nicola had lived in before.

'I understand that, Mrs Knight, and believe you me I am more than glad you're here. As it happens, your timing is perfect. Nicola *needs* to talk to you.'

Pleased that her daughter was ready to talk and maybe work with her to heal their latest rift, Barbara's heart raced with anticipation. Although they had seen more of each other since Morton had walked out, it was still a roller coaster ride between them.

'I've driven across town in the hope we can make our peace, Tony. It is long overdue. And, just for the record, I've never stopped trying to help my daughter, but you'll understand in time, it is not always that easy to reach Nicola.'

Tony nodded. Barbara wasn't sure if it was affirmation or resignation of what she had just said. Either way, it was not going to be a girly chat with her daughter and knowing this, she lowered herself down onto one of the chairs nestled around the light oak table.

Rinsing his mug under the tap, Tony turned it upside down and laid it in the plastic draining rack. 'I'd better go and see what the kids are doing and then we'll be out of your hair,' he said, wiping his hands on a crumpled tea towel. 'I think it's best that it's just you and Nic. The kids can get rid of their energy racing through the park.'

He dropped the tea towel at the side of the sink and Barbara watched him stride out of the kitchen, 'Thank you,' she called, unsure what to say and worried about what Tony was referring to when he said, *I think it's best it's just you and Nic*. Why did he think that?

Trying to work out what new challenge she was faced with, Barbara heard a loud burst of happy giggling from the hall. 'Bye Nana, see you soon,' her grandchildren called out, followed by the slamming of the front door.

Silence followed and she found herself alone in the house with her daughter.

Chapter Thirty-Three

'Mum, what are you doing here? Has something happened?' Nicola said, surprise in her voice as she shuffled into the kitchen. Barbara swung round and for a moment wondered if she had called at the wrong house. The sight that met her came as a shock. Her daughter looked a mess and, like Tony, she had black circles under her eyes, her hair needed a brush through and although the clothes she wore were clean, the pretty green jumper, which she had bought for Nicola's birthday last year, had a hole in the sleeve.

'No, nothing has happened,' Barbara replied, moving towards her daughter, the waft of fragrant soap reminding her that Nicola had recently showered. 'I just wanted to see you and thought maybe we could talk,' she said, and wondered why she felt nervous in the company of her own daughter.

Glancing towards the front door, Nicola's face took on a haunted expression, 'Did Tony ask you to come here?'

'No, why would he?'

'No reason,' Nicola said and shrugged her shoulders. 'I just wondered. It's not like you to turn up unannounced.'

'Are you telling me you don't want me here?' Barbara found herself saying and wished her tone didn't sound so confrontational. She wasn't here to argue, but judging by the way Nicola was looking at her with suspicion it was obvious her visit was not going to be easy. What had made her think that dropping in unannounced was a good plan?

'As I said, I was hoping you and I could talk.' Seeing a puzzled look cross Nicola's face, it was clear to Barbara that turning up on a Saturday morning had been a mistake. 'I'm sorry I should have telephoned first, but...' she hesitated, then ploughed on, 'We did not part on the best of terms and I was afraid if I did ring first you'd tell me not to bother.'

As Nicola continued to stare at her she tried to read what was behind her daughter's troubled eyes. Tony had said she wasn't in a good place and Barbara wondered what demons were stalking her today. Her heart contracted to see Nicola still so obviously troubled, what was going on in her daughter's head that had her moods swinging from euphoria to despair? Although if she was honest, Barbara reflected, she had seen little of the euphoria over the years. There must be periods of good times, she reasoned, because Nicola had met Tony. In the fifteen minutes she had been in the house, her first worry of possible difficulties between Nicola and Tony had slipped away. The vibes she had picked up from him had been those of loving and caring, and yet Nicola's weary eyes screamed something different.

'I've not come to fight,' Barbara said, cautious of what was the best way to approach the conversation she hoped to have with her daughter. Watching her slump wearily down on a chair, Barbara took the seat next to her and held out her hand. 'You look worn out. Grief has many facets and there's no shame in letting it all pour out.'

Staring down at the proffered hand, Nicola ignored the gesture. 'You have no idea have you, is that why you're here Mum, to find out how I'm grieving?' Nicola shot back, her tired expression in contrast to the annoyance in her tone.

Determined not to bristle at Nicola's cutting words, Barbara steadied herself. 'No darling, that is not the reason. I've come to see how we can find a way to end the friction between us. I don't know about you, but I don't want to go on like this anymore.' She wanted to add that Terry's death had galvanised her into finding a way to understand their eldest daughter better, but even as she uttered her words of platitude, she was pointedly aware she was stepping in treacle; afraid of the slightest change in tone or the wrong word slipping out that would create yet another altercation.

'Can I make you a cup of tea?' she asked. Getting to her feet and not waiting for a response, she set about making a fresh pot.

Nicola didn't answer, but watched her mother bring two mugs of steaming tea over to the table. 'Thanks,' she said, and without emotion took hold of the mug. 'Dad's death hasn't changed things between us, Mum. I know I'm still a disappointment to you.'

'I wouldn't be here if that was the case, Nicola. Like all mothers I only wanted the best for you, but... well, things turned out a little different.' She reached over and this time took hold of Nicola's hand, it was cold. In an attempt to appeal to the mature, responsible side of her daughter, she carried on. 'You're a mother now, love, and I'm guessing you want the best for your girls? Want them to have the best they can achieve: good school results; jobs they will enjoy and, one day, partners who will care for them and love them and, most important, that they have a happy life. That is all we ever wanted for you, darling. Happiness and a feeling of worth.'

Nicola picked up her mug and looked down at the tea. She sipped at the warm liquid then shrugged her shoulders. 'My girls will do well,' she said. Placing the mug back on the table she gazed at Barbara and said, 'I'm a good mother, Mum.'

For the first time since she had arrived, Barbara saw conviction sparkle in her daughter's eyes. 'I don't doubt that for one moment, Nicola. Your dad and I had every confidence that you would do well.' Sensing a chink in her daughter's armour, Barbara said, 'We can't turn the clock back, but I would like us to try and find a way back to being a family again. I will try if you will,' she said, her words filled with hope.

Pushing herself to her feet, with a couple of steps she covered the space between them and wrapping her arms around Nicola hugged her tight. 'It breaks my heart seeing you like this. I love you; I always have and I always will. You are my first born and hold a special place in my heart.' She placed her chin on the top of Nicola's hair and breathed in her daughter's fragrance. 'I know we've had more than our share of testing times, but surely we can move forward?'

'It's not that easy,' Nicola said, tears filling her eyes.

'Of course it is,' Barbara said, taking a step back. She dug into her handbag and pulling out a tissue wiped away her daughter's tears. 'I need to know my granddaughters better. And it would be nice to see more of you and get to know Tony. From what I have seen, he seems very caring, so what can be so difficult?'

'I want them to have you in their lives too,' Nicola agreed, taking hold of the tissue. 'I don't want us to always be at each other's throats, Mum. Tony is a good man and he makes me happy. The girls love him too and Taylor is already part of our family.'

'I am glad to hear you are happy with him. So surely that is more reason why we should be close.'

Nicola nodded.

Barbara moved back to her chair, her journey had not, after all, been wasted, she just hoped that whatever place Tony had eluded to Nicola being in would change now they were talking. 'Thank you my love, I know I have not always been patient with you. I will try to be kinder. I promise I won't let you down. With Dad gone, there is just us, you and your family, me, Becky and Uncle Bob.'

'No!' Nicola screamed, jumping to her feet. 'No, not *him*!'

Startled at Nicola's reaction, Barbara gasped, what on earth had she said this time? My God, how wrong she had been thinking a few words and a hug would change things. The road, she travelled with her daughter never seemed to get any easier. She should have foreseen Nicola would not stay calm for more than a few minutes. A firework was less explosive!

'For goodness sake, Nicola, what on earth is wrong with you?'

'What do you mean?' Nicola shot back. 'It's not me there's anything wrong with, but if you insist on *him* still being part of our family, then I never will be and nor will my girls. So accept that from now on I'm officially cut off,' Nicola barked. Grabbing her mug of tea and stomping across the kitchen she sloshed the remains of the drink down the sink and slammed the mug down on the chopping board.

'Nicola, please, the man is confined to a wheelchair. Where is your compassion? He was your father's best friend and has been a wonderful friend to our family. As I've said before, he's family. What has he ever done to you that you should dislike him so?'

Snorting with derision, Nicola snarled, 'If he's family, then ask him about the accident and what *really* happened.'

Unsure where this was going, Barbara strode towards Nicola. As much as she wanted to take hold of her daughter and shake her, she knew it would be a waste of energy. There had been tension between Bob and Nicola for years now and she and Terry had never got to the bottom of it. Bob had never shown any animosity towards Nicola, all the aggression had been directed at him from their daughter. 'Nicola, you know what happened to him. How can you be so callous as to suggest we ask him to rake over that appalling accident again? Why should he do that? Whatever has got into you?'

'Okay! Then ask him about Burley House and Laura Speedwell,' Nicola hissed between thin lips that had turned almost white.

'Laura Speedwell; Burley House,' Barbara repeated, 'Who and what are you talking about?'

'Just ask him, please Mum.'

'But why should I?'

'Because I need you to.'

'Well if you know, tell me now and then we can get whatever this is all about out in the open.'

Bewildered at how her visit was turning out, in an effort to try and calm the situation, Barbara took hold of Nicola's hand. 'Come on love, please sit down, I don't like to see you like this. I've no Idea what all this is about, but I promise you I will find out.' She was at her wit's end. It was like handling a bag of eels, no sooner had she got a grasp when suddenly all hell broke loose and she lost her grip. Sifting through the jumble of words that had passed between them and the anger Nicola felt for Bob, she began to wonder if her daughter had had a teenage crush on him. He had been very good looking when he was younger. She recalled Bob was one for the girls in those days and probably this Laura was one of his conquests. Had Nicola made a pass at Bob and being the gentleman he was, he had let her down gently. It sounded ridiculous, but it would answer why there was such animosity from Nicola. What she didn't understand was why Nicola was so aggrieved after all these years. She sighed at her conjecture and wondered why nothing was ever straightforward with her daughter.

'I can't, Mum. Please do as I ask.'

'Okay darling, if that's what you want, I will speak to him, but only if we can part this morning as friends and promise each other we are going to try to stay that way.'

Nicola stared at her and not for the first time, Barbara wondered if her daughter suffered from something more serious than depression. She didn't like to think of anything more sinister, but it was clear there was something not quite normal at times.

Nicola nodded, whispered 'Yes.'

'Right then, I'll mention this Laura to him if it will make you happy.'

'It will, it will,' Nicola said, a sardonic gleam flashing in her eyes.

Chapter Thirty-Four

Nicola sank down on the kitchen chair, agitated, her resolution to talk to her mother had flown out of the window and all because the very mention of *his* name had the shutters sliding down on the rational Nicola, whilst the door flew open on the angry, bitter woman who lost all reason. Fuming at her inability to control her temper and tongue, she nibbled at her bitten finger nails. Why did she do this? Of course, her mother turning up unannounced had flustered her and her resolve to talk about the things she needed to talk about had evaporated. Instead, she had snapped at her, screaming out stupid questions that should never have left her lips. Thankfully, her mother had hugged her and had agreed to ask the question.

Chewing at her little finger, she just hoped Mum did ask *him* because it really was time to talk about what had happened, what *he* had done, and all the years of shame and torment that had dogged her life and soured her relationship with her mother. Nicola knew the only way to go forward and enjoy the happiness and love she was now surrounded with was to talk. She needed to tell her mother, not only for her own sanity, but for her children and, importantly, for Tony too. He didn't deserve to be living with a Jekyll and Hyde personality. Why he loved her she had no idea, but she was glad he did. And because of that she had revealed her darkest secret to him. Even now, several weeks later, she could still see the shock and pain in his hazel brown eyes as the words had tumbled out of her.

Thinking about how Tony was coping with her shameful secret, gradually convincing her that none of it had been her fault and making her feel whole and worthy; encouraging her to tell her mother and to seek redress, yet never pressurising her, Nicola felt ashamed. She should not have spoken to her mother like she had. Screaming about Laura Speedwell and Burley House was not the way to go forward. It was not the way to show her mother that she, Nicola, was not the belligerent daughter her mother had always seen, but one who had been holding a dirty secret for so long that it flowed like poison throughout her system, making it impossible for her to be the daughter her mother wanted.

To make amends for today she would invite Mum for Sunday lunch. The children would love it and as well as enabling her mother to get to know Tony, she could try and find a way to talk.

With a plan to work too, Nicola made herself a cup of coffee. She would give her mother enough time to drive home and then she would call her.

Chapter Thirty-Five

Driving home on what felt like auto pilot, Barbara picked through the words that had been exchanged during the last hour spent with her daughter. Like so many times over the years, it had seemed she was in the company of two different people. One moment Nicola was calm and coherent, the next volatile and angry. Barbara had arrived at her daughter's home feeling positive and had left feeling drained, but what disturbed her the most was the amount of aggression constantly directed towards Bob. Why? She asked herself once again, and although she had asked Nicola the same question, she had never received an answer that made sense. Where was Burley House and what did it have to do with anything? And who was Laura Speedwell and why did Nicola insist she find out about her? As pointless as it was, thought Barbara, the next time she spoke with Bob she would weave the girl's name into the conversation, if for no other reason than to appease her daughter.

With her mind filled with Nicola, she hardly noticed the disruptive roadworks of earlier. Pulling onto her drive, feeling drained from her visit rather than the queues of traffic, she was tempted to call her daughter. As this thought sat in the forefront of her mind, the image of Nicola's tired face filled with indignation flashed before her and she thought better of it. It would do no harm to put a little distance between them. A few days would help them both calm down. Next week would be plenty soon enough to struggle through the treacle that was the sticky path of her daughter's mind.

Climbing out of the car, Barbara heard the faint sound of the phone ringing in the hall. She calculated whether she could get inside before it stopped then accepting it was unlikely, she locked the car door. If she was honest, she wasn't sure she was in the mood for any more chatting with whoever it might be. As she slipped her key into the lock, the phone stopped ringing. Relieved, Barbara unlocked the door and headed inside. Maybe after all she would call Bob and invite him over for Sunday lunch. It would give her an excuse to cook a decent meal and, at the same time, slip Nicola's question into the conversation. It might go some way to help bridge the gap between them if her daughter knew she had taken her question seriously.

Draping her jacket over the coat hook, Barbara glanced at the red flashing light on the phone warning her she had missed a call. Although not wanting to talk to anyone just yet, she was anxious to make sure it wasn't Becky trying to get hold of her. Because no matter how she felt, her girls were always at the front of her mind; one more than other, she thought. Seeing that the number displayed was Nicola's, she sighed wearily. Was it an apology or another round of questions? Deciding she wasn't up to risking another outcry just now, she lifted the phone and punched in Bob's number. He at least would be civil to her.

Chapter Thirty-Six

With a glass of chilled wine at her elbow, Barbara turned to Bob.

He ignored the glass of wine on the kitchen table and instead stared down at the roast on the carving board in front of him, then gazed back at her and pulled a face.

She didn't miss the amusement in his eyes as he took in the pitiful joint. 'I know it's only a small piece of pork, Bob, but there are only the two of us...' Passing him the carving knife, she wondered if she would ever again be able to have a Sunday roast without feeling emotional.

Bob reached out and took hold of the handle, but Barbara momentarily hung onto it longer than necessary. This was Terry's job, she thought. '*Will I ever learn to live without him?*' It was the little things that seized at her heart, like carving the Sunday roast. It had been traditional for him to do the honours. "It's a man thing," he would say positioning himself in front of the table and posing, as if appearing on one of the celebrity TV cook shows. Then with deftness he would run the blade of the carving knife along the steel to ensure it was razor sharp before slicing into the meat.

'My favourite,' Bob said, removing the knife from her grasp, 'and Terry's too,' he added, as if reading her thoughts.

Maybe having Bob over for lunch hadn't been such a good idea, she mused, as old memories once again wrapped around her. It had seemed so when she had invited him, believing that cooking a Sunday roast would help bring a little normality into her very abnormal world, but it hadn't. This weekend she had manged to get everything wrong. First up, she had turned down a few days staying with Becky and her husband, arguing they were busy people and she needed to sort things out. Becky had disagreed, but had quickly acquiesced. Then there had been yesterday's fraught visit to Nicola, who she later discovered had left her a message, apologising and inviting her for Sunday lunch, but by then she had invited Bob. Yes, she had got it all wrong and knowing this, a stab of guilt pierced at her heart at declining both her girls' offers especially Nicola's.

'Did you ever know a girl by the name of Laura Speedwell?' Barbara suddenly found herself asking as she dropped a knob of butter into a pan of drained boiled potatoes. 'I only ask because Nicola mentioned something about her yesterday,' she added fluffing up the potatoes with a large fork. With no response, she was about to repeat the question, when the sound of steel clattering onto ceramic tile had her spinning round. 'Is everything all right?' she asked, staring at Bob's pale face.

'Yes, yes,' he stuttered averting his eyes from Barbara, 'the knife slipped, no worries.'

'Not too sure about that,' she chided sweeping across the room and picking it up. 'We'll have a visitor now.'

'What?' Bob stammered.

'An old wives saying, my mother used to say it when a knife fell to the floor,' she replied. Rinsing the knife under a stream of hot water she dried it on a clean tea towel and wondered why she was wittering on about some old saying. 'Here,' she said and handed the knife back. Bob reached out and took it, but not before Barbara noticed how his hand shook.

'Are you sure you are all right?' she asked, transferring her gaze from his trembling hand to his pale face. He was never one for much colour these days, but right now he looked like he was about to pass out and she wondered what had brought this on.

'I'm fine, really,' Bob stammered. 'It's the new meds I'm taking. They give me the shakes from time to time. Maybe I'll have to give up carving or stop taking the meds,' he retorted, a false bravado to his tone as a nervous smile twitched on his lips.

A fresh wave of sadness washed over Barbara at seeing her old friend slowly deteriorate. 'They're forever changing your tablets, you need to let the doctors know the side effects, especially shaking like that,' she said, unsure if the name Laura Speedwell had been the real cause. Maybe she had hit on a raw nerve, though perhaps she should not have asked in the first place. Feeling responsible, she apologised. 'I'm sorry Bob, I shouldn't be asking questions while you're wielding a sharp knife,' she said with a smile, taking in the number of slices carved and seeing there was plenty for the two of them. 'I think there's enough for you and me.' She took back the knife. 'Best I take care of this. If you carry on shaking we'll end up with mince,' she added, trying to lighten the situation.

Bob make a sound and Barbara wasn't sure if he was choking or chuckling. 'You always manage to see the bright side and that's why I've been able to cope,' he said pushing the carving board to the centre of the table.

'I wish that was the case,' she said and shaking her head, turned back to the pans on the hob. Perhaps if she had lightened up more and tried to see the brighter side with Nicola, then maybe they wouldn't be at loggerheads all the time. 'So I take it you didn't know this girl then?' she pushed, not really understanding why, despite having apologised. Perhaps it was the way Nicola had insisted she ask him. Maybe it was worth persisting if, in the end, she could reconcile these two people.

'Laura Speedwell, you say?' Bob's voice quivered. He took a deep breath that wheezed noisily down to his lungs and made his nostrils flare before he continued. 'Yes, I did know her, but it was a long time ago, she was an old girlfriend. It's funny you should ask about her.'

'Really?' Barbara's eyebrows arched to disappear under her fringe. 'I don't think you've ever mentioned her before,' she said, spooning creamy mashed potatoes into a small serving dish.

'Haven't I?' he said, a slight catch in his voice.

Barbara glanced at him from the corner of her eye and to her surprise, noticed his face had turned the colour of puce. Goodness, Bob was in poor shape today, she worried. Whatever meds they were prescribing him were causing him unusual anxiety. As for an old girlfriend, what had it got to do with her anyway? She wished now she hadn't asked.

Wiping the back of his hand over his mouth and keeping his gaze on the carved meat, Bob said, 'I was in love with Laura and I'd hoped she would one day be mine.' As he spoke he reached over and gripped the stem of his wine glass. His trembling appeared to have abated slightly. 'Then one day she told me she was pregnant...' Bob paused and lifted the glass to his lips and emptied the contents in one noisy gulp. With a distant look in his eyes, he stared down at the empty glass as if it reflected whatever he saw in his mind's eye. In a strained voice, he continued, 'You have no idea how happy I was to know I would be a father, but like many things in life, sometimes it doesn't work out how you expect it to be.'

Barbara looked on and took in his cheerless face, watching as he wiped the palm of his hand across his clean shaven, chin. Beads of perspiration bubbled on his brow and a couple of drops trickled down his temple. Oblivious of Barbara's stare, he raised his glass to his lips and seeing it empty, he placed it back down.

Barbara wondered what had happened to this Laura, but didn't want to ask as she could see how affected he was talking about her. Once again she found herself apologising. 'I'm sorry, Bob. I can see from the pain on your face I've strayed into personal territory,' she said, cursing her daughter under her breath. She would put penny to a pound that Nicola knew all about this Laura Speedwell. What was her game? Her daughter's apology of yesterday suddenly appeared nothing more than a smoke screen as Nicola continued to play her silly, spiteful games against Bob. To distract her annoyance at being played for a fool, Barbara yanked open a drawer and selected cutlery for their meal.

'No, you don't need to apologise. It was one of those things. At the end of the day she didn't want the baby and went ahead with a termination in a private clinic. I knew nothing about it until it was all over.'

Searching for words, much as she was now rooting for the lunch time cutlery, she avoided turning to face him. He didn't deserve to have her prying into his life like this. Pulling out what was needed, Barbara placed the cutlery on the table. 'It's none of my business and I had no right to ask,' she said, pity welling up inside her. She could kill her daughter for her insensitivity. It was clear it was another one of her tactics to create conflict and misery. What Barbara could not understand was why Nicola wanted to hurt him. What had possessed her to ask such a question? It was becoming more and more clear that Nicola was far more disturbed than she could ever have imagined.

Taking the wine bottle out of the fridge, she twisted at the cork, then filled Bob's glass almost to the top. 'Once again, I'm sorry,' she said, recharging her own glass. She wanted to know how Nicola knew of this woman, but seeing Bob in such a state she felt it necessary to change the subject. She was about to talk about what was on the television that afternoon, when Bob cut in.

'You said Nicola mentioned her?'

'Did I? Yes, but I think we've said enough about this, let's move the subject to something more cheerful. My daughter seems at her best when she's causing pain.' Barbara felt bruised that she had been set up. She had firmly believed her visit yesterday had laid the foundation for bridges to be built, not for narrow parapets to be constructed in order to teeter on the edge playing mind games. She sighed deeply. She would need to calm down before she spoke to her daughter again, if not she would end up venting her anger and any hope of a reconciliation would be lost.

'Don't upset yourself,' Bob said, a sharpness entering his voice, stopping her wading further into the murky waters of her daughter. 'It happened a long time ago and until now, I'd not given it a thought for many years.'

Barbara placed her hand on Bob's shoulder and squeezed gently. Through the thickness of his tailored jacket she felt a layer of fat. The once trim, muscular body had withered away to waste with years of immobility. Her heart ached at the changes. He had born it all without complaint or bitterness. 'You know, we all ought to take a leaf out of your book on patience and kindness,' she said, to raise the mood of their conversation.

Bob reached up and patted Barbara's hand. 'Let's forget about it and enjoy the wonderful meal you've cooked,' he said.

She nodded in agreement. Somehow, his dismissal of the subject only added to her annoyance. 'You're right, Bob, let's not allow the things we can't change to spoil our Sunday.' She turned and picked up her glass. 'Cheers,' she called and raised it to her lips. Now, more than ever she was missing Terry. He had always said the best way to cope was to ignore Nicola when she was in a strop. As the wine slipped down her throat, Barbara could hear Terry's voice reminding her what to do. She would take his advice and avoid her daughter for the next few days.

Chapter Thirty-Seven

It had been three days since Bob had been for Sunday lunch and four since Barbara had spoken to her daughter, though she was still baffled at Nicola's latest attempt at causing mischief. Thankfully, Bob had not been overly worried about talking about this Laura, though she hadn't missed the catch in his voice when he spoke about that time in his life. After he had left she had called Becky, the guilt of turning down her youngest daughter's offer to stay for the weekend had nagged away at her. This time she had readily accepted the invitation to spend some time with them at the back end of the week. 'I'd love to,' she had said and had felt Becky's smile travel down the wire at her response. Her youngest was confident and self-contained, the complete opposite of her sister. Hard to believe they were sisters at times. Yet both had enjoyed the same privileged upbringing, the same opportunities. How could they have turned out so different? It was a question that had often puzzled her.

With a few days to herself before she drove down to the south coast, Barbara decided to visit the local garden centre in the hope it would occupy her enough to still all the thoughts that played around in her head.

Finishing the last drops of her second cup of coffee, her thoughts were broken by the phone ringing. Reaching out she picked up the handset and to her dismay saw Nicola's number. She wasn't sure she wanted to speak to her right now, knowing it would throw a dark cloud over her already sombre mood. With her thumb hovering over the answer button, she knew she couldn't ignore her and stabbed at it.

'Hello Nicola,' she said in a hollow voice, bracing herself for a reference to the question she had been asked to put to Bob.

'Hello Mrs Knight, it's Tony here, Nic's partner. I'm sorry to trouble you, but—'Panic rose and Barbara's stomach muscles contracted, 'What is wrong?' she cut in. There had to be something wrong. Tony had never rung before. 'Is Nicola okay or is it the children?'

'The kids are fine, but it's Nic I'm worried about,' Tony replied, his tone anxious.

He was not alone on that score, Barbara thought, she had been worried about her daughter for years. What had she done now that needed Tony to call her?

'Mrs Knight, are you still there?' Tony's anxious voice drifted down the line.

'Yes I'm here,' she answered. 'What's wrong? I am assuming something is for you to call me?' Until last Saturday she had thought Tony a little aloof, but after her visit, she had warmed towards him having seen love and respect in his eyes.

'It's not so much as what's wrong it's more that she needs to talk to you, especially after Saturday. She's been very upset since then; inconsolable. Please could you come over? I wouldn't ask, but I don't know what to do with her. I've taken the morning off work to be with her until you arrive. Please. She needs your help.'

Barbara heard the beseeching in his voice and felt the fine hairs on her forearms rise. 'What has she done?' she asked, trying not to travel back to the times when Nicola had self-harmed.

'Nothing. If you are thinking about her hurting herself, she hasn't and won't. Right now she just needs to talk to you. It's not that easy to explain on the phone. I'm afraid she is having a breakdown. Please, if you could just come to the house,' Tony insisted.

Barbara did not miss the desperation in his tone and wondered what he knew about the self-harm period? Clearly Nicola had told him something. Did he know about the abortion? she puzzled.

'Don't worry, Tony, I'll leave straight away. Do I need to bring anything?' she asked, scanning the kitchen surface tops for her handbag.

'No and thank you, you've no idea how I feel knowing you are heading over, but please drive carefully, it is not life-threatening.'

Thank God for that, she was about to say when she heard a click telling her the call had ended. Locating her handbag, she grabbed it and hurried to fetch her car keys from the hook inside the front door. What was Nicola playing at this time, was it a genuine call for help or another one of her games?

Chapter Thirty-Eight

Twenty-five minutes after leaving home and breaking every speed restriction across town, Barbara brought her car to a shuddering halt against the kerb outside Nicola's house.

No sooner had she yanked on the handbrake, when Tony appeared jogging down the drive towards her, his face strained and in need of a shave.

She pushed the car door open, climbed out and tried not to panic. Nicola had put her in situations before that had made her heart miss several beats. Whatever was going on, it was important she remained calm. Clutching her bag, Barbara reached out and took hold of Tony's arm. 'I don't know what's going on, but you sounded desperate. What has happened?'

'Thank you for coming, Mrs Knight,' Tony said, breathing in short gasps as if he had been running miles rather than the few metres down the tarmac drive. 'I wouldn't have called if I didn't think it was important for Nic to talk to you. She's fallen apart and I don't know how to deal with her. I'm sorry,' Tony said, sounding defeated.

His distress was plainly evident to Barbara, his pale face was pinched and the dark circles under his eyes she had seen on Saturday, appeared darker. 'Do you have any idea what is causing her such upset?'

'Yes and that's why we need you,' Tony said, a weak smile lifting his strained features. 'I'm sorry to have frightened you.'

'You don't need to apologise, my daughter is a troubled soul at times. Come on, let's go inside. I'm sure we'll have it all sorted as soon as we have a talk, so stop worrying.' Having had years of practice dealing with Nicola's behaviour, Barbara just hoped it wasn't another of her daughter's tricks to create attention or unrest.

Getting here had been hair-raising enough, having jumped every orange light. She had never seen herself as a racing driver and now appreciated how the emergency services felt when they needed to get to someone who clung to life with their last breath.

She followed Tony into the house in a state of bewilderment at the turn of events. Only yesterday she could happily have strangled Nicola for upsetting Bob and making her look and feel such a fool. By contrast, right now she felt sick with worry.

Leaving the front door open, Tony immediately ushered her upstairs.

'I'll bring you up a cup of tea in a few minutes,' Tony said as he pushed open the main bedroom door.

'Thank you,' she said, wondering why tea was the answer to all ills.

'Your mum's here,' he announced, pushing open the bedroom door. Hanging onto the handle, he almost shoved Barbara into the room and before she could utter a word, he had gone, the sound of his feet hurrying down the stairs filling the silence that surrounded her.

She sucked in her breath as she spied Nicola resting against a bank of white pillows, her face as pale as the pillow slips. Her beautiful cornflower blue eyes, which could shine as bright as any star, were more like dark, inky water; dull and lifeless. Even her naturally wavy strawberry-blonde hair, thankfully long again, flopped dull and lank across her shoulders. A wave of sadness engulfed Barbara as she took in the sight of her eldest daughter. All her angry thoughts of the last few days evaporated.

'What on earth has happened?' she asked, in a voice that was barely above a whisper.

'Mum!' Nicola sat bolt upright. 'Did you ask him? Please tell me you did,' she was almost shouting.

Positioned at the side of the bed, Barbara felt the shock waves from Nicola's booming voice. Stunned, she glared at her daughter. Is that all Nicola could think about? *No hello Mum, thanks for coming.* She had almost killed herself driving to get to her side, imagining any number of horrors, and all her daughter could think about was whether she had asked *the* question; a question that had caused both pain and anger. Unsure if she could speak in a civil tone, Barbara sank down onto the side of the bed, feeling as if the last breath of air had been punched out of her.

'Is that why you didn't call me or come round? Or have you not asked him?' Nicola garbled incoherently, her eyes wide and glaring at her with laser like intensity.

Now Barbara could understand why Tony had called her. It was clear he was out of his depth and, at this moment, she knew how he felt. Taking in her daughter's haunted and disturbed look, anyone would be frightened, she thought; Nicola looked unhinged. There was a possibility Terry's death had upset her far more deeply than even she had understood. Grief affected people in different ways and as indifferent as Nicola had appeared over the years, there was little doubt she was suffering deeply. Barbara could not ignore the fact that her own mind had been filled with thoughts of Nicola ever since the funeral. No matter how hard she tried to push them away, awake and asleep her daughter had occupied her mind. Maybe after all she had been too harsh, especially at the funeral when she had seen Nicola drinking to excess. Had she let her daughter down by not recognising her behaviour this time for what it was? Sheer grief. What she was seeing now, it appeared Tony had been right; Nicola was on the verge of a breakdown.

'I'm sorry darling, I had no idea…'

'So he told you?' Nicola screeched, talking over her.

Shocked at the force in Nicola's voice, Barbara asked, 'Who told me what, darling?' She spoke softly, trying to grasp where her daughter was coming from and at the same time her mind racing on how to reach and calm her.

'*Him*! Who do you think I'm talking about?'

'Him? Who's him?' Barbara asked, perplexed and wondered if Nicola was on any medication. After the abortion she had been extremely low and needed anti-depressants. Over the years Nicola's mood swings had been legendary and she suspected her daughter had never truly recovered or forgiven her for making her go through with it. It had been one of the darkest days of her life, Barbara reflected, and although she had never regretted what she'd had to do, the loss of their closeness had been a high price to pay.

'Nicola, are you on any tablets?'

Sucking her cheeks in, Nicola growled, 'Mum, you are not listening! Why won't you just answer the question?'

'Believe you me, I am listening, but before I answer you I would like to know if you are taking any medication.'

'Why, what does it matter?' Nicola snapped, 'but no I'm not. What's important right now is finding out if you asked my question. Mum, believe me, it's important. God, how many times do I have to ask?' Nicola wrung her hands, making her fingers crack at the aggression of her action.

To still the agitation, Barbara grabbed hold of Nicola's hands and leant forward. 'Please darling, look at me.' As she spoke, she fixed her gaze on her daughter's face. To her relief, Nicola tilted her head and with a pitying glance, stared back at her. Thankful she had her attention, Barbara answered the question. 'If by "him" you mean Bob, yes I have asked him, but you knew the answer didn't you?' She kept her voice even and controlled. She had no idea why Nicola would ask about something she knew the answer to or why it was suddenly important to drag up Bob's past.

Yanking her hands away, Nicola stared at her mother. 'You knew, didn't you? You knew all along, and that's why you're ignoring everything, but it won't go away, you know that don't you?'

'Nicola, my love, I honestly have no idea what you are talking about.' Barbara got to her feet, unsure what to say or do next. Gazing down at her daughter, she decided to play along with her for now, but only until she was able to work out what kind of help was needed. 'Whatever makes you say that, Nicola? Of course I didn't know. I was only delaying answering your question because I can't see what can be gained by dragging up something like that, especially when it happened such a long time ago.'

'Yes, it was a long time ago, but that doesn't mean it can be ignored anymore, Mum,' Nicola murmured, her voice now so low that Barbara could hardly hear. 'You know, it's taken me years to find the strength and courage to talk to you. Had it not been for Tony, I would never have said anything, but he told me if I didn't he would go to the police.'

Barbara felt a bubble of panic rise up in her chest. Right now, it was not the police Nicola needed, but a psychiatrist. 'Why would Tony think the police could help, darling?' she asked, thrusting down the panic and keeping her voice calm. As she spoke she strode over to the door, she needed to phone a doctor.

Nicola flung the duvet back and leapt out of bed with such agility that Barbara found herself stepping back.

'Mum, I beg you not to leave, just come back and let's talk, please. I can answer your question.' Tears cascaded down Nicola's face as she stood staring at her mother. 'Please,' Nicola begged.

Barbara pulled her daughter to her. 'Oh my love, whatever it is that's wrong with you, I promise we'll get it sorted. I love you, I'm your mum. Now come on, let's get you back into bed and then you can tell me why you need the police.' Without protest, Nicola complied.

Barbara pulled the heavy duvet over her and seeing Nicola snuggled under the warm covers, said in a soothing tone, 'I'm going to ask Tony to make us a cup of tea. I think it will help both of us stay calm.' She didn't believe anything short of a strong tranquiliser would calm her daughter at the moment, but the need to do something was overwhelming.

Throwing the duvet off as if it was light as a feather, Nicola cried, 'No Mum, no! Not now. Please come back I need to talk to you.'

Feeling her control slipping, Barbara returned to Nicola's side and settled on the edge of the bed. For the second time in as many minutes, she draped the duvet back over her disturbed daughter. With soothing strokes, she pushed Nicola's hair from her tearstained face and tucked the strands behind her ears. Then gently she wiped at the tears that spilled from Nicola's swollen eyes, all the while her mind churning with worry and questions as to what had happened to send her girl over the edge.

'I'll tell you what, shall we try again, tell me what is really bothering you and then I can help.' Not wanting to set off another voluble attack, Barbara kept her voice steady and decided not to mention the police. Though what they had to do with it all mystified her.

Shuffling into her pillows, Nicola leant against the headboard. She bowed her head as if to keep the fear in her eyes from her mother. 'What did he say about Laura?'

Exasperated that the conversation had not strayed from Bob and this Laura, Barbara raked her fingers through her hair in an attempt to stop her from losing the minuscule of control she had left. Walking on a tightrope across high buildings wouldn't need any more concentration than trying to work out what was going on in Nicola's mind. 'Darling, does it matter? Why are you so interested?'

'I only want to know what he said,' Nicola persisted, her attention settled on her chewed fingernails.

Silently cursing at the ridiculousness of the situation, Barbara decided that she would make one more attempt to snuff out this constant need to keep questioning her about Bob. 'Okay, I'll tell you if this can be the end of it. Agree?'

Barbara wasn't sure if it was a nod or simply a twitch as Nicola stared down at her hands, but continued regardless, eager to end this line of conversation. 'He said Laura was an old girlfriend who got rid of their baby.'

Nicola looked up and smirked, but to Barbara it was more like a snarl as her daughter's eyes flashed a look of pure hatred and contempt. It was then that Barbara's mind did back flips and her breath caught in her throat. Was Nicola the "old girlfriend"? *Surely not, please not that?* Then, as if her thoughts had taken on a life of their own, her mind spun out of control down through the years in an attempt to pinpoint when this might have happened, while on another level denying that it could possibly be true. Her thoughts came to a shuddering halt as she remembered the abortion and Nicola's persistent refusal to name the father, and then three days later, when she had been rushed into hospital, her life hanging by a thread. Not Bob. No! No, please not Bob, that *could* not be possible. And yet, like a thunderclap, it all tumbled into place. Was that why Nicola was always so hostile towards him? Barbara's mind recoiled with horror, she did not want to think that he had touched her or been anywhere near her, and as for the abortion. No, she could not go there. She had to be wrong.

Stamping down on all these ludicrous thoughts, she turned to Nicola and in a voice that was filled with trepidation she spoke, 'Nicola, please tell me. Were *you* the girlfriend?' Her daughter glared back at her and for a moment Barbara was sure she saw a glint of mockery in her eyes.

Pulling her hands free Nicola continued to pick nervously at the skin around her fingernails. 'You really have no idea have you?' she said, and this time Barbara didn't miss the mockery. It was like watching the pendulum of a clock swing back and forth as Nicola's moods swung from full on emotion to calm mocking.

'It does seem that way,' Barbara said, 'but I'd like to know. You can share anything with me.' Did she really want to know what her daughter and Bob had been up too? The very idea of him near Nicola made her want to vomit?

He might be a good friend and be part of the family, but having an affair with her daughter was unthinkable.

'It's complicated and…' Nicola trailed off.

'Complicated?' Barbara found herself repeating, and knowing that everything she had thought about her dear friend would be blown to the wind if it was true, yet still she could not stop herself asking, 'Am I to assume that you and Uncle Bob had an affair?' There, she had said it and as much as she needed to get to the bottom of her daughter's breakdown, she did not want this to be the cause. Hoping against hope for a denial, she was to be disappointed.

'It was the parties…' Barbara heard Nicola's voice float into her thoughts. Taken aback at the turn in conversation, she stared at her. Baffled, she shifted uncomfortably on the side of the bed wondering where her daughter's mind was going now.

'That's how it all began,' Nicola continued, her eyes focused on some point at the other side of the room. 'The nurses on the TV said the doctor had chiselled features. Except it didn't end like the TV programme.'

Barbara got to her feet. What had she been thinking, sitting here trying to offer consoling words, when in fact her daughter needed help immediately. She was clearly delirious. Stooping, she reached over and placed the back of her hand on Nicola's forehead. To her surprise it was cool; she was not running a temperature.

'I'm not that sick,' Nicola snorted, 'but I am ill,' she admitted. 'I need help, Mum and now Dad is no longer here I need to tell you. It was me! *I* was Laura Speedwell who went to the Burley House clinic. It was me, but I was never Uncle Bob's girlfriend,' Nicola said in a low voice that still managed to echo round the room.

Motionless with shock, Barbara watched as her daughter's face crumpled into a mass of misery.

Chapter Thirty-Nine

As if frozen to the spot, Barbara absorbed the words her daughter had uttered. Her mind reeled on how Laura Speedwell and Burley House were anything to do with her daughter. Bob had said Laura was an old girlfriend, but Nicola had just admitted she was never his girlfriend.

Confused, she took a deep breath to ensure her voice came out solid rather than a scream. 'Nicola,' she said returning to the side of the bed. 'How could you be her, my darling?' Leaning over she wrapped her arms around Nicola's shaking body. She needed to hold her tight and keep out the fear that was creeping over her. Several minutes passed in silence and Barbara's mind shifted to overdrive waiting for Nicola's response.

Releasing her hold, Barbara looked down into Nicola's face and for a moment their eyes locked. The depth of pain reflected in her daughter's eyes shocked Barbara. She pulled Nicola back against her and felt her daughter clasp onto her as if she wanted her mum to never let her go.

'I'm sorry, Mum,' Nicola eventually said, her voice muffled as she unfolded herself from her mother's embrace.

'You don't need to be sorry, darling, but please tell me what makes you say you were Laura?'

Lifting her head, Nicola glared at her mother through wet strands of hair. 'Because I was, I told you it was complicated and it is. You see, he did it, he did it to me and I couldn't stop him.'

Barbara felt the earth shift around her as if her body was suffering a personal earthquake, 'Who did what to you, my love?' she said, in as controlled a manner as she could muster, as if she was talking about a skirmish in the playground rather than abortions and clinics.

Burrowing her head in her mother's shoulder, Nicola said, '*Him*,' her voice sounding thick as if she was speaking through water.

'And who is him?' Barbara dared to venture, praying that all the jigsaw pieces that had materialised in her head over the last few minutes were not going to reveal the picture that was now frightening her rigid.

'Uncle Bob.'

'Uncle Bob,' she stuttered and wondered if she had heard correctly.

With a display of unexpected strength, Nicola pushed herself away from her mother and moved to the other side of the bed. 'You don't believe me, do you?' she said, agitated. 'He said you would never believe me and that's why he wouldn't stop. It was only because I ran off to live with Brett that he left me alone. The bruise was the start. Look…' In a frenzy Nicola scrambled to her knees and pulled at her PJ bottoms, stabbing her finger on the white flesh at the top of her thigh. 'Of course you can't see it now, but it was there,' she said. 'You remember that dizzy woman, Aunty Jenny? She told you about it the day we came back from a sleepover, the same day as the big ceremony for the new Wendy House.'

Barbara saw nothing more than a red mark made by Nicola's stabbing finger, but that was years ago, she thought, and Nicola was so young.

'He was right all along,' Nicola went on. He said I would be the one that would go to prison for lying if I told anyone.'

As Nicola spoke Barbara witnessed a whirlpool of emotions shift across her daughter's features and felt as if she was being sucked into a vortex from where there was no return.

Struggling to find a lifeline, Barbara stared at her daughter, then without warning, Nicola leapt off the bed and landed, barefoot, on the multi-coloured rug at Barbara's side. The tension in the room inflated to the point it seemed palpable.

Standing stock still, Nicola kept her eyes focused on her feet. 'He did it,' she said in a small voice as if she were regressing to being a child again. 'Even when I said no he kept doing it and wouldn't stop. He said if I didn't let him then he would get what he wanted from Becky.' She spoke in a whisper as if every ounce of her energy had drained away.

No; no, please not this, Barbara silently begged, breaking and aching as she took in the implications of what Nicola had just said. Please, someone tell me this was not what had happened. Please tell me it is not why her daughter had turned from a beautiful intelligent girl into a stroppy, rude young woman. A woman determined to destroy her life along with that of anyone who cared for her? As her thoughts mushroomed, she wanted to believe Nicola was telling the truth, yet nothing she knew wanted her to believe that Bob had abused her daughter. God; Nicola had been only nine years old when they'd built the Wendy House. Barbara felt bile rushing up her throat and swallowed hard to keep it down. She opened her mouth to speak, but the words that would shatter their world into tiny fragments lodged in her throat with the bile. No mother wanted to hear their daughter had been abused. Why hadn't she known? There must have been signs, but she had seen none. *Why?* she asked herself, racking her brain in the hope there was something to help her see what she had missed. As a mother she should have known, but she hadn't. Instead she had trusted Bob Wakefield, seeing him more than a loyal friend, but someone important enough to be a part of their family, never imagining he would go near her girls. Involuntarily she pushed her fist into her mouth as the bitter bile threatened to rise into her mouth, the contents of her stomach wanting to be free of her. What did Nicola mean when she said that he had only left her alone after she had left home to live with Brett Morton, what did that mean? How long had he been touching her? Had he touched her when she was young?

These questions and many more fought for answers, each one slicing through her like a hundred tiny paper cuts.

Eventually she opened her mouth to speak and though her lips moved all she could hear was a gushing sound in her ears as if she were standing underneath a waterfall.

'Mum, Mum, are you all right?' Nicola said, grabbing hold of her shoulders. Hearing Nicola's piercing voice pulled Barbara back to her waking nightmare. She didn't want to believe what Nicola had just told her. More than anything in her life she wanted to believe she had misheard. Now, as she regarded her daughter standing, trembling at her side, she knew Nicola was telling the truth. No one could be in this state if it was simply a fabrication to destroy Bob Wakefield for whatever reason. As terrified as she felt, she needed to know what had happened and when. Bracing herself for what no mother wants to hear, she asked, 'Please can you tell me what happened.'

'You went very pale.'

'No, darling, I don't mean me. I want to know what he did to you and when.' Aware that what she was about to learn would change everything forever, once again she wished Terry was here.

Nicola dropped down onto the edge of the bed, her hands shaking as she continued to pick at her fingers, her right leg twitching nervously as she cast her gaze down. 'He did the things you do when you are grown up.'

'When?' she asked.

Nicola concentrated on pulling the skin from the cuticles. 'When he babysat and sometimes when you had parties.'

Barbara sucked her breath in through her teeth, knowing the next question would be the hardest. 'How old were you?'

Nicola chewed on her bottom lip and without moving her gaze from her fingers, said, 'The first time I was ten.'

Hearing this, Barbara felt the contents of her stomach surge up into her mouth and knowing that no fist would keep this lot down she hurried to the en-suite. Grabbing hold of the toilet lid, she slammed it up and vomited. Several minutes passed as she threw up and retched. Only when there was nothing left to bring up, did she push herself to her feet. No matter how many times she rinsed her mouth out she would never rid herself of the sour taste of betrayal as long as she lived. Then, on legs that felt more like rubber than bone, she returned to Nicola's side.

'The accident was my fault,' Nicola blurted, followed by an avalanche of words that gushed out as if in a frenzy to tell everything. 'I thought he was dead and worse I hoped he was dead, but of course he wasn't, was he?'

Barbara squeezed her eyes shut as every muscle around her heart contracted as if into a tight fist at what her daughter had been forced to endure. The accident had taken up so much of her time and she remembered how she had insisted Nicola visit Bob in hospital. What kind of a mother was she?

'You do believe me Mum, don't you?' Nicola begged, her voice rising to a hysterical pitch, 'because it's true.'

Feeling fit to commit murder, Barbara was starkly aware she had to stay calm, 'My love, of course I believe you, why wouldn't I?

With a wan smile, Nicola placed a hand on her mother's, 'Thank you.'

Clasping her daughter's hand, Barbara needed to find out what her beautiful daughter had been subjected to, yet as much as she wanted to know everything, there was a part of her that did not want Nicola having to relive what he had done.

'I'm sorry to ask, but do you think you can tell me what he did?' Rubbing at the soft skin on the back of Nicola's hand, Barbara waited. It was important she knew everything to ensure she had the strength to help her daughter through what was going to be a frightening and traumatic time.

'Some of it I can, not all, but he did it,' Nicola kept her eyes down as she spoke and Barbara could almost taste the shame that emanated from her daughter.

'Can you tell me about Laura Speedwell and how you came to be her?'

Nicola wriggled free and slipped back under the duvet. 'It's not easy to say now and yet I've spent years telling you in my head what he was doing. I've always been too afraid, but you know, Mum, Tony helped me. He helped me see that I had to talk to you one day and tell you.'

Barbara didn't know Tony well enough, but right now she was more than grateful that he was part of Nicola's life.

'I was nine when he first started touching me and by the time I was thirteen I'd had my first abortion. That's when I was Laura Speedwell. It was his idea to change my name so we could hide and no one would know or ask too many questions or find me. You organised the second abortion for me, but I was too scared to tell you who the father was. I was always scared of what he would do, Mum.

Barbara listened in horror as Nicola gave her a thumbnail account of the years leading up to the abortion and what happened after. Every word that flew out of Nicola's mouth gouged into Barbara's flesh as if she were being thrashed with a barbed metal pole.

'The Wendy House I hated because it was the place he liked to take me. He said it was our little place to go to for fun. He would always take a little picnic for us and then afterwards he would do it.'

Images of the Wendy House, all clean and new, flashed through Barbara's mind, along with the pictures of Terry with the girls on the day of the surprise. It was meant to be a place of laughter and safety not a place of fear and torture. Now she understood Nicola's reluctance to use the Wendy House.

'I'm sorry Mum, I am so sorry,' Nicola finally said, 'please hug me'.

With more force than she had intended Barbara took hold of her daughter and squeezed her tight to her. She wanted to take away all the pain and shame of what Bob had done to her, if only that were possible. But, of course, it wasn't.

'Oh my love, you have nothing to be sorry about. I'm the one who is sorry because I didn't protect you and keep you safe.' Barbara knew she would spend the rest of her life punishing herself for not seeing anything to indicate her daughter was being abused. How could she have been so blind? And how could that dreadful man still call at her house with his words of condolence and kindness, when he had carried out such heinous, unspeakable acts? He had sat at her table, held her hand, even hugged her close to him and all the time he had held an abominable secret; abuse that had been systematically carried out on her daughter over several years. Numb with shock and consumed with blinding anger, Barbara still had one more question to ask before she called the police.

What I don't understand is why didn't you tell me or your dad?'

'Why do you think?' Nicola sobbed. 'I told you, I was scared. You have no idea just how frightening he is. Even now he still threatens me.'

'Threatens you?' Barbara repeated.

'Yes, he tells me that if I say anything, firstly you won't believe me and secondly, he will tell the police I tried to kill him with the accident and then they will take my girls away from me. I have been so afraid of going to prison and what you would do if you found out. You know, fear is far more frightening than anything else I know. After all, sex is just sex when you get used it.'

Barbara winced at how such an intimate act could be described so coldly as "just sex". What had that bastard done to her girl? She felt her life fracture. It was as if a pen had steadily drawn a thick black line down the middle of her life and from this moment on there would be a *before* today's horrific revelations and an *after*.

For several moments Barbara and Nicola sat in silence as if there was a need to absorb all that had been said. The only sounds that drifted into the room were from the occasional cars that drove past the house. Life continued as normal outside their four walls and yet their lives were shattered. How *could* that man have done that to them? He had lived in their lives as if nothing had happened and all the time he had abused and almost destroyed her daughter. As guilty as Bob was, Barbara felt she was just as much to blame. If anything she was more to blame; she was a mother and had not seen any of what had been going on. She had not thought for one moment that something so terrible had been happening under her own roof, because it was so unthinkable. She had thought Nicola's behaviour was just her daughter being awkward; a teenager with hormones running wild. She had watched as Nicola's interest in everything had evaporated to nothing. She had seen her grow into a wilful person destined to walk down the roughest of roads on life's map, ignoring all the opportunities handed out to her. And all the time her beautiful daughter was being brutally abused. Barbara felt sick to the core as the shock of it all started to bleed into her body and she knew that as long as she drew breath, she would make sure he never touched another person again. If it was the last thing she did, she would see that monster brought to justice and made to pay for what he had done.

Nicola leant against her mother. 'Thank you again,' she sobbed. 'Thank you for believing in me. That's all I've ever wanted.'

Chapter Forty

Nicola had always believed that once she had found the courage to reveal her shameful secret the heavy burden that had sat on her shoulders for years would lift. Temporarily it had, but the need to talk to so many strangers about the most intimate of details had taken its toll. Her sleep was still filled with nightmares as flashbacks played throughout her hours of slumber and panic attacks dogged her waking hours. Counselling and medication helped and the loving support of Tony, who continued to struggle with what had been done to her and having to witness her waking nightmares, so much so that he had ended up having to take mild sedatives. Her mother was coping, but only because anger and a determination to bring Bob Wakefield to justice propelled her through each day; her energy fuelled by raw guilt for her ignorance of what had been going on all those years. And, as much as this galvanised her to do what she needed to do, the shame of being so naïve and unseeing would live with her mother for the rest of her life. Nicola just wished she'd had the courage to have spoken to her years earlier, when she was still a child. Then they both would have been spared travelling down the road to hell. Today they would need all their strength and love for each other, for today, at last, Bob Wakefield would face the justice he deserved, at least she hoped that would be the outcome.

'Are you okay?' Barbara asked, her face pinched with anxiety as she reached across the low table and wrapped her fingers around Nicola's clammy hand.

Nicola shook her head, 'Not really,' she replied, feeling the comfort of her mother's hand squeezing her own, 'but don't worry, Mum. Whatever happens in that court room today it is over and we can start to rebuild our lives.'

Leaning against Tony, who sat quietly at her side, Nicola thought back through the weeks of interviews, investigations and collecting of evidence, which at last were at an end. What the judge would make of all the information he had before him she had no idea. The abuse was her word against her alleged abuser's, but thankfully the records from her first abortion, including the DNA sample they had taken, were still available. She had no idea how long medical records were retained. Possibly because they had had doubts of her age, believing she was not the sixteen year old she had said she was, the records had been kept, but whatever the reason, she would always be grateful they were still available.

'The prosecution seem to think he will go to prison. I'm not sure what I think of that, I only ever wanted you to know and to believe me.' Nicola squeezed her mother's hand. 'I am just relieved it is all in the open,' she said, but her heart felt as heavy as stone at how her mother had aged during the last couple of months. Her dad's death had left her mum broken-hearted, but even the aching loss of someone so loved had been set aside since Nicola's revelations. Death, her mother had coped with; the abuse had destroyed her. After that heartrending morning when all her secrets had been flushed out, even before the tears had been wiped away, the police had been contacted. Her mother, galvanized into action, had refused to leave the police station until she had repeated all she had been told. Two plain clothed officers, both male, had taken her mother to a windowless room where a coffee-stained table and four low-back chairs filled the space. They had listened with patience to what she had to say. Afterwards, they had interviewed Nicola, a female officer replacing one of the male officers.

For Nicola, talking to her mother had been one thing, but revealing all the intimate details to strangers proved to be every bit as disturbing as everything she had gone through during her years of abuse. With each response to their questions, both had simply nodded their heads as they had scribbled pages of copious notes. And, despite their initial flourish of interest, she had seen doubt in their faces, even more so after Bob Wakefield had been arrested and denied everything.

Seated in his wheelchair, acting the innocent, his features strained to gain maximum effect, he had played on his disability, going into minute detail about the accident as if that was the main reason he had been taken to the police station. He had insisted on detailing how she had lured him across the busy road in revenge for his having slept with her at sixteen and his refusal to be her boyfriend. Naturally, he had not mentioned stalking her, carefully omitting he had been calling out to her. It was only when medical records were produced from Burley House on "Laura Speedwell" and her uncle, "Ted Wilkins", and after DNAs had been analysed, that he had broken down and admitted he'd had sex with her, although he had denied the years of abuse.

The Wendy House had not escaped the hunt for evidence – although what might be found after so long Nicola could not imagine – meant its destruction had had to wait, however much as she had wanted it obliterated. The creaking, damp and musty Wendy House was thoroughly raked over by men from forensics, dressed in white overalls, with plastic bags over their shoes.

At last the day arrived when they received the all clear. Without delay the place was ripped down; nothing was salvaged. The broken pile was set alight and Nicola and her mother had watched the flames lick at the timbers, scorching and ultimately turning all that had happened in that wooden house to dust. Turning her back on the smouldering ashes Nicola had whispered, 'Sorry Dad.' She knew he would want to reap his revenge on his old friend if he could.

'We're ready for you now,' said a willowy-framed, middle-aged woman breaking into her thoughts. Wearing a light grey skirt with matching fitted jacket, her hair clipped stylishly back from her face, the woman's soft voice belied her formal look. 'We're in courtroom three,' she added as Nicola looked up. Then, with an understanding smile, she ushered the three of them out of the waiting room.

The courtroom was much smaller than Nicola had imagined and less intimidating than those she seen portrayed on TV. She, Tony and her mother were settled into formal upright chairs. In front of them was a low wooden balustrade and on the other side was a long table, several piles of leather-bound books stacked on its surface. There were various other people in the courtroom, some wearing gowns and wigs. The atmosphere was tense. Her mother took hold of her hand and Tony held tightly onto her other one. With her eyes cast down, she heard the familiar squeak of *his* wheelchair filling the quietness of the courtroom.

Nicola felt the tension ripple through every inch of her body and as if pulled by an outer force, she found herself casting her gaze towards him. To her shock she saw he was looking straight at her, tears spilling down his pinched face. As their eyes met, his lips moved, but no sound came out. Then, in a silent cry, he mouthed, '*I'm sorry. I'm very sorry.*'

Years of emotions welled up threatening to overwhelm her, but before she could take in *his* silent apology, a voice from the prosecution filled the silence of the courtroom.

'Bob Wakefield, do you plead guilty or not guilty to the charges against you?' A forceful voice asked and Nicola held her breath.

Without hesitation, Bob replied, 'Guilty.'

Letting out a deep breath, Nicola struggled to her feet and shuffling past Tony she walked out of the courtroom. It was over at last. She didn't know whether to jump with joy or cry out loud nor did she know if she would ever recover from what he had done to her, but one thing she was certain of, and that was she would put every ounce of energy she possessed into making sure she moved forward with her family, and that meant all of her family.

The End

CPSIA information can be obtained
at www.ICGtesting.com
Printed in the USA
LVHW091410311220
675533LV00032B/252

9 781537 125800